The East Asian Region

The East Asian Region

CONFUCIAN HERITAGE AND ITS MODERN ADAPTATION

Edited by Gilbert Rozman

PRINCETON UNIVERSITY PRESS

PRINCETON, NEW JERSEY

Library of Congress Cataloging-in-Publication Data

The East Asian region : Confucian heritage and
its modern adaptation / edited by Gilbert Rozman.
p.   cm.
Includes index.
I. Philosophy, Confucian—East Asia. 2. East Asia—Social
life and customs. I. Rozman, Gilbert.
B5233.C6E37   1991   181'.112—dc20   90-37421

ISBN 0-691-05597-1
ISBN 0-691-02485-5 (pbk.)

First Princeton Paperback printing, 1993

This book has been composed in Linotron Baskerville

CONTENTS

PREFACE

THIS VOLUME is the product of an informal seminar supported by the Mellon Foundation through a grant to Princeton University. From 1985 to 1987 the seminar regularly brought together local graduate students and faculty as well as invited outside discussants to examine various historical and comparative dimensions of the East Asian Confucian tradition. We are grateful to the scores of participants who contributed on those occasions to the shaping of this manuscript. Sarane Boocock, Stephen Chiu, Deborah Davis, Sheldon Garon, Marius B. Jansen, Ryoko Kato, Laurel Kendall, and Andrew Walder are among the many to whom we are in debt. Our preliminary discussions explored many more dimensions than those examined in this book; no doubt others will carry the analysis forward with the advantage of benefiting from our loose ends. We want to express our appreciation also to Margaret Case and Laura Kang Ward of Princeton University Press and two anonymous readers who helped to revise this volume for publication.

The collaborative efforts in this book have been guided by the image of an emerging, though still vaguely defined, field of study. Viewed from a global perspective, it might be called regionalism, since the primary concern is how one region in the world differs from other leading regions. Seen more closely, this field involves the comparative and interdisciplinary study of the countries within East Asia. In this way, we can determine what constitutes the common regional heritage as distinct from the specific national traditions. This differentiation can best be achieved by examining the diffusion of the regional legacy over many centuries and its adaptability in an era of modernization and of state-sponsored movements intended to inculcate a new worldview. Our goal is to analyze a changing regional heritage interacting with national and interregional forces.

The Introduction approaches East Asia through comparisons with the West, led by the United States and Western Europe, and the North, centered in the Soviet Union. This exploratory discussion highlights the special character of the East Asian region, briefly explaining what this region is and how it has developed.

From our overview comparing three regions, we search for a revised typology of societies, reaching beyond the familiar categories of capitalist and socialist, modernized and nonmodernized. In addition to explaining the study of regions and identifying some topics useful for the study of heritage, this chapter concisely reviews the Confucian intellectual tradition, together with stereotypes of individuals and of group relations within the region. It presents a general introduction to the East Asian region.

Future research will likely present a vast panorama of interregional comparisons. Our aim here is merely to trace some outstanding differences and to indicate combinations involving both East Asian traditions and outside elements. We recognize that over many centuries the regional tradition interacted with distinct national traditions and responded to changing societies, that over the past century and a half it has combined with imported traditions and has been transformed by modernizing societies, and that the pace of "internationalization" continues to accelerate. Not only does the region stand out for its indigenous tradition and for its adaptations in the course of borrowing, it also should be seen as a source of convergence. We should consider the impact of East Asia as a leading region that finally becomes an exporter of its own regional legacy.

Throughout this book we ask what is Confucian about East Asia. The Introduction reviews the central concepts in the Confucian worldview and makes interregional comparisons with other worldviews. Part I considers what was essential to Confucianism in each of three countries, and asks when it spread to successive groups in the population. Part II continues by discussing what survived from this tradition, and whether or not it was perceived as Confucian. The Introduction also considers the prospects for Confucian behavior in an increasingly competitive and interdependent world.

We are concerned with Confucianism as it was practiced in diverse settings. We view Confucianism as a set of rituals aimed at harmonizing human relations and more generally as a guide to social behavior. We also see it as a method of governance, relying on a system of education and a clear-cut ordering of the society. It is a worldview, but often not an exclusive one. It is a set of ideals, combined with the means to achieve them at the individual, community, and state level. These concerns lead us to investigate the social history, the sociology, of East Asia.

Part I consists of three parallel chapters, each presenting a chronology of the spread of Confucian values and behavior through one of the East Asian countries. Although China was the birthplace of Confucianism and, unlike Japan and Korea, was not conscious of an imported doctrine, it is important to trace the spread of the attitudes and practices of this worldview even within Chinese society. Only in the second millennium after Confucius' death in 479 B.C. did the practices that had become closely identified with his teachings become widely disseminated among the Chinese people, and even in the third millennium diffusion continued but remained incomplete. In Korea the Confucian legacy was introduced later and did not spread widely until the fifteenth century. In Japan mass acceptance of Confucian principles was accelerated in the eighteenth and nineteenth centuries.

The three chapters on Confucianization in premodern times lead us away from the better studied intellectual history of Confucian ideas to the less explored impact of these ideas on the lives of individuals in various social strata in their family setting, community activities, and education. For each country we seek to determine the timing of the dissemination, the means by which it was accomplished, and the groups most affected. Above all, our concern is with the degree and character of Confucianization. In this way, we can better show what is common to the regional tradition as well as what varies.

Japan was the last of the three to become Confucianized, and it remained less so in the mid-nineteenth century than China and Korea. Yet, because of many factors, including the rapid spread of education and the competitive character of state sponsorship in a country with local government autonomy, Japanese Confucianism acquired a more dynamic form. It was a stronger force for centralization, less encumbered with particular forms of rule and elite selection.

Part II also reviews East Asia's three national paths, but concentrates on the modern era. It is concerned with the fate of the Confucian tradition in an age of modernization and its interaction with capitalism and socialism. While some attention is given to national perceptions of the Confucian heritage, more centers on the actual persistence of the tradition, whether recognized or not, in various spheres of life.

For comparative analysis it is necessary to distinguish different types of Confucianism. Chapter 4 points to five types and compares their presence in China and Japan. It stresses that Japan's Confucian legacy was more favorable for modernization because the traditions themselves were somewhat different. Moreover, Japanese built directly on these traditions, while Chinese leaders were often struggling to repudiate their heritage. In combination with Western liberalism, Confucian attitudes help to accelerate modernization. In combination with the aggressive campaigns of radical socialism and their stifling controls on the expression of traditional attitudes, modernization is slowed in the long run, even if short-term mobilization may give the illusion of rapid strides in the economy. Part II is concerned with the modern fate of a tradition that once appeared to be dying, but in fact proved to be unusually amenable to continued application.

Our objective is to explore some of the broadest contours on the map of East Asian Confucianism. To do that we range over 2,000 years of history, we probe all three of the principal national traditions, and we highlight many features of each society. Already, separate and more in-depth explorations have been launched into some of the cross-national features. Such efforts can be more successful if we appreciate the overall terrain on which these features have developed.

In our effort to find ways by which Confucian traditions contribute to the unparalleled dynamism in East Asia during recent decades, the Introduction emphasizes the advantageous sides of this tradition. Without denying the role of other forces, we highlight how Confucianism operates as an engine of dynamism and as a positive force. At the same time, we are careful to mention some negative sides of this tradition and to point to gains achieved by combining regional traditions. Other chapters generally do not address these questions; instead, they are concerned with how Confucianism spreads or endures, regardless of the consequences for national dynamism. Of course, in the modern era the fate of Confucian values is closely associated with their impact on modernization. The arguments of the Introduction are reinforced in Chapters 4 and 5 as we look more closely at the modern era. Doubts remain that a Confucian-based society in the position of world leader would be sufficiently respectful of democratic diversity and other values best identified with Western traditions. Nothing we write should be construed as support for a new cultural hegemony. In any case, the issue is not what our individual preferences might be, but what traditions prove successful in an age of international integration and rapidly growing dependence on science and technology.

This book presents four general messages to various audiences. To the academic community, we say, "Examine East Asia as a region, analyze Confucianism as its basic worldview, and build a new field of scholarship around a comparative approach to regionalism, especially by focusing on comparisons of the West and the East." To East Asians, we say, "Set aside your exclusive nationalism in order to take a closer look at your regional traditions, and in the case of China reconcile yourself to those traditions while seeking to supplement them with Western traditions." To Westerners, we say, "Be prepared to borrow more from another regional tradition, first by appreciating the strengths of that tradition and then by selectively combining them with your own regional strengths." For others, the primary message is to reexamine your own regional tradition through bold comparisons, which, however painful, may facilitate realistic borrowing in the future.

CONTRIBUTORS

MARTIN COLLCUTT, Professor of Japanese History at Princeton University

PATRICIA EBREY, Professor of Chinese History at the University of Illinois

JAHYUN KIM HABOUSH, Associate Professor of Korean History at the University of Illinois

MICHAEL ROBINSON, Associate Professor of Korean History at the University of Southern California

GILBERT ROZMAN, Professor of Sociology at Princeton University

The East Asian Region

—————————————

THE EAST ASIAN REGION IN COMPARATIVE PERSPECTIVE

Gilbert Rozman

THE EAST ASIAN region (the East) is one of three regions now contending for world superiority, as measured by some combination of economic, political, and military prominence. Long shunted aside in the wake of the global hegemony of Western Europe, the United States, and Canada (the West) and for roughly a quarter century after 1945 partially obscured in the shadow of the Soviet-led socialist bloc (the North), East Asia, through its economic prowess, burst onto the world scene in the 1970s and 1980s. Each of the three preeminent regions boasts its own strengths in world competition: the West remains ahead in scientific innovation and in the vitality of its democratic political culture; the North, now seriously weakened by a one-sided economy and the slow pace of restructuring, long stood secure in its concentrated military might and its capacity for centralized mobilization of resources; and the East is proving successful in its competitive enterprises drawing on an educated and diligent work force. Modernization began with the individualism of the West, was later prodded by the command economy of the North, and has recently been advanced by the organization man of the East. Each region modifies its approach (not always successfully) as different problems of modernization are faced, but a basic regional orientation persists.

These distinct strengths in each region are nourished by different traditions—long-established predispositions expressed as attitudes and life choices. In this book we consider the impact of traditions embedded in the Confucian worldview on modern development in East Asia. In order to do so, we examine the long-term development of social relations in China, Japan, and Korea, and we make some comparisons within this region and between regions. Our goal, which we only begin to achieve in this volume, is to take a regional, historical, and comparative perspective on the importance of Confucianism for East Asian dynamism.

Prior to its recent emergence as a center of the world economy, East Asia was not just another region on our heterogeneous planet.

In population scale, literate civilization, economic vitality, and other dimensions, this region has stood out in successive periods of human history. In a world comprised of thousands of nationalities, hundreds of countries, and more than a dozen regions, East Asia reigns along with Western Europe (and more recently the broader West including the United States and Canada) as probably the greatest and most enduring regional force in world history. At the time of the Roman Empire, China was the only empire comparable in terms of size and accomplishment. In the era of nation states, it took many centuries for Western European countries to catch up to China in urban prosperity, rural enterprise, and mass education—and in some related aspects such as size of the largest cities and literacy rates it was not until the Industrial Revolution that similar levels were reached in the West. Japan was also overtaking China, and Korea had achieved high levels of its own. Not one country, but the entire region excelled in world history.

Among premodern regions, the Middle East and South Asia have known periods of flourishing civilization and are rightly acclaimed as the crucible of some of the world's great religions. Since World War II, the Soviet Union (along with the United States) has achieved unprecedented ascendancy as a superpower able to project its influence to distant regions, and its might was long augmented by its hold over Eastern Europe. Nevertheless, despite periods of extraordinary accomplishment, these regions cannot claim the sustained vitality linking ancient magnificence with contemporary dynamism that distinguishes the history of East Asia. Whether viewed as the terminus of the Silk Road in Roman times, the glory of Cathay in Marco Polo's time, the great civilization of the East in the writings of seventeenth-century Jesuits and eighteenth-century European philosophers, or the economic miracle of our own time, East Asia retains a special splendor and mystery for observers around the world.

While Western civilization has over several centuries penetrated into all corners of the world, East Asian ways, in the eyes of numerous observers, have long remained shrouded in a mystique of inscrutability. When Western powers—in pursuit of colonies, commerce, and converts—were scouring the globe, East Asian countries turned inward, even limiting their contacts with neighboring countries. In far-flung territories Western religions, political institutions, and languages have left an indelible imprint. In contrast, few outsiders have shown much interest in Confucianism, Taoism, or Shintoism, and hardly any have taken the trouble to learn Chinese, Japanese, or Korean. This region has not projected its power or its systems of belief outward, nor have its citizens, to the degree seen elsewhere, clamored for foreign products; in the late eighteenth century the Europeans had difficulty selling their goods to China (and they resorted to covering their trade deficit with illegal transshipments of opium), and again in recent years there have been sizable trade deficits with countries in the region.

By the standards of Western European history—whether one considers war, commerce, religion, or simply the daily movement of people—the East Asian region and its separate countries have been insular. This conclusion holds, to some extent, even in recent decades. From the 1950s well into the 1970s China was more cut off from normal intercourse with the world community than any other major country. Despite Japan's enormous stake in international economic transactions, it has been slow to encourage foreign students to enter its schools and its university programs taught in the Japanese language, or foreign businessmen to enter the inner circles of its corporate boardrooms. No wonder that global understanding of East Asia lags far behind the international significance of this region!

World opinion is at last awakening to the special character of the East Asian region. Observers around the globe now marvel at the dynamism of this region. Some have tallied the statistics on economic performance, exclaiming about the quadrupling or quintupling of GNP over barely two decades since the 1950s or 1960s. Many have reported on the avalanche of high-quality and competitively priced exports that draw foreign customers by the throngs, provoking anguish as well as envy among leaders in other countries concerned with their balance of payments. Appreciation for the achievements of this region can be found in commentaries on superior educational performance, low crime rates, high life expectancies, and an unusual degree of family stability—to mention just several of the many themes that draw superlatives. Increasingly East Asia stands for a rare combination of rapid economic growth and high social stability, extraordinary individual effort and persistent group support.

At the same time, mixed with admiration are often puzzled or condescending explanations that assume that a huge price is being exacted in the stunted development of individual personalities. Critics disparage the lack of personal choice and creativity—the fact that individuals may be asked to make enormous sacrifices for the group with little recourse to customary rights that limit group authority. Political intolerance and fanaticism have led to tragic consequences. Personal networks often degenerate into pervasive favoritism and corruption. While some observers weigh the positive figures concerning this region's development heavily, others downplay them in favor of the costs imposed.

Both responses inevitably introduce the subject of heritage (how the past lives on in the present); yet little has been done to sort out, with an eye to both pros and cons, both region and nation, the effects of heritage on the special place of this region in world history. The significance of regional and national heritage is found, above all, in the distinctive impact of past habits and ways of thinking in an increasingly modernized world. How one assesses the accomplishments of this region depends in part on one's views of the region's past. How one predicts the prospects for the region also is closely related to one's calculations of the durability of the historical legacy.

East Asia is a great region of the past, having been in the forefront of world development for at least two thousand years, until the sixteenth, seventeenth, or even eighteenth century, after which it suffered a relatively brief but deeply felt eclipse. Projecting recent patterns of achievement by countries in the region and by transplanted persons whose families have moved abroad, most observers now agree that East Asia promises to be a great region of the future. It is no longer controversial to assert that this is a region that should be examined closely by all who seek to understand the present course of world development.

The Region as a Focus

It should come as no surprise to Westerners, unaccustomed to looking beyond national boundaries to view Western Europe as a single region, that East Asian peoples have also rarely adopted a regional focus. Indeed, while political and religious regional groupings such as the Roman Empire, the Holy Roman Empire, and Napoleon's army of conquest established a degree of pan-European unity, such regional organizations are difficult to identify in the history of East Asia. While economic and now political integration are sweeping Western Europe, where trade ties have long been close, the large East Asian countries are unaccustomed to a regional division of labor. Japan's abortive East Asian Co-Prosperity Sphere in World War II and its preceding decades of colonization in the region (lasting for 35–45 years in Taiwan and Korea) stand as a rare exception, politically and economically, to the dearth of regional integration. Justification for taking this region as a unit must be sought elsewhere, not in political alignments or in large-scale flows of trade over a long period.

Justification for a regional focus is not hard to find. This focus is evident in the common heritage of the region, which is customarily, although somewhat imprecisely, called the Confucian heritage. We apply this label without disregarding the fact that Buddhism, filtered through China and its already established Confucian orientation, also shaped the regional heritage. Indeed, even where there is some historical association between behavioral patterns and Confucian teachings, the patterns sometimes were not associated with just one philosophical tradition. As explained below, we use the concept of Confucian values broadly to refer to a complex of attitudes and guides to behavior that spread from China. Throughout the region there is general awareness of the common Chinese roots of much of each country's tradition and of the Confucian core in borrowings from China. Nevertheless, especially in Japan, not all of the patterns that we consider are normally identified directly with Confucian teachings.

The East Asian region extends from Japan and Korea in the northeast to Singapore and Hong Kong in the south. This region forms the eastern edge of Eurasia and is located largely in the moderate zone between the vast but sparsely settled northern lands of Siberia, the Russian Far East, and Central Asia, and the tropical southern coastal and island areas of Southeast Asia. The East Asian region can be divided into three: the areas of Chinese settlement—in the second half of the twentieth century under the four separate governments of the People's Republic of China, the Republic of China in Taiwan, Hong Kong, and Singapore—and the two areas of non-Chinese residence, consisting of Japan and the two Koreas. Contemporary political realities result in seven governments, which largely represent the three sustaining national traditions: the Chinese, the Japanese, and the Korean.

Of the areas excluded from the East Asian region described in this book, only Vietnam would have some claim to membership, but this claim is far more tenuous than that for any of the above areas. Within the region are areas central to the tradition and those that were or have become secondary. As relatively recent and small-scale offshoots of China with long periods of Westernized leadership, Hong Kong and Singapore pose problems of interpretation that deserve separate treatment. Comparisons of contemporary variations in North and South Korea introduce another dimension that we scarcely consider below. North Korea remains largely inaccessible, and our initial effort to consider the interplay between socialism and East Asian traditions will have to rely on China, its much larger neighbor to the southwest.

In this preliminary effort to identify the principal lines of development in the East Asian region over a long time span and the ways in which premodern patterns combine with modern forces, we concentrate on the three traditional societies of China, Japan, and Korea and on one modern outgrowth of each—the People's Republic of

China, the state of Japan, and South Korea. In these three core areas one can look at both national manifestations of the Confucian heritage and regional commonalities. One can identify distinctive approaches to the heritage in each country and compare them in order to achieve a general understanding of the region. In addition, through the study of interrelations between capitalism or socialism and these traditions in three countries, one can chart the main lines of modern development.

China dominates the region in population and as the source of the principal elements in the common heritage. It has also, through deliberate government policies, experimented most with breaking away from the heritage. Japan stands out as the most modernized, having most effectively combined the heritage with the needs of modern development. We look also to historical Korea as the other premodern soil on which the general heritage was cultivated and as a vital contemporary society in its own right. Together in recent centuries these three countries have comprised from 25 to 35 percent of the world population. For instance, in the 1850s China comprised close to one third of the world's population, while Japan held about 3 percent and Korea another 1 percent; a century later China was close to one quarter of the total while the other two countries combined remained at the 4 percent level.

Core values of the East Asian heritage emerged in the second millennium B.C. in northern China, a time of agricultural diffusion, city building, and establishment of governments. They were systematized and expanded by Confucius and his disciples amidst the intellectual cauldron of contending schools of thought and warring states in the following millennium. In the first millennium A.D. the Confucian worldview, associated with the Chinese written language and principles concerning government and social relations, spread through the region; Korea and then Japan borrowed extensively from the preeminent civilization of China. In our own millennium—as recently as the fifteenth to nineteenth centuries—the common heritage was still penetrating down from government and elite circles to the common people. It was still gaining new substance from China's own intellectual developments, specifically Neo-Confucianism. It was continuing to combine in new ways with native traditions and with the separate traditions of Buddhism, which had also been transmitted via China. Gradually, through state sponsorship and intense education, backed by supporting social structures, Confucian practices and ways of thinking entered the lives of most people.

This region remained a relatively separate and self-contained part of the world until the arrival of Westerners in the nineteenth century.

Geographical barriers and technological limitations had preserved the separation of this region from the outside. The lofty mountains and vast arid lands of Central Asia and the difficulties of long-distance sea transport served as a formidable buffer. Although breached by camel-loaded caravans and, later, compass-guided ships, the inhospitable terrain and treacherous seas effectively divided Eurasia and made interregional contacts with East Asia for all but nomadic peoples few and occasional. Inner Asian peoples managed on more than one occasion to conquer China, but they lacked sufficient numbers or experience in the governance of a large country to alter, in a major way, China's traditional way of life. Europeans who made contact in the sixteenth and seventeenth centuries soon found their access restricted by suspicious governments. For three centuries after their ships were capable of reaching East Asia, they were unable to penetrate the countries of the region. Only in the second half of the nineteenth century did foreigners, backed by the superiority of their arms, begin to subvert and transform the heritage of the region irrevocably.

It is sufficient to focus on the quarter millennium from the early seventeenth century to the mid-nineteenth century when interregional contacts around the globe undercut many regional traditions, to see that East Asia stands as a glaring exception. During this period Chinese, Japanese, and Korean national traditions became more deeply embedded. Powerful states succeeded in preserving and at the same time redirecting the traditions of their countries. As a result, when the irrepressible forces of the modernizing West imposed their will in opening the countries of East Asia, the contrast between old and new was all the more stark; over the previous two and a half centuries each East Asian state had strengthened the formidable resources that it would bring to bear for the struggle. Only China, under the impact of a deteriorating political system in the nineteenth century, may have lost some of its capacity to respond. Spared from colonization from outside the region and nourished by continuous, state-directed development of their own rich heritages over more than a millennium, the countries of this region were perhaps as well equipped as any in the non-Western world to channel the forces of modernization along a path of their own choosing. They could not resist foreign penetration, but they could draw on their own resources to shape its outcome.

The period between 1850 and 1950 brought a confrontation between the two regions of West and East. The technology of the former was superior; the traditional states of the latter were vanquished. Nonetheless, elements of those societies and manifestations of their common heritage endured. They endured through the depths of despair brought on by war and by the relative deprivation in the face of Western modernization.

East Asia rose from the ashes of war—from Japan's region-wide invasions which brought on World War II and Japan's devastating defeat, from China's Civil War, and from the Korean War. First Japan, then Hong Kong, Singapore, South Korea, and Taiwan, and finally the People's Republic of China (in a restricted range through a few coastal economic zones) began to challenge on world markets. A regional resurgence was in full swing by the 1980s. Not one country but an entire region was leaping to prominence on the world scene. The balance in economic growth and world eminence, which in the late nineteenth century had tilted sharply in favor of the West and later had shifted also to the North under Soviet leadership, was now moving rapidly toward the East.

Typologies of Societies

An incurable habit in the social sciences and in popular thought from the earliest recorded history is to divide the known world into types of peoples and societies. Such stereotyping assumes a life of its own, shaping events as well as public consciousness. Some classifications have been based on religion or race; others, on the predominant form of production or commerce; still others, on regional rivalries. In our time we take pride in having overcome the most superficial and obvious stereotypes by devising classifications that are alleged to convey the essence of a society's functions. Nevertheless, we still find it irresistible to divide the world around us in this way. During the second half of the twentieth century we have become mesmerized by two typologies: the sharp distinction between capitalism and socialism and the vast gulf between the modernized and the less developed countries.

In a simpler era early in this half century, capitalism was routinely associated with the modernized West and socialism signified the orthodox, centralized rule or legacy of Stalin and Mao. The universe of societies could be neatly captured by a fourfold table (Table 1) and by a triangular division of the globe into the capitalist West, the socialist East (in our terms, North and East), and the Third World South (which includes both capitalist and socialist countries and many that are described as a mixed and embryonic form of the two). Recent developments make these typologies appear incomplete. The conviction is growing that attention needs to be given to modifications in

TABLE 1
The Prevailing World Typology, 1950–1990

	Modernized	*Less Developed*
Capitalist	West	South
Socialist	East	South (East)

our prevailing worldview in order to reflect and better understand the main currents in recent world history.

Ever since the 1950s occasional spectacular events have elicited some wavering in the support for the fourfold classification of our world. Four developments have perhaps stirred the most rethinking: (1) Khrushchev's de-Stalinization speech of 1956 and subsequent socialist reforms aroused speculation that socialism and capitalism might converge or, at least, be increasingly driven by similar professional and bureaucratic interest groups; (2) the Sino-Soviet split that came into the open in 1960 and was followed later in the decade by China's Cultural Revolution raised interest in a reclassification of socialism into two varieties; (3) the extraordinary economic growth rates in Japan in the 1960s and early 1970s also heightened interest in the notion that there are two divergent types of capitalism; and (4) the oil shocks of 1973 and 1979 created the possibility of a redistribution of world income that would lift a part of the Third World into the category of developed nations. Over time some of the drama was taken out of these developments: (1) Brezhnev's status quo leadership took the wind out of the sails of reform socialism; (2) the Cultural Revolution was exposed as factional rivalries in which idealism had been quickly eclipsed, and then was repudiated as a decade lost to chaos and ignorance; (3) the 1973 oil shock cut Japan's growth rate in half after a single exceptional year of stagnation and inflation; and (4) the OPEC exporters suffered in the 1980s from lower oil prices and a failure to fuel all-around modernization from this single source of energy. After the drama of each of these challenges appeared to be fading, our worldview kept reverting to its earlier fixation.

In the 1980s it became increasingly clear that at least two of the above challenges refuse to go away. Moreover, the other two challenges have resurfaced in a new guise. Rather than individual challenges, as had occurred over the previous decades, a combined assault on the fourfold typology was gathering force. This collective challenge was concentrated in one region. China's vigorous reform program before 1989 renewed attention to pluralistic models of socialism. Japan's enormous surplus of industrial exports reemphasized the diversity of the capitalist world. Moreover, the speculation that had once centered on Soviet-American convergence reappeared first in discussions of so-called capitalist elements in China's socialist reforms and then in comparisons with Gorbachev's restructuring of Soviet socialism. Finally, the wide-ranging competitiveness of several East Asian economies superseded the glitter of OPEC's monoproduct riches in scenarios of crossing from less developed to modernized. All of the fundamental questions about classifying societies have been coming together in the upsurge of East Asia on the world scene.

A New Typology for the Fourth Quarter of Our Century

A common element runs through the various East Asian challenges to our prevailing worldview. China deviates from socialism, it is said, because of a deep-seated family orientation, a community-oriented departure from centralization, and an emphasis on securing compliance through persuasion even when coercive means continue to be employed—sometimes with brutal consequences. Japan does not fit popular notions of capitalism, we are told, because of its family solidarity, paternalistic group bonds, and cooperative spirit between state and enterprise. South Korea, Taiwan, Hong Kong, and Singapore have duplicated the Japanese "economic miracle," opinion holds, because they share in a regional tradition of diligence, entrepreneurship, striving for education, and (except for Hong Kong) state coordination. What all of these arguments have in common is the idea that East Asian social structure and thought differ from patterns found elsewhere and, furthermore, that what sets one country in this region apart from the world seems to resemble what sets the entire region apart. Striking similarities shine through amidst the many differences from country to country that also need to be noted.

We see no need to tamper with the classification of modernized and nonmodernized countries, especially if one avoids the danger of treating as a dichotomy what is obviously a continuum. We also find the distinction between capitalist and socialist a useful way of perceiving our century, yet we see an advantage in redrawing this dichotomy somewhat so that more distinctions can be made. Above all, we propose to add a third dimension to the analysis in order to capture the East Asian qualities labeled here as "Confucian." If socialism should collapse, we shall be left with two regional variants of capitalism.

Table 2 presents the sixfold typology that results from our approach. At present the capitalist Confucian societies are already rel-

TABLE 2
A Typology for the Fourth Quarter of the Twentieth Century

	Modernized	*Nonmodernized*
Capitalist	West	South
Confucian	East (Asia)	
Socialist		East (Asia)
		South
	North	

atively modernized, while the socialist ones remain relatively non-modernized. Rather than a triangular world, our typology finds greater justification in using all four quadrants. This requires us to relocate Soviet and East European socialism in the newly added North region. (By 1990 the socialist category was breaking down; one area of the North after another was scurrying to join the West.) The East Asian countries are appropriately referred to as the East region.

This book is concerned with the East Asian region and its Confucian heritage. Capitalism and socialism are familiar concepts in our times. What requires explaining is Confucianism—a religion, some have suggested, but with few or no visible believers today; a philosophy, others have argued, but with hardly any conscious adherents. In order to make a case for our typology, we must show how Confucianism spread in history and how it can endure in submerged forms roughly a century after the removal of its formal support. Before we do that, however, we want to elaborate on our typology with its three principal systems of thought and behavior.

Modern institutions and values are not simple outgrowths of particular traditions. Socialism draws on Russian traditions, capitalist and liberal values draw on Western traditions, and modern East Asian values draw on Confucianism, but each does so with much modification in a changing society. East Asia today is not as Confucian as it was 150 years ago; what exists today is the product more of shared consequences of modernization than of a distant heritage suitable for an agrarian society. Capitalism and socialism, however imprecisely these terms are often used, are concepts chosen to characterize modern conditions, while Confucianism is not. Yet, we do not have a better term to collectively describe family patterns, educational practices, attitudes toward the state, and other patterns found throughout East Asia. Also, because Confucianism was not a narrowly defined scriptural doctrine and has substantial implications for ethical behavior in a modernized setting, we think that, with appropriate qualifications, it can be used as a label for contemporary societies.

THE THREE SYSTEMS OF THOUGHT OF EAST, WEST, AND NORTH

At the end of the twentieth century three systems of thought are competing for world supremacy. One is an official ideology, recently rejected by many earlier supporters but still promulgated by die-hard followers and some governments that accept it as the exclusive truth about the development of humanity—past, present, and future. The second is a set of accumulated teachings and social science findings that are widely accepted, but, perhaps because of their pluralistic implications, are set down nowhere as a full-fledged belief system. The third is a philosophy that guided one third of humanity in the nineteenth century and had long been thought to have died out in this century; it lingers in the attitudes and behavior of people rather than as a label for an accepted system of beliefs. These three systems—in some cases overlapping in a single society—are Marxism-Leninism, liberalism, and Confucianism.

Other systems of thought can also be found in the contemporary world. In the West, liberalism continues to encounter some competition from Christian fundamentalism. This force has strong roots in some countries and among pockets of less educated people in others, but often among professed Christians the values of liberalism have displaced or been combined with earlier Christian beliefs. In the northern tier of countries, in addition to an undercurrent of liberalism that survives even among Communist Party members who pay required lip service to the official ideology, there are nationalistic movements that appeal to religious orthodoxy based on Christianity or Islam. Islam also remains a substantial force in the belt of countries from Morocco in the West to the Philippines in the East. Various national and local exclusionary movements, more visibly supported in poor communities than in urban middle-class areas, can be found further south in Africa and in parts of Asia. While Christian fundamentalism, Islamic fundamentalism, and localist worldviews are capable of impassioned resistance, none have been harnessed to modernization as have the three dominant systems identified above.

At the risk of oversimplifying world geography, these systems can be placed on a world map consisting of four quadrants. Liberalism came from Western Eurasia. Through colonization, it spread initially to the Western hemisphere, and became part of the worldview of people of all regions. Marxism-Leninism fully emerged in Northern Eurasia and spread largely to adjacent areas, but gained adherents in all regions. Confucianism originated in East Asia and, because of the absence of any proselytizers, and with the exception of migrants who have settled elsewhere, remains confined to that region. To the south of Eurasia and in the southern part of the Eastern hemisphere, although there are outposts of liberalism and Marxism-Leninism, systems other than the dominant three are most common. Further distinctions are, of course, possible, including identification of the Indian and Islamic worldviews as two of the most significant forces in the southern region.

The contest for world supremacy or successful adaptation in a more closely integrated world draws on different mechanisms of international contact and exchange. Marxism-Leninism has made most of its gains through military means; yet it also had success in the intellectual transfer of ideas. In the 1980s it was on the defensive; there was even a spreading conviction that it is incompatible with advanced levels of modernization and integration into the world economy. Liberalism has held on to some gains previously made through military means. It has been the dominant force in the intellectual transfer, even among those who profess some Marxist beliefs, combining superiority in scientific areas with traditional humanistic teachings and modern pop culture. Yet, high levels of social deviance raise doubts about long-term prospects for sustaining a strong work ethic. East Asia's Confucianism only recently has become a world actor. Without advertising its own values, it is demonstrating through success on world markets the strength of its values and organizational methods.

Political thought figures into characterizations of a region's system of belief. East Asia's one-party rule reflects a dearth of democratic institutions. Student idealists, who rally around nationalistic and anticorruption goals, are an active if inconsistent force for democracy. Elderly politicians, whose behind-the-scenes factions are the key to power broking, operate in an intensely competitive but not democratic environment. Vertical groupings within political parties dominate the highest levels of the policy-making process. Only Japan has found a way, within this context, for national leaders to resign after short terms in office and for rival parties to function as legitimate opposition with an unquestioned opportunity to oppose and defeat the governing party. Taiwan and South Korea are now becoming more tolerant of political opposition too.

The East Asian way deviates from both Western democratic and Northern socialist traditions. In contrast to the United States and many Western countries, East Asian capitalist governments remain in the hands of a single party. The opposition parties are more fundamentally opposed to existing policies. Cliques—normally dominated by elderly leaders—set policies behind the scenes and often benefit from lax restrictions on financing, while bureaucratic interest groups struggle, with at least some success, to maintain the autonomy of their professional operations in economic and other spheres.

Communist systems in East Asia are also twisted from the original Soviet model. Factionalism becomes more personalized (as it is elsewhere in the region), such that lifelong loyalties take precedence over the pursuit of beliefs. Moral commitment endures, especially among students. It can take the form of mobilization behind radical egalitarian ideals, as during the Cultural Revolution, or demonstrations for democratic reforms, as in China's 1986 and 1989 student movements. The unprincipled cynicism that dulled life in the Brezhnev era seems more difficult to sustain in an East Asian society accustomed to moral claims by its rulers, yet patience before unpopular authoritarianism has also been visible among East Asians, who have concentrated on family prosperity or, if necessary, family survival while awaiting a change in national leadership. This is true both of the response to the militarism that has at times weighed heavily in Japan, Korea, China, and Taiwan separated from China, and of the response to communist campaigns and controls that deny traditional values.

Confucianism starts with the assumptions that human nature is good and that virtuous leadership can produce moral and diligent behavior in others. Implied in this worldview is a moral appeal based on successful education—good models, good rituals, good communications, and, above all, good teachers in all settings from the home to the national leadership. Along with this idealism (associated with the teachings of Mencius and with Neo-Confucianism that spread to Korea and Japan) was a deep strain of realism (from the teachings of Hsun Tzu and borrowed from Legalism) emphasizing collective responsibility and hierarchical social control. Marxism-Leninism as developed under Stalin starts with a gloomy assessment of the class nature and political consciousness of most citizens and presupposes leadership that is highly centralized, tough willed, and backed by police vigilance. Communist parties that follow this worldview demand discipline, although ritual fulfillment of obligatory numerical targets often masks a stubborn disregard for responsible task performance. Liberalism places trust in institutions that create checks and balances rather than in human nature. This worldview focuses attention on the rule of law—on the elaboration of rules and procedures that punish wrongdoing and reward efficiency through the operation of market forces. In summary, the East idealizes micro-level, personalized moral suasion, the North claims to rely on macro-level, impersonal discipline, and the West formalizes intermediate-level, regularized

TABLE 3
Three Regions Compared

Historical Core	Western Europe	European Russia	China-Japan-Korea
Geographical Orientation	competition and colonies	expansion	continuity
Control Tendency	balance of power	centralization	moral suasion
Religious Background	Catholicism, Protestantism, sectarian coexistence	Eastern Orthodoxy, assimilation, minority separation	Confucianism, Buddhism, Shinto, Taoism, eclecticism
Social Orientations	individualism	collectivism	familism
	conflict	control from above	harmony
	separation of powers	bureaucratism	paternalism
	market mechanisms	state planning	regulated markets
	freedom for individuals	socioeconomic guarantees	equality by age, seniority
	aptitude	discipline	diligence
	material interest	public requirement	spiritual strength
	legality	duty	heritage
	independence	conformity	loyalty
	leisure orientation	informal economy orientation	work orientation
	impersonal enterprise	large welfare-organizing factory	small, family-based firm
Modern Social System	capitalism	socialism	variants of capitalism and socialism
Major Modern State	United States	Soviet Union	Japan, China

procedural uniformities. In actual circumstances, all three types combine mixtures of many elements and make some use of the methods best associated with their rivals. There are no pure approaches to the complex problems of an ongoing social system, but there are sharply different orientations associated with the three types of systems.

For a Confucian system to operate effectively many factors must be present. The national leader should envelop himself in imagery of legitimacy and virtuous behavior. The government bureaucracy should be seen as a fairly selected professional elite of the ablest and most upright individuals. This meritorious elite should appear dedicated to serving the people. Families should be given the opportunity to educate their children, to enjoy the fruits of their labor, and to pursue various strategies for prosperity. This system can break down when its ideals become little more than empty pieties and leaders shift sharply toward centralized rule. Arrogance breeds obsequiousness and corruption among officials. Local administration, which ordinarily has little scope for maneuver, becomes stultified. Personalized ties and nepotism, which threaten bureaucratic efficiency even in normal times, thrive in periods of overcentralization.

East Asian societies differ in their historical experience with establishing counterweights to the forces that lead to a breakdown and in the presence of either Marxism-Leninism or liberalism as an ideal modern ideology. Under Mao Zedong the combination of Marxism-Leninism, exceptionally weak intermediate levels of government, and prestigious revolutionary authority accentuated the centralized forces that cause malfunctioning. In postwar Japan, the combination of a vacuum of authority, a relatively favorable tradition of intermediate-level government, and liberalism established a strong balance against centralization.

Each of the three systems of thought evolves out of a rich and variegated regional heritage. The original systems of belief—Confucianism, which is over 2,500 years old, Christianity, which is 2,000 years old, and communism, which is just 150 years old—are subject to diverse interpretation. Adherents in earlier as well as contemporary times, and those who seek reform from within the tradition, find diverse meaning in the classical writings and core ideas of their creed. Alongside loyalists to the emperor and sticklers for long-established rituals stood Confucian restorationists, who sought to prolong the Mandate of Heaven by making officials more virtuous, and occasional Confucian rebels, who fought for the victory of a new emperor and a favorable turn of the dynastic cycle. Communist theorists and officials can be differentiated into dogmatic followers of Stalin or Mao, who resist the slightest challenge to previously unassailable doctrines, and pragmatists, who advocate revising theory until it fits the objective conditions of a single country's historical experience. Systems of thought must be seen as imposing constraints without eliminating all choices. Through the study of heritage, the constraints as well as the choices can be elucidated.

THE STUDY OF HERITAGE

Efforts by social scientists to dispense with the study of national heritage have met with failure. In the search for a common path to "civilization" during the nineteenth century, and to modernization or revolution during the twentieth, many belittled the enduring consequences of historical factors. Some assumed that national differences are of little or no consequence only to discover that class struggle and modernization assume unexpected forms in non-Western countries. Under these circumstances, political scientists introduced the concept of political culture to explain enduring orientations toward democracy or dictatorship, sociologists gravitated toward comparisons of traditional social structure to explain different outcomes of revolutionary and modernizing forces, and scholars working in Marxist-Leninist countries began to differentiate models of socialism based on national characteristics. Neither socialism nor capitalism is as all-embracing a category for interpreting a country's development as many once thought. The historical slate is not wiped clean, and particularly in East Asia, its effects are becoming widely visible.

East Asian countries stand out as glaring exceptions to earlier generalizations that were presumed to have universal applicability. The People's Republic of China, both under Mao Zedong at the time of the Great Leap Forward and the Cultural Revolution and under Deng Xiaoping in the era of reforms, defies many long-proclaimed "laws" for the socialist camp of nations. Japan appears as an exception to numerous assertions about industrialized countries. The confusion for Western-oriented generalizers only mounts when the two Koreas and the three "little Chinas" (Taiwan, Hong Kong, and Singapore) are added to the regional picture.

Not only is awareness rising of the continued significance of a country's heritage, there is also heightened acknowledgment that elements of that heritage can contribute to unusual dynamism in development. The way people interact at home, school, and their workplace, the way they view their government and their own society's place in the world, affects their rate of modernization. Even if, for a time, the foreign impact seems to be displacing more and more of the traditional behavior, a process of interaction is at work in which some

elements of tradition may be reasserted and may guide modernization in new directions. On the one hand, we find the peoples of East
Asia sharply divided into contrasting social systems labeled capitalist
and socialist. On the other hand, in the late twentieth century some
elements of a region-wide heritage are being credited as the common
denominator for a resurgence that ignores national boundaries.

The East Asian heritage has rebounded spectacularly. Over the
previous century there were times when it seemed to be succumbing
to outside forces. First, it was besieged by nineteenth-century imperialism accompanied by many of the trappings of Western civilization.
Then homegrown Japanese militarism sought to impose throughout
the region a distorted version of the common heritage. Finally, in the
aftermath of World War II, the region faced on two sides a new and
formidable threat to traditional practices. Nonetheless, neither under
Mao Zedong's radical brand of socialism nor in the early years of the
postwar Occupation of Japan, when foreign control over that island
country was asserted for the first time, was there the general extinc-
tion of national traditions that some had thought possible. Neither
monolithic socialism implanted in China by zealots anxious to root
out "the four olds" nor foreign-imposed, democratizing reforms followed by frenzied modernization in Japan prevented the reassertion
of a vital regional heritage. By the 1980s that heritage, adapted to
modern requirements and guided by carefully selected policies, had
made this region the most dynamic in the world.

In the late nineteenth century and the first half of the twentieth
century, the image within East Asia of both national and region-wide
Confucian traditions declined sharply. This intellectual heritage and
model of social conduct was exposed, along with all the other customary ways of thought throughout the world, as no match for the scientific approach disseminated from the West. From the 1860s to
1880s, and even more in the ultranationalist atmosphere of the 1930s
and early 1940s, Japan turned to its nativist Shinto traditions as the
symbol of the part of its past that leaders insisted should be kept alive
in the midst of modernization. After World War II Shinto nationalism was discredited, leaving a vague concept of "feudalism" as the
negative term for the social relations inherited from the past, which
the democratic movement asserted must still be swept away in Japan's
rush to modernity. In many types of social relations and attitudes the
past lived on in Japan, but it was only gradually, in the 1960s and
especially the 1970s, that these came to be viewed in a somewhat positive light. The label "Confucian" was not widely revived. Instead a
more general term, "Nihonjin-ron" ("theory of being Japanese") became popular.

Chinese were slower to turn against Confucianism, but their process of repudiation lasted longer and provoked more violent emotions. In the first decade of the 1900s, while the Ch'ing dynasty tottered on its last legs, reforms severed the all-important knot binding education in the Confucian classics to imperial examinations and official appointment. After the Revolution of 1911 sentiment against Confucianism mounted, symbolized by the May Fourth Movement in 1919 with its strident rejection of classical learning. Marxism-Leninism began to spread in the 1920s, and after the Revolution of 1949, required political education in its orthodox teachings did battle with persistent Confucian values in the daily lives of the people. The most intense anti-Confucian campaigns came in the peak years of Maoist revolutionary radicalism. Among the onslaughts were attacks in the mid-1960s on the "four olds" and again almost a decade later as part of the anti–Confucius anti-Lin Biao campaign. Only after Mao Zedong's death was a more tolerant image of Confucianism gradually revived. Even so, the notion that vestiges of China's presocialist and precapitalist past largely represent a negative, "feudal" tradition resounds as the dominant message in the 1980s.

In Korea Confucianism was perceived as an obstacle to modern development, as in China, and as an external tradition inconsistent with mounting nationalism and associated with obsequiousness before the foreign Chinese culture. In the decades of Japanese rule, efforts to impose a particular tradition of state Shintoism and imperial rule contrasted to the more tolerant universalistic Confucian traditions. After 1945 a more benevolent attitude toward Confucian traditions mixed with elements of liberalism prevailed in South Korea.

In the 1970s and 1980s writings on East Asia in the West, the Soviet Union, Japan, and China were, in different degrees, becoming more positive in their interpretation of the Confucian heritage. In the West this trend resulted from the continued efforts of sinologists long impressed with the humanistic values of traditional China, from the new cult of Japan among social scientists and journalists, and from the early comparative impressions of the region-wide economic resurgence. In the Soviet Union the shock of the Sino-Soviet split led, by the early 1970s, to a search for the distinctive characteristics of Chinese history. Despite the initial negative cast, an expanded range of historical topics was studied in an increasingly objective manner. By the 1980s, Soviet authors were also discovering the positive consequences of Japanese culture. Within Japan, leaders of the Liberal Democratic Party were affirming more nationalistic goals for education about the positive and distinctive qualities of Japanese history. In the PRC, Chinese academics were holding annual conferences on

Confucianism. Interest in national and regional heritage was mounting in the 1980s.

By the end of the decade a counterreaction could also be detected. In both China and Japan it became obvious that beneficiaries of the existing system were justifying their opposition to reforms as consistent with national traditions. Chinese communist repression of democratic reform advocates and Japan's Liberal Democratic Party defenders of a political system awash in scandal faced new challenges.

The intensified demands for Westernization contain important correctives to existing problems, yet they do not alter the reality of a resilient regional heritage with the capacity to exert a profound influence on future developments.

The concept of heritage—even more so for a region than for a country—poses difficulties of interpretation. It threatens to be vague and all-encompassing. Any overview must somehow chart a course through the multisided, multidisciplinary, multicountry, and multiperiod demands of scholars with an interest in heritage.

One set of publications treats the philosophical and religious thinking, including the principles of Confucianism, that guides social behavior; this is the intellectual side of heritage. Another approach focuses on the social psychology of personality traits and individual-group relations; this is the national-character side of heritage at the level of the individual. There is also the related side of educational transmission at the level of the classroom. Elsewhere, one finds a literature on corporate management and the principles of business organization; this is the practical, business side of heritage at the level of the work-group. One type of reader may be familiar with writings on bureaucracy and the art of government, as seen for example in the administrative guidance given to the society. Another type of reader may follow the ethnographic, micro-level studies of family and neighborhood. These are the community and government sides of heritage both at the level of the settlement group and at the level of the state. Compounding this variety of coverage, there is the problem of tracing in detailed historical treatises how these elements of the East Asian heritage have evolved over many centuries among three distinct populations and, more recently, seven separate states. The disciplines of anthropology, economics (and management), history, politics, psychology, religion (and philosophy), and sociology all seek explanations for aspects of this rich heritage.

Simple answers highlighted in popular books seek to cut through this web of complexity. It is tempting, no matter how ambiguous the evidence, to pinpoint one deep-seated philosophical principle (perhaps a theme in the teachings of Confucius) that induces compliance, one persistent character trait (perhaps from techniques of childhood socialization) that encourages individuals to be diligent, or one pervasive organizational device (usually present in labor-management relations) that leads to the mass mobilization of people. Scholarship demands more: it requires us to examine the multisided character of heritage and to interpret commonalities against a backdrop of diversity. Contemporary characteristics must be seen not as straightforward manifestations of the past, but as part of a changing historical context. Assertions about guiding attitudes should be supported with explanations of how these attitudes came to be displayed in behavior. Our wariness of oversimplification, however, should not deter us from setting a direct course toward the goal of identifying the common regional heritage and its main lines of variation.

THE CONFUCIAN INTELLECTUAL TRADITION

Ideas about how people should behave and how societies should be organized have become associated with many widely cited concepts in the philosophical literature of this region. Perhaps the most all-embracing concept is that of the Way (*dao* or *tao*). This is the perception of some natural order of existence. The idea of the Way implies a linkage between nature and human society: balance and harmony in the former serve as a model for the latter. In turn, there is frequent need (in the minds of some this was reinforced by natural omens) to restore balance and harmony to human society. The utopian Chinese concept of the great harmony (*ta-t'ung*) heightened awareness of the gap between ideal and reality. Sometimes the Way is referred to as the Way of Heaven (*t'ien*). The word "heaven" did not necessarily mean an external force responsible for the existence of the world, or that element of reality capable of determining events on earth. To Mencius, the fourth century B.C. disciple of Confucius who popularized the concept of the Mandate of Heaven, it meant nature or the ethical cosmic order in total. F. W. Mote explains that this makes man the central measure of everything and is an uncompromising statement of humanism. Above all, the Way represents an idealized view of how things should be set right when conditions are less satisfactory than usual.

Depending on how the Way was interpreted, this philosophy could become a force for conservatism or for radicalism. In China it at times became a rationale for rebellion against an emperor who failed to follow the Way and "lost" the Mandate, but more generally it was a force for conformity, to alter behavior in order to make it more consistent with the Way. In Japan, by Tokugawa times, the "way of the warrior" (*bushido*) had come to be seen as a class-specific branch of the Way, and it defined in considerable detail the ideals to which samurai were expected to conform. Japanese placed even greater stress than Chinese on preserving group harmony (*wa*) and fulfilling one's duty (*giri*) and also on open-ended obligations to those to whom one owes an unrepayable debt (*on*). Chinese obligations tended to become less personal and more abstract, as symbolized by the performance of rituals in accord with propriety (*li*); yet in China, too, there have been highly visible examples of extreme personal obligation overruling other considerations.

Among the many caretakers of the Way, the ruler was foremost. His subjects owed him loyalty (*chung*). This implied adherence to social norms and required more specific forms of devotion and sacrifice among Japanese samurai, who were in direct contact with their feudal lords. Duties were not always so one-sided as to preclude responsibility for advising the ruler on how to act in accord with the Way. A powerful motif in China was to rise to official position and through political service to advise the emperor. The concept of benevolence (*jen*) called on those with power to concern themselves with the well-being of others. The Way implied a society tempered by loyalty, propriety, benevolence, and a concern for harmony. Stability would rest more on moral suasion—and community maintenance of behavioral standards—than on coercion.

Another motivating force in East Asian thought was the ideal of the superior man (*chun tzu*). In principle, this was not an ideal restricted to a small nobility, but a goal with at least some applicability to each individual. Implied in this concept is the perfectibility of man. At the very least, human nature did not stand in the way of self-improvement, and in mainstream Confucian thought it was seen as a positive force. Rather than otherworldly fatalism, this philosophy called upon human volition, knowledge, and courage to achieve superior behavior. The focus was on the individual, within the context of the family or the teacher-student relationship, to seek self-improvement through self-examination and corrective action. In China and Korea the ideals of good behavior were conveyed in abstract themes associated with the concept of righteousness (*i*). In Japan the ideals tended to be identified with one's attitude toward one's actions, imprecisely conveyed in the term spirit (*seishin*). In all three countries popular currents of thought stressed making one's mind pure. This required both mental adroitness and powers of concentration, some of which were encouraged by Zen meditation, and the acquisition of knowledge. The concept of wisdom (*chih*) stressed rationality, education, and informed judgment. To achieve this state, Chinese and Koreans were admonished, they should learn the lessons of history, the ultimate source of authority in social issues.

Confucian thought kept expanding through syncretic forces. The original teachings of Confucius were reinterpreted by his followers over several centuries in the Warring States era of intense philosophical competition. This was followed by the amalgam of Taoist, Legalist, and Confucian ideas—known as Han Confucianism—that served the centralized needs of a great empire.

Elements of Buddhism were later incorporated into official thought in China, accompanying the aristocratic splendor of the T'ang dynasty and obliging Confucian teachings to expand their concern with life-cycle rituals to counter the glitter of Buddhism. Mass dissemination of Confucian rituals and values gained new force in the Sung dynasty following a commercial and administrative opening of the country to mass participation. The ascendancy of Neo-Confucianism from Sung times represented a new wave of thinking about the philosophical roots of behavior. Other amalgamations reflected the interaction of non-Chinese conquest dynasties, most prominently the powerful centralizing force of the Mongols in the Yuan dynasty. In the late imperial period, especially the late Ming and the Ch'ing, there were additional accommodations to a more mobile, cosmopolitan population, especially to new interregional commercially based interest groups. The actual contents of Confucian thought were gradually changing over more than 2,000 years, but the basic concerns with family, education, service to society, state-supervised harmony based on ethical conduct, and individual self-cultivation persisted.

In Japan, Confucian thought reached a peak in two periods: (1) first, in the initial wave of borrowing from T'ang China, when the fundamental principles of Confucianism were accepted and at the same time twisted to conform to the greater localism and hereditary officeholding in Japan; and (2) later, when Neo-Confucianism was considered to be a powerful force for legitimating stable, central government in the early Tokugawa period when warlord military bands were in the process of being converted to peacetime bureaucracies. In both periods Confucianism became identified with a need to strengthen central control and to maintain previous forms of hierarchy.

THE FORCES OF CONFUCIANIZATION

Practices identified with Confucian ideals spread among the populace of China, Japan, and Korea. The following chapters describe how this occurred. Despite variations from country to country, we can identify important commonalities.

The diffusion of Confucianism occurred gradually, through state sponsorship, from the top down. The process was syncretic, not to the exclusion of other religious and philosophical traditions, although some were eradicated as a threat or channeled by state suppression. The process accelerated as the society became more bureaucratized, literate, and entrepreneurial. Confucianism, as we are familiar with it, reflects the interests of the educated bureaucrat, the operator of a family farm, and even the director of a merchant house. Because the needs of centralized state building, education, economic activity, and corporate solidarity persist in modern times, demands for modernization may reinforce its impact. This continuity is easy to overlook because a period of transition dramatizes the removal of old institutions which had come to symbolize Confucianism in practice.

Rituals and texts provide the most obvious evidence of Confucian beliefs. Rulers observe annual ceremonies, to the point that their lives may become highly regimented. The spread of specified rituals associated with family life to wide segments of the population indicates the extent of Confucianization. Yet, even when Confucian texts are read by large numbers of people, their rituals may remain a mixture of various traditions. In modern times, as the texts are discarded and the rituals become simplified or abandoned, the attitudes associated with them may endure.

In the final analysis, as much as one must resort to measures of ritual behavior and familiarity with texts to estimate the degree of Confucianization, the true measure of its impact is in the extent to which people's lives are guided by Confucian ideals. Even if the point is reached at which consciousness of the Confucian roots of particular attitudes has faded, the continued presence of such attitudes can be taken as a sign in a single country or a region that the tradition endures. It is how individuals respond to family, school, community, workplace, and the state that best informs us of their worldview.

STEREOTYPES OF INDIVIDUALS

Popular stereotypes can help to draw attention to qualities associated with individuals across much of East Asia. Of course, even the most widely disseminated stereotypes fail to fit some people under any circumstances, and many people in particular periods of a country's development. Region-wide stereotypes obscure variations among countries and local variations within countries. They seem to apply least

well to twentieth-century China—because of structural barriers resulting largely from governmental policies, one suspects—but perhaps
on an individual level best of all to overseas China. To the extent that
they apply as generalizations, they need to be explained: What historical conditions gave rise to them? What contemporary structures sustain them? What countervailing tendencies threaten to undermine
them? We list here many stereotypes for the East Asian region as a
preliminary step toward answering questions of this sort about them.

A number of qualifications may help to keep our list of stereotypes
in perspective. Descriptions of East Asian regional or national character tend to focus on Japanese more than on other peoples, on older
rather than younger generations of our time, on men more than on
women (although the gap in public life has shown signs of narrowing), on educated and securely employed persons more than on mar-
ginally employed, and on periods of rapid economic growth. (It
should at the same time be kept in mind that the most traditional
forms of behavior not directly dependent on upward mobility are
more often associated with women and with less-educated, rural residents, who have been least affected by rapid growth.) Descriptions
of traits are considered to have wider applicability than to the groups
they seem to fit best, particularly when seen in a worldwide comparative perspective.

East Asians are said to be characterized by self-denial, frugality,
patience, fortitude, self-discipline, dedication, rote learning, and aptitude for applied sciences and mathematics. They are thought to ex-
cel in tasks that require unstinting effort over a long period in which
gratification or reward is delayed. Persistent devotion to memorization or repetition of a task finally results in a skill becoming well-
learned. This predisposition prevails whether the skill is mathemati-
cal computation, musical performance, artistic craftsmanship, or
applied industrial technology.

Our impressions of how youths are socialized reinforce these stereotypes. In the formative years, the child is taught to be dependent,
to submerge the self within the group, and to learn to serve the
group. He or she learns to conceive of the self not as an abstraction,
but in reciprocal terms appropriate to specific relationships. There is
no independent ideal of an individual prepared to conquer a succession of worlds. Instead, one's identity is changeable, depending on
the others who are present. Linguistically, in Japanese, this flexibility
is reflected in the many terms employed to designate "I" and "you."
In the countries of East Asia individualism is portrayed negatively, as
a cause of selfishness and anarchy—as a barrier to the achievement
of the goals of the community or the state. In China the Marxist-

Leninist critique of bourgeois individualism along with structural support for the work organization reinforces the anti-individualist strains of Confucian thought.

Following a family upbringing that downplays individualism, years of schooling assume great importance for inculcating East Asian habits of behavior. The school insists on diligence—intensive rote learning often accompanied by chanting in unison or regurgitation of detailed knowledge on tests. Parents and teachers make the child conscious of difficult examinations far in the future to which preparation must be geared. Moral education, whether Confucian or communist, teaches the ideals of self-sacrifice and self-cultivation within a context of hierarchical relationships. Individuals grow up mindful of the approved lessons of history, proud of the glorified achievements of their country's past, alerted to the future obstacles to collective and individual goals, pessimistic about the prospects for easy success, and convinced that extraordinary commitment is necessary to prevail. Competition reaches a peak; virtually all students who show promise are drawn into the frenzy. While observers have noted pathological consequences, and some of the material memorized seems to be of little long-term value, the attitudes formed have lasting significance.

Are individuals inspired or coerced into the self-sacrifice and endurance expected of them? Observers are divided in their answers, often impressionistic rather than based on systematic study, to questions about motivation. Modern Westerners tend to view with suspicion the means employed to develop East Asian character traits; they place a high price on the resulting losses to the individual. Their criticisms often assume that the norm of humanity is an innately self-serving individual, who is happiest when he is least restricted. Contemptible mechanisms of a repressive nature crush man's natural instincts. While granting that these mechanisms may not be direct coercion by agents outside of the family, the Western critics find a more subtle inculcation of fear or irrationality. According to this perspective, fear normally takes the form of intense mental pressures that induce guilt or shame, leaving their victims handicapped in expressing their spontaneity and creativity. The result, it is assumed, must be a rather unhappy, tension-ridden conformist. Fear of group displeasure and ostracism may also be accompanied by the direct threat of force, associated especially with prewar militaristic and postwar communist ideologies.

Along with fear, irrationality figures into Western perceptions of the causes of conformity. An inability to think clearly and identify one's self-interest is widely ascribed to otherworldly religions, which insist that earthly pleasures be subordinated to the prescribed steps necessary to achieve salvation or to appease supernatural forces, whether gods or ancestors. By extension, the same reasoning may be applied to this-worldly irrationality in the form of a belief system that glorifies behavior on behalf of the nation or other entity that does not serve the self-interest of the individual. Whatever the explanation, many Westerners take for granted that a high price is exacted in eliciting the personal behavior found in East Asia. Even when the behavior is admired, those who exhibit it may be pitied.

Other observers see a different set of forces at work in the emergence and persistence of stereotypical East Asian character traits. The root of the matter is not fear or irrationality—at least, no more than in most societies—but a different set of assumptions and rewards to guide behavior. Lacking a concept of original sin, Confucian philosophy professes optimism about the perfectibility of man, whether human nature is seen as basically good or bad. It takes a positive outlook on the family's and teacher's ability to guide an individual into seeking to serve the family's interests. The individual is not sacrificing but fulfilling himself by learning to cooperate. Parents teach children, largely through positive reinforcement, to find gratification through long-term undertakings in which great effort must be invested. They learn to feel moral through self-control.

Historical factors led to the character traits observed in East Asia. Through a long period of Chinese history—in some matters for 2,000 years and in others for at least most of the past millennium—ordinary peasants could buy and sell land, participate in nearby market transactions, and aspire to education that gave some opportunity to prepare for nationwide examinations and possible appointment to public office. This opportunity structure contrasts sharply with the conditions for large numbers in Europe, especially serfs and, in some periods, nonaristocrats in general. In Japan, while the framework of a closed elite class persisted, the opportunity structure improved markedly in the Tokugawa era. Hayami Akira has coined the expression the "industrious revolution" to describe the changing work habits of ordinary Japanese by the early nineteenth century. Such historical explanations suggest that individual character traits need not be mysticized into a kind of unchanging national character or dismissed as an outcome of seemingly repressive forces.

Japanese are not model citizens able to adopt only what is best for their own lives and for their society. In the 1980s many examples could be found of Japanese deviations from the ideal. Although they led the world in life expectancy, the Japanese often exhibited behavior that seemed to disregard health needs. Smoking rates remained among the highest in modernized countries, especially as teenagers—

including even larger numbers of girls—began to light up. Fast-food outlets were quickly giving Japanese local commercial centers an American appearance, although their products (however convenient) posed a threat to Japan's dietary advantage. In education, glaring shortcomings were also in evidence. Despite widespread recognition of the importance of learning English, Japanese children who returned with an excellent command of the language after living abroad were routinely allowed to forget their English. Schools made no provision for maintaining conversational skills, and parents feared ostracism or bullying of their child if nonconforming behavior were manifested. The craze for mindless comic books among youth of all ages (to be sure, relatively harmless compared to diversions in other nations) also seemed out of place in a society in need of well-informed citizens. After only a decade of educational revival, Chinese leaving for science graduate programs abroad already seemed to be challenging Japanese students in their ability to analyze international problems. While these problems of Japanese life may not seem to be as serious as problems in other modernized countries, they are indications that Japan does not have a monopoly of successful strategies and is not a sure bet to lead the world in an age of knowledge-oriented, internationalized, and healthful life-styles. East Asian individuals may yet face an environment in which less conformist and more creative responses will become the key to success.

STEREOTYPES OF GROUP RELATIONS

Individual traits are learned in the context of groups. The willingness of individuals to subordinate themselves to the group helps determine what they will learn from the group. Especially the family, the school, and the workplace (or rural community) shape the individual's development.

East Asian group members are noted for the following qualities: group orientation, acceptance of authority, deference, dependence, conflict avoidance, interest in harmony, seniority consciousness, and dutifulness. More specific manifestations of these qualities are found in various types of groups. Within the family, East Asians are famous for filial piety, ancestor reverence, patriarchal authority, female subordination, respect for the elderly, intergenerational continuity, long-term planning, and fear of collective dishonor. These characteristics are commonly lumped together as "familism" or the extraordinary preoccupation with family solidarity and interests. Within the workplace, East Asians have become identified with enterprise paternalism, lifetime employment, organized recruitment from schools and communities, company spirit, seniority wages, and enterprise unions. Analogues have been discerned between these group characteristics of modern enterprises and both family and rural community organizational traits.

Group members are expected to make a commitment more exclusive and binding than in other societies. Whether a new bride or a new salaried employee, a member is chosen with care based on clearly stated criteria. Community sentiment stands in the way of easy departure from the organization, with the possible exception of those who have joined for a short-term or trial period. Even in nonfamily groups relations are relatively diffuse; the organization may make broad claims on its members without worrying about contractual agreements that require members to perform only specified tasks.

Groups organized in this manner have the potential to make long-range plans and to adapt quickly to changing circumstances by redirecting labor and revising goals. They count on a carefully chosen, loyal membership or work force to make them competitive. Once in the organization, new members find themselves deeply embedded in hierarchical relationships, where business and personal obligations overlap. This overlap can be traced back to the tradition of family businesses.

The classical Chinese family (*chia*) and the modern Japanese enterprise (*kaisha*) popularly epitomize region-wide characteristics. This is not to say that the Japanese family (*ie*) and the modern Chinese enterprise (*danwei*) do not differ in substantial ways, but that the traits for which this region is best known bridge the obvious differences. Imperial China glorified filial piety, absolute patriarchal authority, and ancestor veneration. Family loyalty took precedence in virtually all situations. Family-centered patterns formed the roots of modern developments. Contemporary large Japanese corporations provide secure employment for the relatively well-educated males who are offered jobs on the preferred track. Hired directly out of school, most male employees of large firms remain with one firm until the formal retirement age. Wages are based largely on education and seniority. A paternalistic ideology equates enterprise loyalty with family solidarity. The extension of kinship terms to non-kin organizations can be found in many contexts.

Westerners are quick to condemn the extreme signs of individual submission to the group, such as the samurai's willingness in premodern Japan to die in defense of his lord's honor, or the requirement that the *danwei* approve decisions about marriage, divorce, and childbirth in contemporary China. On the whole, they criticize the lack of recourse to individual rights as a way to limit group authority.

Nevertheless, they may also praise the concern shown for vulnerable group members, such as the elderly, within the family and the secure environment provided for most individuals.

Group solidarity combined with family farms may be attributed to natural conditions and deliberate state policies. The natural environment throughout much of East Asia permits rice farming based on intensive cultivation and a degree of community cooperation, especially in the allocation of water resources. The state, especially in recent centuries, sought to restrict intermediate organizations that could stand in the way of the family farm as the backbone of tax payments and civil order. Religious sects, landholding organizations, and other groupings were usually tolerated only if they operated on a small scale.

Educational methods in East Asia, past and present, are noted for their stress on following a well-charted, but demanding, course of study. Ultimately the individual is responsible for his own learning, although he is made aware of role models who have followed the same path, he is placed under the strict authority of the teacher, and he is mastering the basics in concert with numerous students throughout his country. The classroom is a potent force for combining performance with conformity. Stress on moral education and rote learning heightens its effects as a socializing force. In China communist political education carried to an extreme the school's demands to transform the individual in the interests of the group. In Japan it is said that the school takes children who have been indulged by their mothers and teaches them the need to subordinate their interests to the group. The high prestige of formal education increases its effectiveness in socialization.

The aura of Confucian values looms high over East Asia. Observers around the world have come to view this region as an imposing sociological phenomenon in which human relations have been molded to maximize collective action. Two related images appear before us. First, the East Asian concern for family and community means that individuals work hard to satisfy the expectations of the group—to prevent others from losing face. This may require them to submerge their individual yearnings in the interest of harmony and the pursuit of collective goals. Second, the East Asian tradition of central imperial authority or hierarchical samurai loyalty establishes a framework for concerted national action. On the international arena—whether in forging export markets or in mobilizing for war—the centralized potential of these vertically organized societies produces a formidable adversary.

Confucian Influences Broadly Construed

Confucius' writings and those of his early disciples are no more a guide to the practical application of ideas construed as Confucian 2,500 years after his death than are the writings of Greek philosophers or the Bible a guide to modern Western behavior or the writings of Marx a guide to contemporary socialism. While partisans in ongoing debates about the fundamental meaning of a system of thought or religion may take a narrow approach to the ideas of its founders, our concern is with a broader set of ideas that came to be identified as the living tradition. These are ideas about the individual's behavior within society, about organization into groups, and especially about social institutions such as the family and the government. We learn about them as much through the study of how the society functioned as through writings detailing correct forms of behavior.

In East Asia any effort to isolate Confucian teachings from other influences on social relations faces an obstacle not found when analyzing societies in the West and the North. Religions for almost all people were not exclusive. One could simultaneously follow Confucian, Buddhist, Taoist, or Shintoist practices, varying the choice according to the situation. Recourse to Taoist or Shintoist customs in order to harmonize daily life with natural and supernatural forces, to Buddhist mourning ceremonies to give reassurance about the complexities of death, and to Confucian precepts to guide social relationships did not arouse accusations of religious heresy. Confucian principles often became part of an eclectic approach to life, not easily dissociated from the other intellectual influences.

Certain social relationships and social institutions constituted the Confucian sphere of influence. There were areas much discussed by the intellectual figures in the Confucian tradition and readily labeled by contemporaries and historians alike as the products of a Confucian civilization. While, depending on the country and the period, we might find some institutions difficult to classify as Confucian or non-Confucian, there is a core that most fully embodies this heritage, especially in the final centuries of the premodern era. The principal institutions in which Confucian values were manifested include the family, the educational system, and the government. There are other levels in which Confucian values operated, but in which the predominance of these values appears to be more controversial; three that figure into our discussion are the community organization, the workplace (in which many were employed for commerce or handicrafts), and the organization of members of the elite. These different levels of organization, often associated with different social classes, help to account for types of Confucianism. We explore variations in the tradition not from the point of view of rival intellectual currents, but from the background of different institutional settings.

The Worst and the Best of East Asia

Personality traits and institutions, like modern technology, can be adapted for good or evil. The individualism associated with Western countries leads both to extraordinary feats of creativity and to severe problems of crime and social deviance. The mobilization methods that drove Soviet citizens into labor camps, collective farms, and other coercive institutions may have had some short-term positive effect on the wartime response that contributed greatly to the defeat of Hitler. In the past and the present, East Asian characteristics have been identified with both great achievements of mankind and notorious injustices or failings.

Individual self-sacrifice for the good of the group is common throughout the world, but in Japan it took the exaggerated forms of altruistic suicide through harakiri and kamikaze pilots. In the second half of the twentieth century much is still expected of Japanese gangsters, Chinese student activists in campaigns, and other East Asians to prove their devotion to the group. While female subordination is characteristic of agrarian societies, China stood out for high rates of female infanticide and the painful practice of footbinding. Authoritarian states are no rarity in world history, yet for hundreds of years before the late nineteenth century East Asia was remarkable for the comprehensiveness as well as the durability of such regimes. Kim Il Sung's unbridled control over North Korea for four decades, and his efforts to pass control on to his son, may be considered an overlay of regional traditions and Stalinist borrowing.

Contrast these symbols of notoriety with the no less significant glories of an often humane regional civilization. China's imperial examination system engaged millions of boys and men at most times over the past 1,000 years or longer in intensive learning and contemplation of the principles and history of social relations. In modern times the extraordinary aspirations for learning throughout the region can be linked to the attitudes spawned by this Chinese system. Japan's extraordinary craftsmanship of silks and swords, to name only two of the best-known products, was an indication of the pride in one's firm that is highly developed in contemporary quality-control circles. East Asian history abounds with evidence of respect (but not full-fledged rights) for the common man—the farmer who works in the field—

and perhaps the dignity bestowed from this starting point in perceiving human relations accounts, above all, for the mass participation in modern development at an early date.

Combinations of the Three Systems

Modern Japan received a massive transfusion of liberalism through the postwar Occupation and the persistence of a democratic political system. This shifting of the balance away from the hierarchical, family-centered, and collectivist side of the Confucian tradition served the needs of modernization. An emphasis on democratic participation has lessened the authority of the state and its leaders. It has made education more creative. Individualism is not as extensive as in other highly modernized, capitalist societies, but the postwar balance (shifting further to the side of liberalism through the effects of modernization) has proven remarkably successful.

In Maoist China communist policies reinforced elements of the Confucian heritage that led to one-sided development. Hierarchy pressed upon democracy. Collectivism left little room for individualism. Behind the facade of efficient planning and formal bureaucracy existed the reality of personal deals based on connections. A society of *guanxi* and backdoor networks combined the shortcomings of Soviet socialism under Brezhnev and Ch'ing dynasty Confucianism. Elites, drawing on political connections, traded favors. Market mechanisms were so badly weakened that arbitrary administrative fiat reached into almost all corners of life. The Chinese communists assailed many traditions, but ended up relying on collectivist, family-centered, community-oriented, nepotistic, and personalized associations to an extraordinary degree. Even so, freed from some old bonds and given, for a short time, a stable environment in which to achieve, Chinese in the 1950s brought immense talent to education, public service and other spheres of life. Socialism mobilized the Chinese people in colossal numbers and achieved some successes, especially in the periods 1949–58 and 1962–65, but for more than a decade prior to the December 1978 reforms it also stifled the great strengths of the Confucian tradition—a thirst for education, enthusiasm for entrepreneurship, a channeling of talent into government service. The Maoist program countered some weaknesses visible in China prior to 1949, especially the inequity of land distribution and the inadequacy of public order, but it trampled on the essence of the Confucian heritage. Meanwhile, it strengthened elements associated with that heritage—particularly collectivism and reliance on personal connections—with negative consequences for modernization.

Reform socialism has, at its best, been more sympathetic to tradition. In contrast with the Cultural Revolution, it supports entrepreneurship on family farms and small-scale individual or family enterprises and it favors selection of a meritocratic intelligentsia through rigorous schooling and testing. The results for the economy were stunning through much of the 1980s. Yet, the reform side has continued to face opposition from advocates of an orthodox brand of socialism akin to Brezhnev's post-Stalin centralized system. The intelligentsia face restrictions through political criteria, and entrepreneurship in industry remains peripheral to centralized planning. Confucian socialism is still struggling against orthodox socialism to carve out its own style of "socialism with Chinese characteristics." In the absence of firm evidence that a high level of modernization results from the current combination, it is at least arguable that elements of liberalism may be essential to establish a long-term balance for continued modernization. After the repression of student demonstrations in June 1989, the danger was great that socialist elements would stand in the way of liberal ones. The Japanese gains from postwar reforms may be relevant to other Confucian systems that are making the transition to a higher level of modernization.

Modernization and cultural diffusion in an increasingly interdependent world diminish regional differences. Building on the best in one country's past is not sufficient; the ability to borrow and adapt the best of all regions is becoming more vital to success in world competition. New combinations will appear. As countries that have borrowed most heavily since the mid-nineteenth century and managed to retain many of their own traditions, East Asian states may have the most to teach us about the possible combinations that result. To help us to understand these options, we should gain a clearer awareness of the contrasting starting points in regional and national development along with the impact of various forms of capitalism or socialism on each. In our introductory study we cannot carry this analysis to its conclusion. We cannot even delineate the main lines of variation with the subtlety and qualifications that many who are knowledgeable about one region or another would prefer. What we can do is to highlight some major variations that merit comparative study. Table 3 is our necessarily simplified attempt to draw attention to certain variations as a first step toward deeper analysis.

PROJECTED CHANGES IN THE THREE REGIONAL SYSTEMS

In the next decades we can anticipate increasing innovation in each of the systems and heightened competition among them as well as among separate countries. Facing more dire straits, the socialist countries are showing the most inclination to reform in the 1980s. Western capitalist countries, especially the United States, are also gradually awakening to the need to reform in some spheres. We can add to this picture the uncertainty in each East Asian country despite recent economic successes. China's economic reforms remain incomplete and not matched by major political or ideological reorganization. South Korea suddenly shifted to the course of democratic elections and party politics, while North Korea faces a succession problem (such a problem led to the collapse of radical socialism in its neighbors). Japan is being pressured to open its society to massive increases in imports, new leisure orientations, and "internationalization" of thinking, while its personalized politics caused the LDP to stumble in 1989.

Each system has its own characteristic manner of change. The socialist system changes through a coalition of reform-minded leaders, aware of the overall needs of their country, and intellectuals or interest groups discontented with the overly centralized system in which they live. They must struggle against entrenched bureaucrats, whose departmental interests and personal privileges will be placed in jeopardy by the proposed reforms. Reforms come from above, and their success depends on whether the bureaucrats can be outflanked and replaced and whether the masses can be persuaded that the loss of guarantees and subsidies will be justified by the gain in material incentives and consumer orientation. A single leader, together with his major intellectual advisors and political allies, plays an enormous role in revitalizing a socialist society.

Western capitalist societies are more immediately responsive to public opinion. Bureaucratic interests are much weaker, creating the potential for great volatility in short-term policies while the basic system remains well protected by constitutional guarantees. Amateur government in the United States easily leads to cosmetic approaches to serious problems and a lack of leadership, but it also heightens the opportunity for flexibility. The decentralized intellectual community does not often succeed in persuading the masses, and elected officials oriented to the next election and the public opinion polls do not develop a well-thought-out plan of action.

East Asian societies have difficulty making reforms for other reasons. Bureaucrats are more secure, their positions based on high educational qualifications and professional competence. Public opinion is less fickle; it is more trusting of behind-the-scenes political maneuvering and paternalistic decision-making by a small group of officials. What is often missing is creative leadership. As a result of party and bureaucratic career patterns, emphasizing seniority and consensus-building, fresh ways of thinking do not readily rise to the surface.

Only in extreme conditions will there be a mass shift in the consensus within the governmental elite. Then the presence of experienced and able officials with mass acceptance of their leading role can result in rapid and effective change.

East Asian societies usually have the advantage of being able to carry out reform through their bureaucracies. This is reform through bureaucratic consensus, in contrast with the Soviet style of reform through vigorous leadership by one or a handful of leaders, or the Western method of public opinion appeals. The East Asian political system can break down, however, when a separate elite, based on military experience, diminishes the role of bureaucratic consensus. Mao's revolutionary elite, coming off its military victory in 1949, substituted Soviet principles of government plus the claim to superiority based on revolutionary purity gained over years of struggle. As a result, men with little education or experience, rising with factional support through the levels of a civilian bureaucracy, kept interfering with the governance of China. Military governments in Taiwan and South Korea were much more in conformity with regional traditions, but, mainly outside of economics, they adopted some policies that weakened their claim to legitimacy. Liberal ideals of participation from below coupled with the effects of rapid modernization are creating a climate for political reform in East Asia.

We can expect some convergence among the three approaches. The socialist system is responding to calls for more educated and competent bureaucrats who face more supervision and turnover. Decentralization and democratization are popular slogans. Voices in the United States are appealing for more professional government, attracting better people to public service and giving them a greater say in helping to make their country more competitive. In East Asia new signs of cooperation and pragmatism among opposition parties suggest that democratic alternatives will become more viable; although that process can be interrupted as it was in China.

Other signs of convergence among the three systems will, we believe, result from four factors: (1) modernization; (2) borrowing; (3) economic integration; and (4) internationalization of information and other aspects of life. Modernization is seen in urbanization, industrialization and the rise of the service and knowledge-oriented sectors, aging populations, and many other structural changes. Parallel to each other, countries are experiencing these modernizing changes and are coming to resemble each other more. There is every reason to expect this long-term process to continue and the three regional systems to become more alike. Nonetheless, the basic differences among them are likely to remain for the foreseeable future. They can affect rates of modernization and lead countries that are not competitive to speed up the process of convergence through borrowing.

The Japanese borrowed extensively from the liberal tradition under the Occupation reforms and in a less concentrated form throughout recent decades. China borrowed heavily from the socialist tradition in the 1950s and, more selectively and with less acknowledgment, from the liberal tradition in the 1980s. The Soviet Union now is easily overtaking China in the same reform direction. If recent trends continue, Western countries will be obliged to look seriously at ways to borrow from East Asia. We are entering an age of accelerated reexamination of existing institutions as governments carefully watch trade statistics, economic growth indicators, and other signs of comparative success and failure.

The growing economic integration around the world means that even when major reform programs are not the source of borrowing, continuous small-scale adjustments will bring us closer together. Large numbers of people will experience life under a foreign system. Companies will reorient production toward international markets and with an eye toward countering foreign penetration of their domestic markets. Consumer tastes will tend to converge. Whereas a decade ago China was little connected to international markets and the Soviets acted as if there were a capitalist bloc economy and a socialist bloc economy, these two major holdouts are now emphasizing trade with advanced capitalist economies. The level of economic integration is accelerating rapidly.

Perhaps the biggest change of all in the 1980s was the broadened flow of information across national boundaries. Beijing's "open door," Moscow's "glasnost'," and Tokyo's rapt interest in the "information society" are all signs of a new era. Through satellite television, home computers, videocassette recorders, and many innovations still on the horizon, we can expect to enjoy much greater access to information about the world around us in the near future. As a result, we will presumably become much more international in our outlook. In a nuclear age of space weapons we become more dependent on each other. As the "Cold War" psychology of knowing one's enemy through stereotypes gives way to more complex interactions, we most likely will become more alike in our knowledge and our attitudes.

Paradoxically, as the three major regions become more homogeneous, the impact of regional variations will have to be faced more directly than ever before. Regional variations are likely to take on added importance over the next decades. The forces that lead to more homogeneity also lead to more interest in the consequences of our differences. Integration of the world economy, uninterrupted flows of information, serious negotiations to reach disarmament agreements and forestall military conflicts are among the forces that make us aware of how much our differences matter. The world is moving from separate blocs to integration. Competition is accelerating. We are becoming more conscious of who our competitors are and how they succeed.

The key question for the next decades is not whether Western capitalism or Northern socialism will prevail, but whether the latter will remain distinct, and especially whether the former can compete with East Asian Confucian traditions. This will be the most serious nonmilitary challenge to the West and the North in modern history. Our goal should be not so much to win as to ensure that the gains are spread to all regions of the world and that the process of growing integration gives every nation a fair chance to compete. It will not be easy to set up a stable system that smooths this transition and to reorient our own thinking to improve our competitive chances.

Potential Effects of the Emergence of East Asia as a Leading Region

Western capitalist and especially Northern socialist traditions gave rise to complacency and arrogance, limiting the impetus for reform. There is ample reason to expect a similar result from East Asian Confucian traditions. Traditional Confucianism, especially in China, had this effect. China failed to look at the outside world and to note its advances. Japanese in the 1930s and early 1940s also succumbed to the hubris of identifying their own way of life as the model for East Asia and believing that it should be imposed by force. Willingness to believe in their own moral superiority was a factor also in China's Cultural Revolution, on both the individual and the national level. The classical image of the self-satisfied mandarin who was reaping the rewards of success for numerous years of concentrated study still has relevance today.

Will successful East Asian states and private interest groups prove themselves capable of statesmanship, compassion, and tolerance befitting world leaders? So far, humanistic and social science education in these countries does not seem sufficiently developed to prepare adequate numbers of people with these qualities. In none of these countries does scholarship on the contemporary world meet the highest international standards of objectivity and depth.

Another concern is the unsettled political climate of East Asia. Whereas the major powers in the West and North emerged victorious from World War II with secure boundaries and political systems, the countries of East Asia still face uncertainties about their future boundaries, political forms, and international standing. China awaits the return of Hong Kong and expects to regain Taiwan as well, but relies too much on intimidation to make this a welcome outcome. The two Koreas remain in limbo at a high state of tension. Japan has yet to take its rightful place as a world political force commensurate with its economic standing. It remains unclear what political conceptions will guide the increased international role of East Asian countries. Moreover, in comparison to the West, the divisions in outlook within this region seem more pronounced and intractable. How will regional economic integration be reflected in new political alignments? Deng Xiaoping's shift to an "open door" and "independent" foreign policy and Nakasone's reassertion of Japan's international role while relying on close ties with the United States are only the first steps toward a new international presence for this region.

A major strength of East Asian countries is their capacity to export. We can therefore expect that they will be a force in favor of shifting world competition from military to economic concerns. Although still to some extent protecting their own markets, they are likely advocates of open markets and of freer trade. On the whole, they will see themselves benefiting from new disarmament agreements between the two military superpowers. More than any other region, East Asia is likely to support greater world integration. China's current system will encounter many contradictions from these trends. Some time must pass before we can be confident that the deeply ingrained socialist pressures against an open society will be overcome, yielding a country that can compete successfully and can accept intellectuals as full political partners.

Politically we must be concerned about the impact of differences between East Asian and Western traditions on international relations. East Asians may seek to temper competition with the guidance of a central hand. They could become a force for a more centralized world order. Yet, in the near future, divisions within the region and the gap between the aspirations of China's leaders and the country's level of modernization will delay any prospect of a Confucian consensus. In the long run, such a consensus would dramatically challenge long-standing Western assumptions about the system of states.

On a world scale, Confucianism may prove insufficiently rigorous in opposing the hegemony of one country or one ruling elite. Abuse of power, corruption, insufficient circulation of political elites, excessive demands for loyalty, are all characteristic of East Asian history. To a degree uncommon in the West, they may permeate assumptions about future international relations and threaten democratic institutions at home.

Problems of adjusting to the rise of East Asia will be increasingly noticeable in the West and the North. We will learn to question our own methods more and to pay much more attention to the world around us. There will be intense pressure to root out inefficiencies in our own societies, not excluding the indifferent quality of political leadership that has often plagued our response to problems. Renewed attention will also be directed toward our children and how well they are served by family, school, mass media, and other institutions. The Gorbachev reforms are but the beginning of a long-term process of reexamination in both socialist and capitalist countries. We must learn to be more competitive—at an individual level, as in the selection of candidates for upward mobility, at the enterprise level, and at the national level.

When the world perceived a division into capitalism and socialism and the two blocs were largely separated from each other, the pressures to compete—apart from in the military sphere—were rather faint. As we are becoming aware of a threefold division (temporary, if socialism should collapse) and a more integrated environment, the pressures to compete or decline are mounting precipitously. The rise of the East Asian region means the emergence of a competitive world on a scale rarely imagined in the past.

PART I

Confucianization
The Deepening of Tradition

Chapter 1

THE CHINESE FAMILY AND THE SPREAD OF CONFUCIAN VALUES

Patricia Ebrey

It is already well known that the Chinese state and the ruling class of literati had strong commitments to the values identified as Confucian in the Introduction. There have been many studies of the history of Confucian ideas, the history of education in the classics, the competition of Taoism, Legalism, and Buddhism for the allegiance of the elite, the importance of Confucian ideas in government organization and policy, the role of Confucian ideas in the ethos of the educated class, and the establishment of Confucianism as a state orthodoxy. Rather than retread that familiar ground, in this essay I examine a different historical issue, the process by which ordinary, uneducated Chinese came to share many Confucian values and practices. This process was, I believe, in one fundamental respect unlike the process of "Confucianization" in Korea and Japan, for much of what has come to be called "Confucian" by outside observers was in China simply the dominant set of social and cultural values, associated especially with the ruling class, and not an alien ideology that could be inculcated only by formal teaching.

In examining the "Confucianization" of ordinary people, I will concentrate largely on family practices and attitudes. Historically these were the social relations considered most relevant for the general population. Over the centuries officials and scholars who wished to promote proper social relations and thereby a harmonious society thought first of filial piety, brotherly harmony, wifely submission, and the ritually correct marriage and funeral practices that would instill them. Confucians did not call these attitudes and practices "Confucian social relations" but ethics and propriety (*wu-lun* and *li*); they saw their task not as "Confucianization" but as "transformation" (*hua*). Although not indifferent to more abstract Confucian virtues such as loyalty, sincerity, and integrity, they believed these values were best nurtured by attention to family behavior—a filial son will be a respectful subordinate and a loyal subject. As it says in the *Analects* (1.2), "Rare are those who are filial to their parents and deferential to elder brothers yet are fond of causing trouble to their superiors." More-over, Confucian scholars firmly believed that the need to cultivate family virtues was universal. Not everyone became a student or an official, but everyone had relatives whom they should treat in ethi-cally correct ways.

Traditional Confucian scholars are not alone in seeing family be-havior as the central feature in the moral life of ordinary people. Modern observers have also often explained the values of working people called "Confucian" in the Introduction by reference to the ideas and practices of the family system. For instance, Chinese will-ingness to work hard and defer rewards is often explained by refer-ence to family organization:

> The importance of the future generations can be seen by the anxiety of the parents to see their sons married, and to accumulate property for their children. With this in mind they work hard and live thriftily so that they can save some capital for the prospective children. They feel guilty when unusually good food is eaten or extra money is spent, not because they cannot afford these things, but because they want to have some-thing to leave to their descendants.[1]

Much the same point is often made about the behavior of Chinese emigrants:

> The Chinese peasant had a definite place in the temporal continuum of kin. . . . His world view was, therefore, historical and kin-centered, and in this context his industriousness and thrift served ends transcending his individual life. His primary goal was not individual salvation, but lin-eage survival and advancement. Protracted labor and extreme thrift were the means to these strongly sanctioned ends.[2]

Other scholars have argued that Chinese attitudes toward author-ity are based on father-son relationships: "From such a childhood pattern of relations with family authority seems to grow the adult concern for the presence of a strict, personalized, and unambiguous source of (political) authority who will impose order on potentially unruly peers and provide a clear source of guidance for all."[3] In the vocabulary of traditional Confucians, the mixture of fear, respect, and dependence that Solomon saw as characterizing sons' relations

[1] Martin C. Yang, *A Chinese Village: Taitou, Shantung Province* (New York: Columbia University Press, 1945), p. 45.

[2] G. William Skinner, *Chinese Society in Thailand: An Analytical History* (Ithaca: Cornell University Press, 1957), p. 92.

[3] Richard H. Solomon, *Mao's Revolution and the Chinese Political Culture* (Berkeley: University of California Press, 1971), p. 52.

toward their fathers had a name—filial piety—and they would not have been surprised to learn that filial sons make willing subjects.

Family values and practices are important also simply because they were shared. The relative success of the Chinese in the twentieth century in reestablishing a strong state, in improving educational institutions, in promoting new political ideas, and in mobilizing people for industrialization probably owes much to a strong core of common culture shared by nearly all Chinese, a very large component of which related to the family. Because Chinese already shared so many assumptions about human relations, it was possible to get them to share even more through compulsory education in standardized curricula.

A further advantage of focusing on family practices for an examination of "Confucianization" is that something can be said about them. It would be desirable to know what Chinese peasants over the centuries thought about rulers, officials, and government methods and whether these attitudes were in any specific sense "Confucian" before mass education in the twentieth century, but there is very little in the way of evidence. Whatever ideas they held would not have made much of a difference in their behavior. Nor did literati care much about what peasants thought so long as they were not rebellious or insubordinate. Ordinary people, however, were fully empowered to act in family roles, and thus the degree of "Confucianization" of family practices can be judged in terms of what they did, even without evidence of how they conceived of their actions.

Labeling Chinese family practices "Confucian" may seem to imply that they were a product of ideology that spread from the intellectual elite to ordinary peasants through indoctrination from above or imitation from below. This, I believe, is too simplistic a view. An underlying assumption of this paper is that values and attitudes did not spread simply by becoming known. Family relations can be analyzed into mental or cognitive elements (ways of categorizing people and beliefs about desirable behavior), but they did not spread simply by publicity. It is clear that the verbal formulation of social values was conveyed through many means (preaching, circulation of tracts, elementary education, and so on). Yet I would contend that the social, economic, and political structure played an enormously important part in making it possible for certain ideas to gain acceptance and adherence. For instance, filial piety, in its manifold meanings, was repeatedly urged in school texts, magistrates' lectures, popular religious tracts, plays, and so on. But would this barrage of indoctrination produce "filial" children in our society? Or, more to the point, did people in China become more filial over the course of history as the society was more thoroughly saturated with this message? The perceived need for this indoctrination and the degree that it achieved its purpose cannot be separated from the family as a political, economic, and religious unit. At least as important in fostering the practice of filial submission was the evolution of a patrilineal and patriarchal family structure throughout the society. This in turn depended on the development of the state and economy. Often a practice related to family life may have spread first simply as a ritual act or as an accommodation to a changing social, economic, or political environment. The belief that the practice was preferable may well have taken some time to gain hold.

To trace the development of the Chinese family, I will concentrate on a few key features that were widespread in all strata of society by the nineteenth century. I have organized these into two groups, those that made the Chinese family patrilineal and those that made it patriarchal. In sociological terms, these were the features that established the structure of the Chinese family.

PATRILINEALITY (concepts of descent and kinship)

a. Everyone had patrilineal surnames. These were crucial to their sense of identity.

b. Nearly everyone practiced patrilineal ancestor worship as a domestic rite and as a key feature in funerals and seasonal festivals (some also practiced it as a descent group rite).

c. There was widespread and very strong belief in the need for a male heir for anyone who reached adult status. Therefore everyone had to marry, and if no children were born turn to other strategies—concubines, adoption of relatives, or adoption of strangers—to acquire an heir.

d. Kinship obligations were recognized to a wide range of kin, asymmetrically distributed (heavily patrilineal). This was particularly expressed in mourning obligations.

e. Exogamy rules reinforced patrilineal concepts by forbidding marriage with anyone of the same surname.

PATRIARCHY (property and authority structures)

a. Property, especially land, was conceived largely as family property rather than individual property. Thus it belonged to the men of the family, and when it was divided sons received approximately equal shares.

b. Fathers had great legal authority over women and children, including the rights to marry children, sell them, and dispose of their labor. Especially important in this regard is that there was no real age of emancipation—the only issue was coresidence. Women in a household were jural minors, usually looked on as comparable to younger children, though husbands were not supposed to sell wives.

c. Women were seen as morally and intellectually less capable than men; their roles were to revolve around obedience and nurturing and the highest virtues for them were chastity and fidelity. This was softened by a belief in complementarity: men were not ritually or socially complete without wives.

d. Marriage was arranged relatively early and began in the home of a senior relative.

Some of these features have a clear basis in the Confucian classics, but others did not; the classics do not advocate equal division of property among sons, ancestor worship by commoners, or early marriage. Such practices are "Confucian" not by derivation from the classics but because they came to be accepted as standard, orthodox practices that the Confucian elite in time agreed were suitable for everyone. In the West, canonical sources were treated in a similarly selective fashion: certain Old Testament commandments such as "Honor thy father and mother" were endlessly reiterated, yet practices accepted as normal in the Bible, such as polygyny and the levirate, came to be labeled barbaric and un-Christian.

How did it come about that there was a high degree of uniformity in the ideas and practices underlying the late traditional Chinese family across classes, regions, dialect groups, and economic systems? In some parts of the world (such as France) inheritance practices varied from one prefecture to the next; in other places (such as India) large segments of the society followed matrilineal descent reckoning while the majority were patrilineal. It is probably more common, in comparative terms, for societies to show diversity in family practices, and therefore the relatively high level of uniformity found in China should not be taken as natural.[4]

In examining the spread of these ideas and practices I will try to assess the relative importance of such agents as schools, texts, govern-

---

[4] I do not mean to imply that there was no variation in Chinese family practices, only that this variation tended to be restricted to areas in which several alternatives were all considered acceptable and the choice of one or the other did not undermine the basic structure. For instance, the incidence of uxorilocal marriage (bringing the husband into the wife's family), little daughter-in-law marriage (adopting a young girl as a future bride for one's son), and well-developed descent groups with estates, formal rules, and so on seems to have varied considerably over different regions of the country. Yet variation of this sort seldom seems to have had much impact on other aspects of family organization or attitudes: three neighbors who had arranged different sorts of marriages for their children still were patrilineal and patriarchal in the ways described above.

ment and literati-led preaching, popular religion, and state regulations in the spread of Chinese family values and practices. Popular
religion is important because religious attitudes toward ancestors
provided much of the ideological substructure of the family system.
Through performance and observation of funerals and ancestral
rites, people learned about the need to get spirits settled and the need
to provide for them thereafter. Thus the spread of ancestral rites
throughout the society and the political acceptance of this development marked a major stage in Chinese family history. There is, of
course, a large Confucian literature on the subject of funerals, ancestral rites, and duty to ancestors. However, this theorizing almost always lagged behind the actual changes that were occurring in society.
In Korea ideas about ancestor worship may have come as part of a
total package of Neo-Confucian family practices. In China there
never was a large-scale politically encouraged change of system, and
ancestral rites and funerals remained closely tied to popular religion
into modern times.

The state had a pervasive effect on the organization of the family
through its law codes, control of social mobility, and direct efforts at
indoctrination. Chinese law dealt with family matters in several ways.
Status differences within the family were strongly reinforced in criminal law; for instance, it was a much more serious offense for a
nephew to strike his uncle than for an uncle to strike his nephew.
Marriages and adoptions, to be fully legal, had to conform to the requirements of the law. Property law regulated inheritance and placed
legal restrictions on holding and transmitting property. It has been
well demonstrated for other parts of the world that patterns of inheritance affect family structure. Do sons and daughters all inherit?
Are shares equal? Can an heir get his or her share early or only at
the death of the father or father and mother? The authority of family
heads, the relations among siblings, the ties to close relatives, and
even age at marriage are all shaped by the way family property is
controlled and distributed. The effect of property law is, however,
largely limited to those with some property: a landless laborer has
relatively little control over his adult son, for he has nothing of a material sort that the son needs, nor can he direct his son's labor if the
son must go elsewhere to seek work. Thus periods when the government fostered small proprietorships would help spread a small-
holder mentality and patriarchal family structure. Naturally the government has always played a major role in institutionalizing property
law. During some periods it denied full rights to pass land on to children (in various "equal-field" schemes). Systems of taxation also

changed—sometimes favoring undivided patrimonies; sometimes, early division.

Social stratification, again very much shaped by the state, is relevant to the history of the family system because it affects the process by which ideas and practices cross class lines. In socially fluid periods, people of rich peasant origin could marry into long-established elite families, bringing with them customs and habits of thought that could in time influence the old elite. At the same time, in relatively fluid periods, it was easier for people who aspired to high status to imitate the manners and customs of their betters, leading to a trickle-down of customs from the elite. Marriage practices are particularly relevant here: since child-raising was largely performed by women, when wives could be taken from lower social strata there would be more homogenization of social customs than when high social status depended on having a mother and wife of eminent families.

The family practices of ordinary people were shaped not only by these cultural and institutional background factors, but also by the direct efforts by scholars and officials to educate commoners. What they wished to teach commoners and how they attempted to do it naturally varied over time, depending on philosophical priorities, challenges to influence on commoners, and the intensity of elite-commoner interaction. "Good" or "persuasive" local officials set examples, posted placards with warnings or advice, opened schools, gave lectures, and used their courtrooms to foster trust and respect. Scholars wrote books of advice, guides to family rituals, and moral tracts; they promoted forms of local organization considered morally uplifting, especially village compacts and descent groups, sometimes contributing money to them; they helped found and fund local schools. Generally speaking, the saturation of the population by these educational efforts increased over time. It was greatly advanced in Ming and Ch'ing times by the examination system, which produced a vast surplus of educated men, many of whom remained in the countryside.

One means of indoctrinating commoners was the publication and dissemination of texts, but the importance of texts cannot be totally subsumed under educational efforts. By late Ming and Ch'ing times, when the publishing industry was highly developed and a substantial share of the population could read well enough to use books, texts in and of themselves could play major roles in the communication of values throughout society. Popular novels and stories came to circulate all over the country, communicating much the same ideas to diverse readers. In widely separated places the same guides to rituals and etiquette were consulted by local literati, ritual experts, and scribes, and used to frame the social behavior not only of the educated but also of the illiterate who consulted them.

I am confident that all of these factors (and many others) were important in the evolution of Chinese social relations, but I cannot describe their operation over the sweep of Chinese history in any detail. What follows, therefore, is no more than a chronological sketch in which I try to identify when family practices and ideas appeared, where in society they appeared, and the agents by which they spread.

ANTIQUITY

To analyze how ideas and practices changed and spread, some sort of baseline is needed, and for convenience I will use the time of Confucius and the other Chou philosophers. Well before this time ideas about ancestors and ancestry had been developing in their "modern" direction. Already in the neolithic period, people in north China were intensely concerned with the dead; they devoted large shares of their resources to the burial of the dead and made efforts to communicate with them. K. C. Chang believes that ancestor worship of one sort or another was already present.[5] For much of this century it has been argued that the earliest cultures in north China were matrilineal. Whether or not that inference is accurate, by Shang times patrilineal descent was clearly established, at least for the ruling house and related lines. Succession to the throne, however, was not so strictly from father to son as in later periods, and in early and mid Shang half the successions were to brothers or other close collaterals.

In both Shang and Chou times, political legitimacy was very much entangled with the cult of royal ancestors. Kings buried their predecessors in awesome tombs, communicated with them through libations, sacrifices, and divination, and expected their ancestors to be able to help them in their worldly affairs. In the Chou period, rules for elaborate differentiation in ancestral rites according to political rank were codified. In the form preserved in the *Li chi*, kings were obliged to offer sacrifices of several kinds of meat to their founding ancestor and four most recent ancestors each month; lords, officials, and officers (*shih*) could make progressively fewer and less varied offerings to progressively fewer ancestors. Commoners were not to make sacrifices of meat, but they could offer vegetables to deceased fathers once each season.

Ancient naming practices are confusing and somewhat obscure. In

[5] K. C. Chang, *The Archaeology of Ancient China*, rev. ed. (New Haven: Yale University Press, 1968), p. 103.

Shang times, noble clans had names (*hsing*) by which the consorts of kings were identified, but the custom of referring to people by a family name and a personal name was not yet established. Diviners were referred to by single-character names that often referred to a place and so could be used by others, related or not. Moreover, *hsing* may not yet have been units relevant to marriage; one scholar thinks marriage was allowed with a woman of common clan (*hsing*) identification so long as she was of a different descent group (*tsung*).[6] In Chou times, *hsing* did define the set of people one should not marry, and other family names (*shih*) were used in referring to people. That is, nobles had not only a "clan name" (*hsing*) based on common descent from a distant, perhaps mythical, ancestor, but also a local "family name" (*shih*) that did not always indicate kinship connection. In the *Tso chuan*, when the king sent off a relative or official to build his own town, the king would grant him not merely land but people organized in descent groups (*tsu*) and a name (*shih*) for the polity he would establish. The grantee would keep his original clan name (*hsing*). At other times, "family names" (*shih*) were based on an office, a place, or some distinction, such as being the grandson of a duke. Thus, more often than not, those named Kung-sun (grandson of a duke) or Ssu-ma (marshal) were not related to each other.[7]

The Chou royal lineage and the descent groups of the feudal lords and patricians always had a main line of successive heirs, each of whom generally was the first son of the wife. This line was favored politically, socially, and economically over collateral lines. The social and diplomatic ties between feudal heads of states were regularly couched in kinship terms: Were they both of the royal Chi clan? Were they founded by brothers or by brothers-in-law? By mid-Chou, great families (main lines and their closest collateral lines) were major forces in the politics of the various states.

A link between ancestral rites and male progeny was made by the Chou nobility. In a poem in the *Book of Songs*, the "Impersonator" of the ancestor tells the observers that as the sacrifice was done perfectly the lord will have long life, filial sons, and in time grandsons (poem 247). The vessels used in ancestral rites were frequently inscribed with the wish that sons and grandsons for many generations to come would cherish them. Late in this period, Mencius declared that the

[6] K. C. Chang, "The Lineage System of the Shang and Chou Chinese and Its Political Implications," in his *Early Chinese Civilization: Anthropological Perspectives* (Cambridge, Mass.: Harvard University Press, 1976), pp. 84–85.

[7] M. V. Krukov, "Hsing and Shih (On the problem of clan name and patronymic in ancient China)," *Archiv Orientalni* 34 (1966): 535–53.

worst of unfilial acts was a failure to have descendants (*Mencius* 4A:26).

In theory, at least, neither descent groups nor families had much family property at their disposal. Patricians had fiefs or offices with attached lands, which commonly passed to heirs (normally only one), but these privileges were not supposed to be private property, to be sold or divided, but political responsibilities undertaken by family lines with the concurrence of their lords. Younger sons could remain dependent on the main line, get their own fiefs or offices from the lord, or travel elsewhere in search of employment. Thus, among patricians the family as a unit of production and consumption was not clearly demarcated; the key political and economic unit was not the coresident household but the wider descent group (*shih* or *tsung*) focused on the main line.

The vocabulary with which family relationships would be discussed for centuries to come was articulated in the classical period. Well before Confucius or Mencius, there were words for filial piety, deference to elder brothers, and other role-specific virtues. In the very early Chou period, a declaration preserved in the *Book of Documents* asserted that the worst criminals, worse even than murderers, were

> sons who, instead of serving their fathers respectfully, greatly wound their fathers' hearts; fathers who, not being able to cherish their sons, hate them; younger brothers who, not bearing in mind the evident intention of Heaven, do not respect their elder brothers; and elder brothers who, forgetting the tender regard in which they should hold their younger brothers, are unfriendly to them.   (*Shu ching* V, 9, 16)

Despite the repeated stress on family virtues, there is no reason to think the people of ancient China were especially exemplary in their family behavior. Rather, one should probably conclude that the structure of the family among the patricians generated tensions that people thought could best be overcome by moral effort—that is, because not all adult sons were obedient and adult younger brothers compliant, and these frictions threatened the unity of the family, filial obedience and fraternal compliance had come to be highly valued.[8]

---

[8] Han Fei Tzu took the existence of unruly sons as so common that it could be used to illustrate the problems faced by rulers: "Now if ruler and subject must become like father and son before there can be order, then we must suppose that there is no such thing as an unruly father or son. Among human affections none takes priority over the love of parents for their children. But though all parents may show love for their children, the children are not always well behaved. And though the parents may love them even more, will this prevent the children from becoming unruly?" (Burton Watson, trans., *Basic Writings of Mo Tzu, Hsun Tzu, and Han Fei Tzu* [New York: Columbia University Press, 1967], p. 101).

Confucius is particularly associated with the concept of filial piety, the *Analects* (1.2) even containing the statement that the basis of human goodness (*jen*) is filial piety and brotherly deference. Confucius also made several comments on the nature of filial piety, such as "The son who during the three years of mourning manages to carry on exactly as his father did may be called filial" (*Analects* 4.20). In the next few centuries, when many established principles were challenged, the desirability of filial piety and deference of juniors was assumed by all, even by men such as Mo Tzu and Han Fei Tzu. Han Fei Tzu, in fact, devotes a full chapter to it (chapter 51 of *Han Fei Tzu*), and sees its cultivation as useful to the state because it leads to loyalty. Confucius' followers went further, however, than other schools of thought in also promoting carefully defined ethical relations to a wider range of relatives. Elaborately graded mourning obligations were specified in the *Li Chi* for patrilineal relatives descended from a common great-great grandfather and for the closest matrilateral and affinal kin. These mourning rules conform well to the descent groups of Chou patricians, with their distinctions of seniority both of generation and within a generation among brothers, and their weak sense of separation into households. The *Li Chi* also fully articulates the distinctions between men and women in household affairs and ritual, stressing over and over their hierarchical but complementary roles (see especially the "Nei tse" chapter).

The Chou was a strongly hierarchical age, and most sources imply a great gap between the values and practices of the elite and those of the laboring population. The notions of patrilineality, the structure of kinship groups, the rituals of marriage, funerals, and ancestral rites, and the ethics of family relationships described so far are all those of the elite. Often there is good reason to think they were not even imitated by the lower social levels. As Mo Tzu argued long ago, most people could not even consider performing the lengthy seclusion on the death of their parents that Confucians argued was essential to filial piety. But what peasants did is not well documented. Some scholars think peasants' marriage practices differed greatly from those among the patricians, with betrothal much less formal and less under the control of parents.[9] Less thorough patriarchal control is certainly plausible given that during most of this period peasants did not have land they could buy or sell; without family property that could be increased or lost the need for patriarchal control of family production would be relatively weak.

[9] Henri Maspero, *China in Antiquity*, trans. Frank A. Kierman Jr. (Amherst: University of Massachusetts Press, 1978), p. 72, 406 n. 24.

Did commoners practice ancestral worship in Chou times? Maspero says they did not, as they had neither clan names nor ancestors. Granet, however, argues that the underlying belief in ancestral spirits and an eternal family substance was already present, but that ancestors were not clearly differentiated as individuals and their worship was merged with local seasonal agrarian cults. Schwartz argues that basic ideas about ancestors and their worship were among the most fundamental of the shared cultural orientations of early China and colored Chinese views of sociopolitical and cosmic order on many levels, but he offers no evidence about practices.[10] It seems possible that by the time the *Li chi* was completed, some commoners (or commoners in some parts of the country) made offerings to ancestors. The tone of the rules cited above is not to institute ancestral rites where none then existed, but to set limits on their practice according to status, since effective access to ancestors was a political resource. Taking these diverse sources together, I would hazard the guess that commoners believed in the spiritual power of ancestors and made efforts to maintain worshipful contact with them, but did not follow all the practices of the nobility, such as use of impersonators.

At the same time that common people may have begun to differentiate ancestral from other cults, an agnosticism was gaining hold among the highly educated. Confucius and Hsun Tzu appear to have been skeptical about the divinity of ancestors and their participation in sacrifices. Confucius said he made offerings to the ancestors *as though* they were present (*Analects* 3.12) and urged a disciple to keep at a distance from spirits (*Analects* 6.20). Hsun Tzu said that "sacrificial rites originate in the emotions of remembrance and longing for the dead." For gentlemen who understand this purpose, "they are a part of the way of man; to the common people they are something pertaining to spirits."[11] As was true with many scholars in later centuries, religious impulses thus were not the main motivation for Hsun Tzu's performance of these rites. Yet because Confucius had a nearly mystical belief in the power of ritual to create harmonious social relations, anyone inspired by his teachings would wish to conduct ancestral rites and funerals with due solemnity and care, no matter what he thought of ghosts.

To what types of families or kin groups did commoners belong in Chou times? Maspero says unimportant, indistinct ones: among the

---

[10] Maspero, *China in Antiquity*, pp. 67, 72, 406 n. 25; Marcel Granet, *The Religion of the Chinese People*, trans. Maurice Freedman (New York: Harper and Row), pp. 52, 53; Benjamin I. Schwartz, *The World of Thought in Ancient China* (Cambridge, Mass.: Harvard University Press, 1985), pp. 20–39.

[11] Watson, *Basic Writings*, pp. 109–10.

peasantry there was "a kind of gregariousness, a group life in communities within which individuals and families were submerged and did not count." Granet, basing his argument on Chinese kinship terminology, infers a type of village clan with distinctions only of age and generation, an inference I do not find convincing, because there is no evidence peasants used the kinship terminology in the classics.[12] One senses, reading the writings of late Chou philosophers, that among peasants the small family of parents, children, and sometimes grandparents was well established as the unit of production and consumption. Mencius, for instance, frequently refers to the difficulties peasants faced in supporting their parents and their children (e.g., *Mencius* 1A:5.4, 1A:7.21). Beyond this small family, however, one sees little sign of descent groups or other organization based on patrilineal kinship. Outside of the family, writers mention neighbors and small settlements of several families (eight, in the idealized "well-field" system). Perhaps, if peasants did not use surnames, there was as yet little tendency to use patrilineal kinship to structure community life. At the end of the classical period, when the state of Ch'in wished to exert greater control over the population, it discouraged complex households (ones with more than one adult, married man) but did not take any measures against clans or other groups using kinship as a basis for local organization.

The role of the state in shaping the family behavior of ordinary people certainly began in the ancient period. The land tenure system and social hierarchy described here were all, in part, political creations. Rulers preserved and perpetuated traditions of ancestor worship and gave them associations with both sacred and secular power. The rulers also—at times, at least—attempted to mold the behavior of ordinary people. As Schwartz has recently argued, one of the most fundamental of early Chinese ideas is that the moral and social life of the entire populace can be shaped from the center, through the actions and examples of a universal king.[13] Confucius and Mencius

---

[12] Maspero, *China in Antiquity*, p. 67; Marcel Granet, *Chinese Civilization*, trans. Kathleen E. Innes and Mabel Brailsford (Cleveland: World Publishing, 1958), pp. 154–55.

[13] Schwartz, *World of Thought*, pp. 52, 414. A good example of this attitude is found in a passage in the *Tso chuan* (Hsi 27): "When the Marquis of Chin first returned, he taught the people for two years, hoping to use them [as soldiers]. Tzu Fan said, 'The people do not yet understand duty and are not settled in their livelihood.' Thereupon the marquis sent help to King Hsiang [as an example of acting on duty] and adopted measures to benefit the people. When the people became prosperous, the marquis wished to use them. Tzu Fan said, 'The people do not yet understand trustworthiness, or how they will be employed.' Thereupon he attacked Yuan as an example of trustworthiness. The people then in trading did not seek to get the advantage and fulfilled their promises. The marquis then asked whether they could be used. Tzu Fan said,

stressed how rulers could transform the people through example and ritual once their needs for adequate food and shelter had been met.

In Confucius' conception of a society regulated by ritual, people occupying a great variety of stations and roles would deal with each other in the ways appropriate to their situations, thereby continually maintaining and creating the social system without the use of force. The family was a primary arena in which this would take place, enhancing the social and political importance of correct behavior there. For instance, Confucius said, "When gentlemen are generous to their own kin the people will be incited to human goodness. When the elderly are not neglected, the people will not be fickle" (*Analects* 8.1). Mencius also stressed the need to educate people in more formal ways, claiming that in ancient times the sage rulers had established schools in every village whose purpose was to teach ethics (*Mencius* 3A:3). He also said that the sage king Shun, recognizing that people without education were no different from the birds and beasts, appointed a minister "to teach ethics, that is, the principles that between father and son there is affection, between ruler and subject duty, between husband and wife distinction, between elder and junior priority, between friends faithfulness" (*Mencius* 3A:4,8). Other early thinkers, especially the Legalists, proposed methods of regulating moral and social behavior through clear laws and predictable punishments and rewards. The *Kuan Tzu* states:

> Those who would shepherd the people cause men to refrain from evil acts and women to refrain from illicit affairs. . . . Since they desire their people to be correct, they must prohibit even the slightest manifestations of evil. Slight manifestations of evil are the source from which great evil springs. If these slight manifestations of evil are not prohibited, it is impossible to expect that great evil will not bring harm to the country. . . . When the people, even in minor matters, are meticulous in observing propriety, practicing righteousness, cultivating integrity, and displaying a sense of shame, and even the slightest beginnings of evil are prohibited, such is the basis of good order.[14]

'The people do not yet understand ritual or have a public spirit.' At that the marquis organized a great hunting expedition to illustrate ritual, setting up officers to regulate all of the responsibilities. When the people heard their orders without being confused by them, he employed them. The marquis then went to the border of Ku and relieved the siege of Sung. Becoming hegemon through a single battle was the result of this civil education."

[14] W. Allyn Rickett, *Guanzi: Political, Economic, and Philosophical Essays from Early China* (Princeton: Princeton University Press, 1985), pp. 96–97.

For centuries to come, both Confucian and Legalist ideas about education would affect the efforts undertaken by the state to shape popular behavior.[15]

THE WARRING STATES AND HAN (450 B.C.–A.D. 220)

The last few centuries of the classical period witnessed rapid social and economic change; the society that appears in the sources for the Han period differs in fundamental respects from either the idealized portrayals of early Chou in the classics or the society one can glimpse in the writings of the philosophers. In terms of the emergence of the "modern" family, perhaps the most crucial development was the increasing prevalence of the small family (*chia*) as a unit of consumption and production under the authority of a family head. The small family gained ground during the Warring States period and became universal by the early Han. In the Han the government promoted the status of family heads by policies such as granting them titles, recognizing their legal authority over their wives, children, and other juniors, and making them responsible for the fiscal obligations of the family. The state also promoted the small family by economic and political policies that strengthened the independence of small holders. Even tenants, who may still have been very numerous, were more like small holders than Chou serfs and tenants, with greater prospect of improving their financial situation through diligent savings or migration to undeveloped areas.[16]

In terms of the spread of family practices across class lines, perhaps the most striking change is that by this period everyone had family names (now universally called *hsing*). The most plausible explanation for this development is that when the Ch'in government registered the entire population, the hodgepodge of terms by which people were called were all classified as *hsing*, to be passed down to their patrilineal descendants indefinitely. With surnames, people easily identified with their patrilineal ancestors and patrilineal descendants, making it much easier to see themselves as part of a continuum of descent.

[15] On early educational philosophy, see Howard S. Galt, *A History of Chinese Educational Institutions* (London: Probsthain, 1951).

[16] See Ch'ü T'ung-tsu, *Han Social Structure*, ed. Jack L. Dull (Seattle: University of Washington Press, 1972), pp. 20–24; Hsu Cho-yun, *Han Agriculture: The Formation of Early Chinese Agrarian Economy 206 B.C. – A.D. 220)* (Seattle: University of Washington Press, 1980), pp. 15–35; Chen Chi-yun, "Han Dynasty China: Economy, Society, and State Power," *Toung Pao* 70 (1984): 127–48.

A third crucial change was the marked decline in the importance of hereditary transmission of office and title. Already in the Warring States period, philosophers had argued for the merit principle in assigning office, and under the pressure of competition many of the states were making ever greater use of it. In the unified empire, offices were assigned in a bureaucratic fashion, incumbency seldom more than a few years. Income from offices could be invested in land, which could then be passed on to children. In the past, offices and fiefs could be transmitted to only one son. Land in the Han could be divided, and equal division among all heirs became the established custom, apparently among all strata of society.

This custom of partible inheritance had great consequences for the subsequent history of the Chinese family, but its origins are obscure. It is conceivable that in the Chou period elite families had divided whatever property could be divided (such as money) among all sons, a practice that they then extended to land when it became readily divisible. But division of land when it was a family's most important asset was a very different matter from division of clothes or jewels. It fundamentally undermined the primacy of the main line, leaving eldest sons with little more than extra ritual responsibilities. On the other hand, it is also conceivable that equal division of land started among peasants in areas where land was relatively abundant, which appear to be the areas where the easy buying and selling of land was first established (i.e., Ch'in). But wherever equal division first appeared, one must still explain why it spread so thoroughly. I can think of no economic, political, or religious reason why Chinese custom could not have developed in another direction. A connection between ancestor worship and property inheritance has been shown for many societies, but the Chinese practice of ancestor worship need not have led to multiple heirs, as one heir could receive the property and continue the rites (which was, after all, the system of the Chou nobility celebrated in the Confucian classics). Politically, one can see why an authoritarian government might enforce equal division—as a means of curbing the growth of landed magnates who could challenge its rule. But did this actually occur in China? I know of no evidence that the Han government had a policy of enforcing equal division for typical landlords.[17] Comparatively speaking, however, partible inheritance is very common in peasant societies (the single-heir system of England and Japan being more exceptional), and so

[17] The Han government did undermine the independence of its own nobles from the imperial family by requiring the division of fiefs after the first fifty years of the dynasty (Ch'ü, *Han Social Structure*, pp. 166–67). The Han government also took other measures designed to curb the power of local magnates (Hsu, pp. 43–46).

the spread of partible inheritance in China, while not inevitable, should perhaps be looked on as a normal development in a society of small farmers.

Mobility—social, economic, and geographic—was high in the Warring States and early Han, and played a role in facilitating the changes in family practices described above. Serfdom was steadily undermined and by the Han was completely gone. From then on peasants could buy land, fall into debt, migrate, and so on. The Chou nobility suffered heavy blows in the warfare of the fourth and third centuries B.C. and the concerted efforts of the Ch'in government to undermine it. In the Han a new elite emerged, which readily absorbed the sons of local landlords whose grandfathers had been peasants. Even if the reality of social mobility into the elite was never as great as the myth of it, there can be little doubt of a great transfusion of new blood into the expanding Han elite. Moreover, the belief in social mobility in and of itself was highly significant. It legitimated efforts to imitate the rituals and behavior of higher social levels in efforts to "improve" oneself or one's sons. Social mobility also affected people's notions of families' goals. It became common to think that whether a family declined or prospered depended on hard work and managerial success. No lord, village, or kin group could guarantee a family's economic survival, but neither would any of these entities prevent its advance.

The relative fluidity of stratification in the Han made it much easier for ideas and practices to spread across class lines. This was undoubtedly a two-way process. Han observers such as Wang Fu thought the custom of extravagant burials was spreading from the high-ranking to wider and wider segments of society who imitated them.[18] But certain attitudes and practices of the Han elite were quite unlike those of the elite of the Chou period and may possibly have originated among peasants. Among these I would tentatively place division of property among all sons, faith in the possibility of getting ahead through hard work, and ancestral rites without the use of an impersonator.

Ideas and practices cannot always be assigned either elite or commoner origins. Some of the most fundamental cultural developments of the period probably were a result of the interactive modification of ideas and practices as they passed back and forth across class lines. I have in mind here particularly the tremendous growth in the cult of

[18] Patricia Ebrey, "Economic and Social History of the Later Han," *Cambridge History of China*, vol. 1, ed. Michael Loewe and Denis Twitchett (Cambridge, England: Cambridge University Press, 1986), pp. 609–12.

filial piety. Filial piety was already extolled by Confucius and other members of the Chou elite. In the Han it came to be considered a political virtue, tied to loyalty to the emperor, and manifestation of it in extreme forms was declared to be an adequate basis for recruitment to government office. Han views of parent-child relations were more one-sided and authoritarian than classical Confucian ones,[19] which may reflect not only political needs but also the new patriarchal family structure. The text of the *Classic of Filial Piety*, which espoused the Han view of filial piety, came to be a common primer, used to inculcate generations of students with the ideas that caution, restraint, and obedience will allow one to avoid disgrace to parents and to maintain the livelihood whereby to support them. In this text Confucius is credited with saying,

> In serving his parents a filial son renders the utmost reverence to them while at home. In supporting them he maximizes their pleasure. When they are sick he takes every care. At their death he expresses all his grief. Then he sacrifices to them with full solemnity. If he has fulfilled these five requirements, he is truly able to serve his parents. He who really loves his parents will not be proud in high position, insubordinate in an inferior position, or quarrelsome among equals. If he were proud in high station he might be ruined. If he were insubordinate in an inferior position he might incur punishment. If he were quarrelsome among his equals he might end up fighting. Thus, unless these three evils are eliminated, a son cannot be called filial, even if every day he supplies his parents the three choice meats.   (*Hsiao ching* 14)

Confucius also explained how filial sons become good subjects:

> The gentleman's service to his parents is filial; the fidelity involved in it can be transferred to his ruler. His service to his elder brothers is deferential; the obedience involved in it can be transferred to his superiors. Self-disciplined at home, he can transfer his good management to official life. Through these means when his conduct is perfect at home his name will be perpetuated to later generations.   (*Hsiao ching* 14)

Besides ties to the state and political loyalty, the cult of filial piety had links to lower social levels and perhaps to popular religious beliefs. Filial piety was, generally, an inexpensive virtue that people of meager means could strive to demonstrate; in numerous tales, the filial sons or daughters were explicitly portrayed as people of modest station. In these tales, devotion to serving the whims of peculiar par-

[19] Dau-lin Hsü, "The Myth of the 'Five Human Relations' of Confucius," *Monumenta Serica* 29 (1970–71): 27–37.

ents generally brought natural or supernatural rewards. Through these tales, the educated elite may have absorbed religious attitudes of popular origin, such as awe at the powers of extreme self-denial. Han notions of filial piety also affected ways of serving the dead. In the name of filial piety, men often risked their health to perform extended or exaggerated mourning for parents. By late Han, large stone tombs were built by all those who could afford them, and mortuary art suggests very strong popular beliefs in ghosts and the ability of descendants to ease their parents' afterlife. Even relatively low members of the elite sometimes built stone ancestral temples near their parents' graves to be able to make offerings to them. Some of these actions were "show," but the strength of the religious attitudes should not be missed.

Did the cult of filial piety enhance filial piety in the daily life of ordinary people? I see no way to answer that question. But the circulation of stories of the miracles of filial piety certainly publicized the concept of filial piety in the lower strata of society. However people acted, they were now more likely to have a knowledge of the ideal.

By the Han, patrilineal descent was sometimes used by commoners as a basis for local organization. During periods of strife, especially at the fall of Wang Mang and the fall of the Later Han after 184, the histories frequently refer to groups of kinsmen who fought together. These groups seem often to have been assembled for the special purpose of local defense. Yet even if they were *ad hoc* units, their formation does testify to a readiness to select kinship (and not mere propinquity) as a basis for organization.

The Han period also was one of great geographical expansion, encouraged by the state. As their successors would continue to do for centuries to come, local officials assigned to areas with a large non-Han population fostered "Confucianization" by trying to eradicate deviant family practices, such as casual divorce and the levirate. Their work in opening schools to train a local elite in the classics also helped spread the ideas behind Chinese family customs.[20] Whereas in many aspects of cultural life one can detect a mixing of southern and northern elements, in family life aboriginal practices that were contrary to the classical tradition or Han practices seem to have largely died out.[21]

[20] Hisayuki Miyakawa, "The Confucianization of South China," in *The Confucian Persuasion*, ed. Arthur F. Wright (Stanford: Stanford University Press, 1960), pp. 31–34.

[21] A possible exception is the practice of exhuming bodies after they have been buried a few years and then reburying the bones. This custom, which was well entrenched in Kwangtung and Fukien in recent times, may date back to pre-Han customs of the area (J. L. Watson, "Of Flesh and Bones: The Management of Death Pollution in Can-

Local officials' educational efforts were not confined to areas with
large non-Han populations. Already in Ssu-ma Ch'ien's *Shih-chi* there
are biographies of "good" magistrates who inspired people to correct
their ways through decent treatment, advice, lectures, placards, and
judicious legal decisions. Such officials were seen as a major force for
"civilization," which probably meant largely what is being called
"Confucianism" in this volume.

I have devoted considerable space to the Han period because the
development of Chinese patriarchy (the small family under the authority of a family head with division of property among brothers)
was just as important in the evolution of the Chinese family as the
formulation of ethics, ancestral rites, and patrilineality in antiquity.
This Han family system was the product of an imperial government,
mobile society, and agrarian economy. By the end of the Han the
foundation of the modern Chinese family had been laid. All the items
in the list of key features of the Chinese family system given above
can already be seen among the Han upper class. (It would take several more centuries before all of them were common among peasants.)

PERIOD OF DIVISION AND THE T'ANG (220–906)

The centuries after the Han saw a reversal of many of the developments described above—in small proprietorship, political support for
family heads, and the idea and practice of social mobility. Small proprietorship was already in retreat in the late Han, and over the next
four centuries it may have reached its lowest levels during the imperial period. Moreover, the relatively weak governments of this period
did not respond to these economic changes in ways that would favor
a "small-holder mentality." Generally they paid less attention to family heads as a basis for governing, allowing local officials more autonomy in how they collected taxes or recruited labor. At the end of the
fifth century a radically new land policy was promulgated in the
north that would distribute small holdings to all those able to work
them, but prohibited the recipients from passing on the crop lands
they received to their children. This "equal-field system," which
lasted into the eighth century, gave family heads more freedom from
control by masters, but limited their control over their progeny. Thus
during much of this period farmers found it difficult to build up
their property and "advance their family"; either they had serflike

---

tonese Society," in *Death and the Regeneration of Life*, ed. Maurice Bloch and Jonathan
Parry [Cambridge, England: Cambridge University Press, 1982]).

dependency on the owner of a manor, or they made use of land temporarily allotted them by the state.

The laws of the T'ang, the first set to survive in large quantity, show that even if the "equal-field" system acted to limit patriarchal control over adult sons, the government was not intentionally trying to weaken family heads. In the code family heads had full authority to arrange their children's marriages, which could be at relatively young ages (13 *sui* for girls and 15 for boys). So long as a man and his wife lived with his parents, the younger couple was subject to the older one. Nor could they leave or divide the property without the consent of the parents. Should violence occur in the family, the junior was held responsible or judged more severely. Legal support for patriarchal authority may well reflect widely shared ideas about family life. These ideas are congruent with both ethical emphasis on filial submission and the practical needs of farmers to control their labor force and ensure its continuity. The legal code also drew on classical ritual traditions in setting up complex incest and exogamy rules prohibiting marriage with a wide range of kin, but whether these rules reflected common practice in the T'ang is unclear.[22]

The fourth through seventh centuries were a particularly aristocratic era. Among the elite, patrilineal ancestry was much discussed and governments several times compiled genealogies of all the great families in the country. Just as high mobility of the early Han led to an infusion of previously peasant ideas and customs into the educated class, the low mobility of this period made such transmission difficult. Manners and deportment were continually scrutinized, and no one of social pretensions would wish his behavior to appear vulgar. While peasants were apparently drifting away from the family system of the Han, among the educated elite the old ways, especially the old rituals, became a sign of high social status, of "Chineseness" (in an age of alien rulers), and of "Confucianism" (in an age of Buddhism and Taoism).[23] Maintenance of distinct family practices was made easier by restrictive marriage practices. High social status had to be confirmed through marriage to other families of equally high prestige. Thus an aristocratic family would rarely have a daughter-in-law likely to introduce customs common at lower social levels.

---

[22] It seems likely that they did not in any complete way, as officials were confused by the prohibitions on matrilateral cross-generation marriages. See Hung Mai, *Jung-chai sui-pi* (Shanghai: Shanghai ku-chi ch'u-pan she, 1978), p. 318.

[23] David Johnson, *The Medieval Chinese Oligarchy* (Boulder, Colo.: Westview Press, 1977), pp. 33–88; Ebrey, *The Aristocratic Families of Early Imperial China: A Case Study of the Po-ling Ts'ui Family* (Cambridge, England: Cambridge University Press, 1978), pp. 56–58, 96–100.

It was during this period of diminished social mobility and retreat in small holdings that Buddhism and Taoism spread widely in the society. Buddhism in particular articulated distinctly "anti-family" values: freeing oneself from social entanglements and "leaving the family" to become a monk. It even promoted cremating the dead rather than constructing tombs, the site of so much family piety. To the extent that Buddhist and Taoist deities became the focus of popular piety, ancestors may have seemed somewhat less important or powerful.

Buddhist and Taoist clergy had remarkable success in reaching ordinary people. They preached to people, led them in worship, and helped them perform funerals and masses for the dead. Paradoxically, the effect of the clergy on commoners was not entirely negative for the "Confucianization" of Chinese society, since the social ethics they preached to lay commoners was largely filial piety and related virtues, and they helped commoners fulfill ritual obligations to their dead parents.[24] Their preaching is the earliest case of educated men personally contacting commoners in efforts to inspire them to moral effort.

The growth of Buddhism probably led to some reduction in the scale of burials, but it did not herald any major decline in ancestor worship. It was during the T'ang that people of various social stations began to make seasonal visits to their ancestors' graves and offer sacrifices to them there. For centuries graves had been places where individuals might go to make reports to deceased parents; and they had long been associated with filial piety, as filial sons not only devoted their fortunes to their construction, but spent the mourning period at their side. From this period on, graves also had a new function: during spring and fall festivals they were a place where all the descendants of a dead man met and made sacrifices. Among common people this appears to have been the earliest and the most important kind of *group* ancestor worship.[25] It was also the first type of *sacrifice* to ancestors that the government explicitly permitted commoners to perform.

Education, partly under the influence of institutional Buddhism, expanded greatly during the T'ang period. This can be seen from the great quantity and variety of educational texts that survived in Tun-huang. Even the primers used in schools run by monasteries often taught Confucian social ethics. The most common of these were

[24] Kenneth K. S. Ch'en, *The Chinese Transformation of Buddhism* (Princeton: Princeton University Press, 1973), pp. 14–55.

[25] Ebrey, "The Early Stages of the Development of Descent Group Organization," in *Kinship Organization in Late Imperial China, 1000–1940*, ed. Patricia Buckley Ebrey and James L. Watson (Berkeley: University of California Press, 1986).

the *Family Instructions of the Grandfather*, the *Classic of Filial Piety*, the *Thousand Character Text*, and the *Essential Teachings for Beginning Learners*. The *Family Instructions of the Grandfather*, which survived in forty-two copies in Tun-huang, urges filial piety in simple verse:

> The filial son, in serving his parents
> Visits them in the morning and looks in on them in the evening.
> He knows if they are hungry or thirsty,
> He knows if they are too warm or too cold.
> If they are sad, he commiserates with them.
> When they are happy he rejoices with them.
> If his parents are ill
> He refrains from eating good food,
> And does not seek his fill.
> He does not seek comfort in his lodging,
> Find pleasure in music,
> Or watch entertainment.
> He pays no attention to his body,
> And does not keep his clothes in order.
> When his parents are better
> It is not difficult to rectify these lapses.
> A student, in serving his teacher,
> Shows the same respect he shows to his father.

Some basic manners were also taught:

> When his father goes out to walk
> The son must follow behind.
> If on the road he meets a senior
> He puts his feet together and joins his hands.
> In front of a senior
> He does not spit on the ground.
> If a senior gives him wine
> He must receive it with a bow.
> If a senior gives him meat
> He does not give the bones to a dog.
> If a senior gives him fruit
> He keeps the pit in his hand.
> He must not throw it away—
> Doing so would be a great violation of ritual.

The principles of women's conduct were also explained:

> A bride serves her husband
> Just as she served her father.
> Her voice should not be heard

> Nor her body or shadow seen.
> With her husband's father and elder brothers
> She has no conversation.
> She is filial in her care for her father-in-law's family
> And respectful in serving her husband-master.[26]

As students advanced, they learned the finer rules of etiquette, such as how to vary polite language when addressing someone very superior, slightly superior, a peer, or an inferior; how to write a condolence letter or conduct a condolence call; and how to conduct weddings and funerals. Guides to such etiquette also survive in great quantity in Tun-huang.[27]

The basic Chinese family system probably had not changed much between Han and T'ang times. But by the end of the T'ang several serious challenges to this system (from Buddhism, the equal-field system, and aristocracy) had been faced, and basic family values and practices had survived without major alterations. By the end of this period, Buddhism was actually playing a positive role in promoting "Confucian" family ethics among the uneducated attracted to its doctrines.

SUNG AND YÜAN (960–1368)

The Sung, like the Han, was a period of great mobility—social, economic, and geographic. With the abandonment of the "equal-field" system in mid-T'ang, full private control of land was resumed. Tenantry was common, but its conditions varied greatly. In areas that were only beginning to be developed, tenants were often bound with servile dependency on their landlords. In other areas, however, small independent farms were common, and social and economic mobility high.

With an expanding economy and the invention of printing, the size of the educated class steadily grew. According to Chaffee, only about twenty to thirty thousand students attempted the civil service examinations in the early eleventh century. A hundred years later approximately eighty thousand did. And by the middle of the thirteenth century, when Sung controlled only south China, it seems that four

[26] Chinese texts in Paul Demieville, *L'oeuvre de Wang le Zelateur suivre des Instructions Domestiques de L'aieul, Poèmes populaires des T'ang (VIIIe–Xe Siècles)* (Paris: Institut des Hautes Etudes Chinoises, 1982), pp. 644–48, 672–76, 698–700.

[27] Ebrey, "T'ang Guides to Verbal Etiquette," *Harvard Journal of Asiatic Studies* 45 (1985): 581–613.

hundred thousand or more took each exam.[28] For every man who attempted the civil service examinations, there must have been quite a few who spent enough time in school to learn to read or write but who did not continue long enough to master the classics.

The expansion of the examination system gave renewed publicity to the idea of meritocracy and associated ideas of social mobility. Whatever the actual odds of a son of a peasant or townsman passing the examinations and becoming an official, the belief that such a possibility existed was a powerful force motivating not only education but also other efforts to improve one's class standing. If a peasant could rise to become an official, he could certainly rise partway to become a small-scale landlord or teacher. Families had reasons to plan carefully for long-term goals of advancement, to be achieved by grandsons if not by sons.

This expansion in the size of the educated class also changed the way ideas and values spread through society. It became more likely that every county if not yet every market town had schools and learned men. Ordinary peasants would be more likely to have contact with them—as tenants, kinsmen, neighbors, and so on. As in the Han, high social mobility meant that many scholars and officials were sons of landlords whose grandfathers had been peasants. These men inevitably retained some of their families' customs relating to child-rearing, husband-wife interaction, daily manners, weddings, and funerals, and introduced them to their new social circles. During the first century or so of Sung rule the very highest officials tended to marry among themselves, thus perhaps preserving greater distinctiveness in family practices. By the Southern Sung, however, even the highest-ranking officials were marrying their sons and daughters into local families.[29] Although there was still a considerable cultural gap between peasants and the educated class, it is unlikely, considering marriage patterns and social mobility, that the differences between "high" and "low" gentlemen were nearly as great as in the previous period.

Because such a high proportion of the educated class participated in the civil service examinations, the state had unprecedented opportunities to shape the intellectual activities and orientations of the elite. This was well recognized at the time, and led to bitter controversies about the usefulness of requiring poetry, memorization of the classics, and essays on policy, and about which classics or which commen-

[28] John W. Chaffee, *The Thorny Gates of Learning in Sung China: A Social History of Examinations* (New York: Cambridge University Press, 1985), p. 35.

[29] Robert M. Hartwell, "Demographic, Political, and Social Transformations of China, 750–1550," *Harvard Journal of Asiatic Studies* 42 (1982): 365–442.

taries were approved. The Sung state established more government
schools than any earlier dynasty, aiming for one in each prefecture
and county. Students at these schools received not only free tuition
but also often stipends for living expenses. Many of these government schools had attached primary schools.[30]

Private education also flourished at both elementary and advanced
levels in the Sung. One of the most important primers of late imperial China was written in the late Sung period. Besides teaching simple vocabulary, such as numbers, directions, and the names of grains,
the *Trimetrical Classic* taught basic ethics:

> In human relationships—
> Between father and son is obligation,
> Between husband and wife obedience;
> Elder brothers are friendly;
> Younger brothers are deferential.
> Between seniors and juniors there is rank order;
> With friends there is cordiality.
> A ruler shows respect;
> A subject shows loyalty.
> These ten duties
> Are shared by all people.[31]

At least as influential as the *Trimetrical Classic* was the *Book of Rewards and Punishments*, a tract associated with religious Taoism. It
taught that gods or spirits observe people's behavior and mete out
appropriate rewards and punishments to them in their own lifetime
or to their descendants. Descriptions of good and bad behavior were
not much different from Confucian ones. Good people "exhibit loyalty to their ruler, filial obedience to their parents, true friendship to
their older brothers. By conducting themselves with propriety, they
influence others. They take pity on orphans and are kindly toward
widows; they venerate the elderly and are warm-hearted toward the
young." Evil people by contrast are "perverse, without human-heart-
edness, vicious, and selfish." "They are rude to their teachers and rebellious toward those they are supposed to serve." These people lie,
cheat, and enjoy watching others suffer. They even "treat the spirits
of their ancestors with contempt."[32] Thus, as C. K. Yang wrote, "in its

[30] Thomas H. C. Lee, *Government Education and Examinations in Sung China* (Hong
Kong: Chinese University Press, 1985).

[31] Chinese text in Herbert A. Giles, *San Tzu Ching*, 2nd edition, revised (New York:
Ungar, 1963), pp. 45–49.

[32] Ebrey, *Chinese Civilization and Society: A Source Book* (New York: Free Press, 1981),
pp. 71–73.

relation to the moral order, religion played the role of supernatural sanctioning agent."[33]

Despite the fact that Buddhist and Taoist clergy reinforced basic Confucian ethics, leading Confucian scholars of the Sung were committed to combatting Buddhism's and Taoism's hold on commoners. By providing clergy who would conduct funerals and ancestral rites, Buddhism and Taoism had penetrated deeply into the family life of ordinary Chinese. The Confucian elite, in an effort to compete, reformulated Confucian family rituals so they would be suitable for people of all social stations. From this period on, the classical limitations on ancestral sacrifices by commoners were abandoned, and a single code for gentlemen (*shih*) and commoners generally accepted. The Neo-Confucian movement also led to a renewed interest in patrilineality as the primary basis for family organization. Based in part on an accurate reading of the classics, in part on a yearning for stability, Neo-Confucian scholars called for a revival of the ancient *tsung* system, an end to uxorilocal marriage and adoption of anyone but agnates, and the chastity of widows, who should remain with their husbands' families.[34]

Scholars and officials continued, of course, to encourage all of the old family virtues—filial piety, harmony, and deference. As before, local officials posted placards warning of the punishments to be meted out for irregular practices. The government regularly rewarded outstanding examples of well-run families, especially those that did not divide for several generations in a row, sometimes coming to encompass several hundred people. Such families were considered exemplars not only of filial piety and brotherly deference, but also of effective leadership and successful financial management.

These government efforts all had precedents in earlier dynasties, and on the whole probably were more important in shaping people's ideas of what is admirable than in shaping their behavior. More innovative and perhaps more effective were the efforts of educated men, simply in their capacity as private citizens, to find ways to influence local commoners through new types of organizations. The three that had the greatest long-term impact on the family system were descent groups, village compacts, and charitable schools. The creation

[33] C. K. Yang, *Religion in Chinese Society* (Berkeley: University of California Press, 1961), p. 278.

[34] Ebrey, "Education Through Ritual: Efforts to Formulate Family Rituals During the Sung Dynasty," in *Neo-Confucian Education: The Formative Stage*, ed. Wm. Theodore de Bary and John W. Chaffee (Berkeley: University of California Press, 1989), and Ebrey, "Conceptions of the Family in the Sung Dynasty," *Journal of Asian Studies* 43 (1984): 219–45.

and endowment of descent groups were tied to efforts to reassert the primacy of patrilineal kinship. Ideally, educated men were to assemble all their local agnates, in most cases including people of modest means, even peasants; they were to lead them in joint ancestral rites and encourage them to cultivate all of the standard family virtues and rituals. As mentioned above, since T'ang times local sets of agnates had often been assembling once or twice a year for ancestral rites at graves, and in many places these sets of agnates seemed to have developed a sense of group consciousness on their own. From late Sung on, with an infusion of elite leadership, such groups increasingly took on other activities, such as compilation of genealogies and construction of ancestral halls.[35] In some areas of the country, large, well-organized descent groups became major forces in local social and political life. Even where they did not become politically powerful, their ritual activities helped standardize family practices and certainly strengthened the notion of patrilineality as relevant in social and religious life.

Village compacts were not a form of kinship organization, but rather of village organization, based strictly on residence. Yet their purpose, as outlined by Sung theorists, was to educate villagers in Confucian interpersonal relations, especially filial piety and deference to seniors.[36] To the extent that they brought members of the elite and commoners together they must have helped foster a common ethical vocabulary. Charitable schools, similarly, had no direct tie to the family. However, by bringing knowledge of the Confucian classics to local elites, they fostered social mobility through education, and led to an increase in literacy; thus they promoted transmission of family practices across class lines.

Printing also had an educational effect of considerable magnitude. During the Sung and Yüan periods publishing grew enormously. Gradually handbooks and guidebooks of various sorts came to be published in large quantities, aimed at as broad an audience as possible. Many of these books contained guidelines for family matters, such as long or short versions of the *Family Rituals* compiled by Chu Hsi; diagrams of the grades of mourning; tables of first-, second-, and third-person terms of reference for kinsmen (how to refer to a father's brother, how to address him, and how to refer to oneself when addressing him); sample letters to relatives of all sorts for a wide variety of occasions (especially deaths); selections from earlier

[35] Ebrey, "Early Stages of the Development of Descent Groups."

[36] Monika Ubelhor, "The Community Covenant (hsiang-yüeh) of the Sung and Its Educational Significance," in *Neo-Confucian Education: The Formative Stage*, ed. Wm. Theodore de Bary and John W. Chaffee (Berkeley: University of California Press, 1989).

writers' advice on managing family affairs or cultivating family virtues, and so on. Books, of course, are powerful tools in cultural standardization. Villages that boasted no one with a high-level classical education might still have someone with a copy of a reference book and the ability to consult it to see what grade of mourning one should wear for a sister's son or the wife of a second cousin. All along, the educated seem to have had a basic grasp of the mourning grades and what they meant both in the rituals of mourning and as an indication of kinship closeness. I suspect that these fairly complicated ideas did not really become a part of the common Chinese culture until reference books of these sorts were printed in large quantities and circulated throughout the country.

Enough is known of the family practices of the upper class in the Sung to see similarities to the family dynamics of recent times. Authors of books of advice, most notably Yüan Ts'ai, describe problems of child-rearing, managing money, avoiding quarrels, and so on that are much like those faced by farmers' families in the twentieth century. For instance, Yüan Ts'ai argued that only scrupulous equality will allow adult brothers to maintain a joint family, that men and women have different views about family property and their obligations to sons and daughters, and that a father must watch his treatment of his sons to avoid either spoiling them so they grow up willful or being so harsh he incites their resentment.[37]

Large parts of China were under alien rule during the Sung-Yüan period, under the Liao (916–119), Chin (1115–1234), and Yüan (1215–1368) dynasties. These alien rulers, each in distinct ways, posed challenges to the Confucian tradition, most notably to Confucian ideas of government. However, none of them tried to change the family behavior of ordinary Chinese commoners or the value structure that gave such a high place to filial piety, wifely submission, and family solidarity. Even in the affairs of government, Confucian principles gradually gained acceptance. Indeed, it was under the Yüan that Neo-Confucianism became a state orthodoxy and Chu Hsi's commentaries to the Four Books made required reading for examination candidates.[38]

MING AND CH'ING (1368–1644)

Most of the developments of the Sung-Yuan period continued in Ming-Ch'ing times, even gaining strength. Descent groups became

[37] Ebrey, trans., *Family and Property in Sung China: Yüan Ts'ai's Precepts for Social Life* (Princeton: Princeton University Press, 1984).

[38] Wm. Theodore de Bary, *Neo-Confucian Orthodoxy and the Learning of the Heart-and-Mind* (New York: Columbia University Press, 1981).

more common, books of all kinds became even more available, schools became more widely accessible, and the government became more intrusive in advertising proper behavior.

Another important trend of the Ming-Ch'ing period was greater autonomy for tenants. Servile dependency nearly disappeared in this period. Moreover, in south China tenants often gained permanent tenancy rights, rights they could sell to third parties or transmit to children. As a consequence, a larger and larger share of the population gained family property that provided the basis of patriarchal authority over family members. As discussed already, full expression of the "traditional" patriarchal Chinese family system is difficult without family property. Thus greater control over the resources they needed for family survival may have made peasants more receptive to the teachings about proper family behavior that now reached them with greater regularity.

The growth of the examination system and the intensification of efforts to educate the general population were closely intertwined developments. Steadily through this period, the number of men taking the civil service examinations increased, as did the proportion of them who could not be employed as officials. Educational efforts aimed at ordinary people depended on the vast supply of educated men, and the degree to which similar messages were conveyed throughout the country by these educated men was due very largely to the standardization of their preparation for the examinations. Hsiao Kung-chuan noted that the first step in ideological control of the rural population was ideological control of the gentry.[39] With regard to the proper principles, values, and rituals of family life, the examinations did indeed bring about a high degree of uniformity among the educated. Candidates for the examinations learned that Chu Hsi was the standard authority on the meaning of the classics. From his writings they learned a strict view of proper family relations and family arrangements; they also readily consulted his handbook for the performance of cappings, weddings, funerals, and ancestral rites, the *Family Rituals*. Thus whenever asked about the proper thing to do, they would be likely to give similar answers.

The educated who lived in rural areas were often asked about the proper forms to follow. By the nineteenth century, at least, funerals throughout China showed remarkable uniformity in their basic structure. Recently scholars have argued that this uniformity was largely due to the existence of standardized texts and an elite who inter-

---

[39] Kung-chuan Hsiao, *Rural China: Imperial Control in the Nineteenth Century* (Seattle: University of Washington Press, 1960), p. 184.

preted them in comparable ways.[40] Even though many of the experts who conducted funerals were Buddhist or Taoist clergy, neither Buddhism nor Taoism was a unified church with standardized ritual manuals, and Confucian forms in mourning and sacrifices to the dead were followed even when clergy directed funerals and added their own rites. Confucian funeral rituals demonstrated the importance of ancestors and the ties between the living and the dead, and served continually to teach the young the principles of the family system, especially the need for filial heirs. Thus, as Confucians had long argued, attention to ritual form served to teach moral principles. The Confucian elite in their capacity as experts helped create uniformity in form and practice; the similarity in basic understandings was a by-product.

This is not to say that the government and scholars did not also directly teach Confucian ethics. Throughout the Ming-Ch'ing period the *Trimetrical Classic* and the *Thousand Character Classic* were common primers, and from them generations of schoolboys learned the vocabulary and basic premises of Confucian family ethics. As elementary education became more common—by the nineteenth century reaching a third to a half of all boys—sayings from these books became proverbial, known to almost everyone.[41] By the late Ming, scholars often took an interest in the education of ordinary people and wrote simple didactic tracts. Religious leaders and religious organizations were also issuing many such tracts, which taught general Chinese ("Confucian") social ethics as well as religious principles.

The Ming and Ch'ing governments also took an active interest in the moral improvement of illiterate adults and instituted compulsory public lectures for this purpose. In Ch'ing times every locality was to have a place for twice-monthly lectures by a specially appointed local scholar who would speak in the vernacular. His topic was to be one of the "Instructions" in the "Sacred Edict" of the K'ang-hsi emperor, which ordered the population to behave properly, obey parents, control children, respect seniors, avoid lawsuits, and so on. For instance, one lecturer elaborated on the maxim "Demonstrate ceremony and deference in order to improve popular customs" in this way:

> Though everyone knows how to talk of ceremony and deference, they do not all practice it. Why don't they practice it? Because at present they only know how to use the rules of ceremony to reprove others, not how

---

[40] James L. Watson and Evelyn S. Rawski, eds., *Death Ritual in Late Imperial and Modern China* (Berkeley: University of California Press, 1988).

[41] Evelyn Sakakida Rawski, *Education and Popular Literacy in Ch'ing China* (Ann Arbor: University of Michigan Press, 1979), pp. 8–20.

to correct themselves. For example, if we are quarreling, you'll say I'm
impolite and I'll say you are. One will say, "Why don't you yield to me?"
And the other will reply, "You haven't yet yielded to me. Why should I
yield to you?" At length the animosities become so complex that they
cannot be disentangled. What gain is there in that? You should think a
little and say, "Although he is without proper manners, where are my
manners? Although he hasn't yielded to me, in the beginning why didn't
I yield to him?" If both parties would admit part of the blame, wouldn't
numerous disputes be avoided?[42]

Even though charismatic preachers were undoubtedly rare, these lectures must have had some effect on popular thinking, an effect comparable to that of civics instruction in public schools in the twentieth
century. That is, the important point is that everywhere in the country the same models of behavior were held up for praise or blame,
and whatever people actually did, at least they knew what was considered right.

And some people certainly acted on the basis of the models held
up for public praise. This is perhaps best seen in the case of widows.
Throughout the country commemorative arches erected with government permission honored widows who had remained chaste for
decades or who had committed suicide. These displays inspired many
young widows, even in families of modest means, to renounce remarriage or even commit suicide. Men's and women's understanding of
marriage and wifely roles was undoubtedly influenced by this public
admiration for steadfast widows.

Why did the educated class accept the idea that young widows
should not remarry? Other things Ch'eng I or Chu Hsi said about
family practices (such as their proposals to reinstate the primary line
and not divide property) found no such acceptance. A contributing
factor may have been the examination system that created an educated class larger than the economy could really support. Not only
did those aspiring to higher status wish to distinguish themselves
through exemplary family behavior, but they needed to manage their
family property with great care, making them only too happy to as-
sign a younger son to be the heir of a cousin and his widow. Widow
suicide was especially prevalent in southern Anhwei and coastal Fukien, areas that were highly commercialized and produced many officials, creating an extremely competitive environment and a high
level of frustration among aspiring scholars.[43] And, quite uncon-

[42] Ebrey, *Chinese Civilization and Society*, p. 205.

[43] Susan Mann, "Women in the Kinship, Class, and Community Structures of Qing
Dynasty China," *Journal of Asian Studies* 46 (1987): 37–56.

sciously, the custom of widow chastity may have helped limit the rate of growth of the upper class by taking some women out of the child-bearing population.[44]

CONCLUSION

At the beginning of this essay I asserted that the "Confucianization" of Chinese society was not simply the product of indoctrination or trickle-down from the elite, and identified four agents as particularly important: popular religion, the state, the educated elite, and books. By way of conclusion, I would like to review the relative importance of different means of spreading ideas at different times.

First let me underline how significant the state was in shaping the development of the Chinese family system and especially in fostering a high level of uniformity across class, ethnic, and regional lines. It seems likely that surnames spread through government policies of registering the population. The small family as a unit of production and consumption under the control of a family head was fostered by government taxation policies, laws of land tenure, and legal standards of authority and responsibility. Small proprietorships were likewise made more prevalent than they otherwise would have been by repeated government attempts to foster them. The growth of the educated class, from Sung times on, certainly owed much to printing but perhaps as much to the government's expansion of the examination system. The Ming and Ch'ing states also took an active interest in popular education, not only through schools, but also through lectures and other attempts at proselytizing.

Generally speaking, the earlier the historical period, the less crucial indoctrination by either the state or the educated elite seems to have been. From Han times on, scholars publicly praised family heads who could hold complex families together; but the reason that peasants favored a patriarchal family structure probably had more to do with the political economy of the time and the common need to pay taxes and avoid debts than with the successful communication of these exemplary models. Similar family values have emerged in many other peasant societies and probably would have appeared in China even if no efforts were made by the elite to publicize their conceptions of ideal family heads. An even stronger case can be made for the practice of relatively early marriage, which was more often discouraged by scholars than advocated. Early marriage is common in peasant so-

[44] Cf. Ts'ui-jung Liu, "The Demography of Two Chinese Clans in Hsiao-shan, Chekiang, 1650–1850," in *Family and Population in East Asian History*, ed. Susan B. Hanley and Arthur P. Wolf (Stanford: Stanford University Press, 1985), pp. 20–21, 28.

cieties in which married children live with parents; it has more to do
with the family head's need to maintain authority over his sons and
ensure a supply of family labor than with moral ideals. Still, because
this practice reinforces parental authority, its widespread practice is
an important feature of the family system.

There is evidence, however, that by the Ch'ing period ideas were
spreading from the top down, both through varieties of indoctrination and through imitation. For instance, the value placed on widow
chastity is unlikely to have begun among peasants. It was rooted in
Confucian teachings, especially Ch'eng I's statement that giving up
one's chastity is worse than giving up one's life. This concern for fidelity had connections with the situation of the educated class, but
had no roots in the daily life of peasants. Moreover, there seems little
doubt that this ideal became recognized by peasants (even if not often
copied) because the large educated class in Ch'ing times made a considerable fuss about it. Whatever the psychological, political, and economic reasons members of the elite promoted this value, the general
recognition of it in society was a product of publicity.[45]

Texts in and of themselves also played crucial roles in the spread
of certain ideas and practices. Knowledge of the ritual rules for exogamy and mourning is perhaps the best case. Ordinary people's desire to know the correct practice was fostered by the legal codes, the
spread of descent groups, and the whole panoply of educational efforts that regularly reminded them that there were correct ways to
define and treat kin. But agreement on what the correct ways were
was possible only with the wide circulation of texts drawing on a common tradition. In this case the tradition was based in the ritual classics
and refined and updated by scholars whose works the government
certified as orthodox. Even those who could not read knew that these
texts were authoritative and asked others to consult them when
needed.

Basic Confucian ethical values, especially those that became orthodox during the Han dynasty, certainly were fundamental to the Chinese family and social relations generally. A more problematic issue
is the impact of Neo-Confucianism. My suspicion is that Neo-Confucian ideas changed daily behavior more in unintended than in intended ways. Let me give two examples.

Ming and Ch'ing lineage and descent group documents regularly
cite the writings of Ch'eng I, Chang Tsai, and Chu Hsi on the impor-

---

[45] For a different view, see Jennifer Holmgren, "The Economic Foundations of Virtue: Widow-Remarriage in Early and Modern China," *Australian Journal of Chinese Affairs* 13 (1985): 1–27.

tance of organizing kin, establishing *tsung* (the ancient type of descent group), making offerings to "first ancestors," setting aside inalienable "sacrificial fields," and setting up ancestral halls. One might therefore think that these ideas were a major force in stimulating the development of descent groups, which began to take off just shortly after they were articulated. However, while these ideas were important in providing a vocabulary that legitimated the efforts of educated men to provide leadership to groups of their local agnates, the groups themselves generally came into existence for other reasons; in stimulating their emergence, the new ideas about the *tsung* were not as important as the religious significance of graves and grave rites. These ideas about graves were not derived from Confucianism, though Ch'eng I and Chu Hsi gave them grudging acceptance as "of no great harm." Moreover, the terminology derived from Ch'eng I and Chu Hsi was later used to sanctify institutions quite unlike those they had envisioned. For instance, Chu Hsi held to the ancient system of sacrifices back only four generations and his ancestral hall was a household altar presided over by a direct heir of the great-great grandfather chosen by primogeniture, and not at all similar to the group ancestral halls of later descent groups.

The Chinese practice of adopting a male heir in the absence of sons of one's own, choosing a man or boy from outside the descent group, if need be, could similarly be seen as proof of the overwhelming influence of Confucianism on the Chinese family. By Ch'ing times even poor peasants made great efforts to secure male heirs. It was not enough for a sonless couple to have a daughter stay at home and have her husband and sons support them in their old age; one of the daughter's sons must become their descendant. Without a daughter, or where uxorilocal marriage was considered the greater evil, adoption was the regular recourse. These adoption practices can be looked on as Confucian because the classics stressed the importance of ancestral rites, and without a male heir these rites could not continue. But on closer analysis adoption seems to have spread despite the classics and Neo-Confucianism. The classics explicitly limited ancestral sacrifices by commoners and gentlemen, but both took to performing them well before Neo-Confucian scholars such as Ch'eng I and Chu Hsi accommodated this development. And Chu Hsi never was willing to set aside the classical principle that ancestors are pleased only by sacrifices from their own descendants, or at least people of their own descent line. Adopting a daughter's son, he argued, was totally unacceptable. If there were no suitable agnatic adoptees, then a line simply dies out. Its spirit tablets could still receive offerings for the canonical four generations, but at the altar of a collateral relative, and in his *Family Rituals (Chia li)* Chu Hsi regularly describes how the tablets of heirless collateral relatives should be handled. Moreover, Chu Hsi even urged someone who discovered that he had been adopted to leave his adoptive parents and search for his natural parents so that he could serve them.

What was the effect of Chu Hsi's strictures on Chinese adoption practices? They undoubtedly motivated some of his more committed followers to search for their natural parents or let an uncle's line die out. Moreover, they probably contributed to the strengthening of legal prohibitions of nonagnatic successions. But they did little more than slow down the rate of nonagnatic adoptions among the educated elite and had even less impact outside it.

The agency for the spread of Chinese ideas about adoption does not appear to be indoctrination. None of the instructions in the *Sacred Edict* or the *Trimetrical Classic* stress the necessity of adoption. Descent groups often reiterated this rule against nonagnatic adoption, and when they had estates tried to keep "outsiders" from gaining shares. In fact, the Ming and Ch'ing law codes even forbade leaving property to an adopted heir of another surname. Peasants explained their desire for a son in terms of their need for someone to care for them in old age and after death. Other societies have found different solutions to the problem of childless old age, so this, by itself, is not a complete explanation. The need for an heir after death, however, seems to have been compelling.

My contention is that this component of the "Confucian" family system gained near-universal recognition because the practice of ancestor worship had become the core of the religion of most Chinese. Adoptees were needed to serve as chief mourners and preside at sacrifices, but in the rituals as actually practiced, not as imagined in the classics. Chinese funerals and ancestral rites can certainly be termed "Confucian" if by that one means that they bear specific resemblance to the practices described in the classics and practiced by aristocrats in the Chou period. But the development of funeral rituals in China was not simply an outgrowth of the research or philosophical musings of writers on the subject; it had a logic very much its own as a kind of popular religion, influenced no doubt by a great many factors—ideas about ghosts, afterlife, and geomancy, changes in family organization and rules of succession, the development of descent groups, perhaps even the indigenous non-Han customs in parts of the country. By Sung times it was widely accepted that Buddhist clergy could perform rites for one's ancestors, so why not another substitute, such as a nonagnatic heir? Neo-Confucians wrote at length about rituals, but anyone who reads what they wrote cannot fail to see that popular ritual life (including the ritual life of the educated elite, their main concern) was largely beyond their control. Ssu-ma Kuang and Chu Hsi both wrote manuals for the practice of family rituals, and both deplored the prevalence of Buddhist or merely vulgar practices. Their works certainly had an impact, especially on standardizing what was considered correct practice. Yet even in the late Ming and Ch'ing, literati who tried to follow its prescriptions on funerals saw themselves as confronting solidly entrenched ritual practices very much at odds with the *Family Rituals*. Among the well educated, ancestral rites often were highly formal, done in the traditional ways because they were the proper thing to do, not because the celebrant sensed any real communication with his ancestors or feared his ancestors' wrath if he neglected his duties. As mentioned above, a skepticism about the participation of ancestors in the rites dated back to the late Chou, and did not necessarily dampen feelings of obligation toward ancestors or beliefs that the rites should be performed. Yet among ordinary people, beliefs in ghosts and the powers of the dead were clearly very strong. Funerals did not merely commemorate the dead, they dealt with powerful forces and had to be conducted properly for the soul to gain peace. And the steps taken had major consequences for descendants—a belief well attested to by the use of geomancy to choose burial sites. Anyone who was a full participant in this culture—who performed sacrifices, participated in the steps of funerals, and shared the ideas about the dead conveyed in them— would not be indifferent about having an heir to serve him in death.

Exactly how ancestor worship developed in China has never been adequately studied. I suspect that the transmission of beliefs and practices was not entirely congruent. In the realm of beliefs, indoctrination played little or no role. Belief in the spiritual importance of one's close ancestors is apparently very ancient, and may generally have been stronger among the less educated. The elite might well have become indifferent to these ideas had it not been for the many channels through which ideas could spread upward (through social mobility into the elite, through the family context where wives and servants had different backgrounds and less education, and so on). By Ming and Ch'ing times the Buddhist and Taoist sects propagated their ideas through the written word, publishing popular tracts of many sorts. The religious ideas about the dead intrinsic to ancestor worship, however, were apparently not spread by tracts of these sorts.

The *practices* of ancestor worship seem to have spread in a different fashion. Some practices, such as worship at graves and geomancy, appear to have begun among ordinary people and from there spread to the elite. But a remarkable number of practices were based on elite ritual tradition, such as use of wooden spirit tablets and written prayers, and clearly spread from the top down, by direct imitation of the observed behavior of the elite, institutionalization of them in descent groups, or use of ritual guides. Once the classical limitations on ancestral rites by commoners were officially discarded, scholars fully encouraged the performance of orthodox practices, believing that such practices instilled appropriate family virtues and behavior. Ordinary people undoubtedly found their performance of these rites a meaningful experience, but what it meant to them depended also on their other beliefs and experiences.

Did Neo-Confucianism have a great impact on any aspect of family life? My tentative answer would be yes, but that the greatest impact was in conveying basic Confucian principles to ordinary people. Neo-Confucian reformers took a new interest in the daily life of commoners in response to the challenge posed by the Buddhist and Taoist clergy, who not only preached to commoners but also officiated at their funerals and ancestral rites. In response to this challenge, Neo-Confucian reformers proposed and initiated new institutions—such as descent groups, village compacts, and charitable schools—that brought the elite and commoners into regular contact and that often taught a fairly accessible vision of orthodox family behavior derived from classical Confucianism and general elite culture. They also prepared handbooks of family rituals that could be used by local officials or local educated men to guide ordinary people toward orthodox practices. Some of the preaching done in these contexts may well have fallen on deaf ears, but contact itself was important, facilitating the spread of cultural ideas and habits. The level of this contact seems to have steadily increased during Ming-Ch'ing times and may well account for the relatively high degree of uniformity in Chinese family practices observed in nineteenth- and twentieth-century China.

The topics I have touched on here could all have been dealt with in much greater detail. More research needs to be done on the development of ancestor worship, the relationship of land tenure to family organization, the changing use of surnames and surname categories, the uses of ritual manuals, and the education of ordinary people. I will have accomplished my purpose, however, if I have shown that "Confucian social relations" as practiced by the majority of people in China were the product of a particular type of economy, elite, and religion. I will leave it to other scholars to decide whether the level of "Confucianization" of the Chinese peasantry at the end of the Ch'ing was what has given Chinese areas (including Taiwan, Hong Kong, and Singapore) advantages in economic growth, or whether Confucian ideas previously confined largely to the elite and common only after the introduction of modern education were crucial. I will, however, point out that these areas have not had a common educational system in the twentieth century, suggesting that even if modern education was important, its success was conditioned by common cultural values predating the twentieth century.

The contrasts between the historical process by which "Confucian" ideas were spread in China, Korea, and Japan (see the next two chapters) are so striking that it is surprising so much can be identified as common in the worldview or culture of these countries today. In Korea, "Confucianism" was a foreign import that was used to get both the elite and, eventually, commoners to change some of their most basic social institutions, such as their methods of transmitting property. In China, to the contrary, it seems that "Confucianism" was continually stretched to accommodate changes that came from other sources, such as the state's fiscal measures or popular ideas about ghosts or geomancy. In Japan, "Confucianism" was largely associated with schools and those who attended schools, and until the introduction of compulsory education was not a large part of uneducated people's daily lives. Even ancestral rites were performed as Buddhist rites.

These historical contrasts raise questions for those dealing with the contemporary situation elsewhere in this book. What are the implications of the differences in the institutional bases for "Confucian" values in these three countries? Does deference to authority owe more to the family system in China, but more to political structures in Korea or Japan? If so, will there be differences in the experiences of these countries as the economic basis of family life changes or political structures are altered? If today the Chinese seem less concerned with loyalty to groups beyond the family, could it be that the lower-level Confucianism of the family was that much stronger among Chinese peasants than among Japanese or Korean peasants, making it more difficult to inculcate a higher-order (previously, elite) version that put loyalty to the ruler or state above family goals? Could a major difference between China and Japan be that by the time universal, compulsory education was introduced in China, Confucianism was no longer orthodox and only a dilute version (everyday ethics) was taught?

Chapter 2

THE CONFUCIANIZATION OF KOREAN SOCIETY

JaHyun Kim Haboush

To SPEAK of the "Confucianization" of Korean society assumes that Korean society had not been Confucian, that this society underwent visible changes by adopting what can be identified as distinctively Confucian features, and that these changes affected a significant portion of the population. Korea fits this description rather well. In many crucial areas of life, ancient and medieval Korean society maintained practices that bore no resemblance to Confucian practices. By about the eighteenth century, however, Korea had become a normative Confucian society. Other religious traditions did not disappear. Buddhism and various folk religions remained major forces, especially among women and the lower classes. Nonetheless, measured by such standard criteria of Confucianness as patrilineage with its attendant ancestral and mourning rites, the universal acceptance of ethics concerned with the five social relations, the supremacy of the civil bureaucracy, the recruitment of officials through a civil service examination, and the uniform adoption of a Confucian curriculum in educational establishments, Chosŏn Korea in the eighteenth and nineteenth centuries can be described as very Confucian.

In fact, Korea offers an interesting comparative perspective in the larger East Asian context. Unlike China, where the Confucian system was an indigenous evolution, in Korea Confucianism began as an alien value system whose required practices often conflicted sharply with the native way of life. Despite this, by the eighteenth century Korean society was in its own way as Confucianized as Chinese society. In Japan, Confucianization was far less complete, as explained in Martin Collcutt's following chapter.

One should bear several things in mind when discussing the "Confucianization" of Korean society. One is the issue of Chinese influence on the process. At its most Confucianized, Korea differed significantly from China in many practices. Given indigenous Korean familial and social structures—a rigid class structure, the relative importance of women in the family, and a polity in which a small elite exerted tremendous influence over the throne—it is not surprising that Confucianization would proceed in a distinct manner. Nevertheless, from the beginning, Confucianism in Korea developed in close association with the culture in which it originated. Korean written culture began with the use of Chinese ideographic characters, which were most likely introduced through the Confucian classics. Chinese classical language remained the main mode of written communication for educated Korean men until the nineteenth century. Korea was almost continuously influenced by cultural and political developments in China, where Confucianism, both as philosophy and as social and political practice, was constantly evolving and changing. What Koreans selected for domestic use from the vast repertoire ranging from the classics to the latest developments in China depended on Korean awareness and interpretations of these sources and the needs and ends that they were intended to serve in any given period.

The process of Confucianization in Korea was long, enduring almost the full span of Korea's written history. The characteristics of Korean Confucianism in each era were closely related to the changing Korean perceptions of what Confucianism was and what role it should play; these changes also reflected the Korean commitment to the Confucian value system. Confucian influence began incipiently, followed by a period during which Koreans, making no particular cultural or ideological commitments, pragmatically borrowed specific aspects of the Chinese system. During the Chosŏn dynasty, however, when the Korean commitment to Confucianism deepened, the Confucian system was no longer perceived as merely Chinese. Korean Confucians came to view Confucianism as the font of truth from which all civilized peoples should draw sustenance. They correspondingly regarded the Confucianization of Korea as a transformation to a truly civilized moral order.

With this conviction, Korean Confucians launched a massive social undertaking to transform Korea into a normative Confucian society. Thus, while they were deeply concerned with differences and conflicts between Confucian and indigenous customs and mores, their concern was not that Korean practices differed from contemporary Chinese practices but rather that they differed from the ideal represented in the texts. Although eager to imitate Chinese practices they thought suitable, Korean Confucians were critical when they thought the Chinese deviated from the ideal norm. China, which did enjoy some privileged access, did not hold a monopoly on the "truth."

It was not long before Koreans regarded themselves as more faithful to the Confucian tradition than the Chinese. At first it was their disapproval of the popular Wang Yang-ming school that led to this view.[1] But when the Manchus replaced the Ming dynasty in 1644, Koreans considered civilization to have been lost in China. They saw themselves as the last custodians of civilization. Occupied as it was by the "barbarian" Manchus, China lost any claim as a role model. The task was no longer "Confucianization," but the maintenance and transmission of Confucian norms in as pure a form as possible.[2]

Studying the process of Confucianization by determining which segment of the population came to embrace which aspect of Confucian life—political, social, intellectual—and by identifying the agents and means of change, one sees that Korea exhibits a course quite distinct from that of either China or Japan. The process expanded from a small governing elite to include commoners and slaves, and from the public sphere to the private sphere. During the Chosŏn dynasty pressure was applied to all aspects of life at once through vigorous social legislation. The change was slow at first, but momentum soon gathered, accelerating the process.

Several fundamental changes warrant attention. One is the influence of the Confucian meritocratic ideal as it applied to the indigenous class structure. Another is the Confucian influence on government and political culture. Lastly, the patrilineal restructuring of the family on the Confucian model was perhaps the greatest normative change in Korean society. I will address these issues in a chronological discussion of the Confucianization of Korean society. I will concentrate on the interplay between indigenous structures and Confucian influence.

ANCIENT KOREA

The first Korean exposure to Confucianism is usually dated the second century B.C., when Han China set up the four commanderies in the Korean peninsula. The Han Chinese must have brought the Confucian classics with them to their colonial posts. Most likely, Koreans acquired knowledge of Confucian political administration by observing Chinese practice and applied this knowledge in transforming the peninsula from tribal federations to the centralized states that finalized into the three kingdoms of subsequent centuries. It was Koguryŏ, situated in the north and the first to develop, that displayed

[1] Martina Deuchler, "Reject the False and Uphold the Straight: Attitudes toward Heterodox Thought in Early Yi Korea," in *The Rise of Neo-Confucianism in Korea*, ed. Wm. Theodore de Bary and JaHyun Kim Haboush (New York: Columbia University Press, 1985), pp. 399–404.

[2] JaHyun Kim Haboush, *A Heritage of Kings: One Man's Monarchy in the Confucian World* (New York: Columbia University Press, 1988), pp. 23–25.

Confucian influence in the early centuries. A National Confucian Academy was established in 372, and in 373 a code of administrative law was promulgated, creating a new centralized bureaucratic structure. The southern state of Paekche followed suit. Not until the early seventh century did Silla, in contention with Koguryŏ and Paekche for control and conquest of the peninsula, make serious attempts at adopting Confucian features of government. What Silla sought through Confucianism was a measure of centralization, a patriotic code of conduct for its ruling warrior class in peace and war, and transmission of the arts of government to this class.

The impact of Confucianism on the three states was limited, as the overriding religious ethos was Buddhist (the Korean states having converted between the fourth and the sixth centuries). Confucianism was deemed useful as a model for political organization within strict limits. The three states, for instance, evolved into monarchies with somewhat centralized bureaucracies incorporating such standard features as the six ministries.[3] The concept of meritocracy, however, did not accompany the adoption of a Confucian bureaucracy. In each state, the bureaucracy seems to have been staffed exclusively by aristocrats. In Silla, where we have clearer knowledge, each bureaucratic rank was pegged to bone rank, which was in turn determined at birth by the ranks of both parents.

That Confucian practice was confined to the public sphere in Silla is illustrated by the way in which Confucian social ethics were incorporated into the codes of conduct for the *hwarang*, the knightly organization consisting of aristocratic youth. The first three codes reiterated three of the five Confucian social relations—loyalty to the ruler, filial piety to one's father, and trust between friends. These were seen as useful in upholding political and social order and in maintaining the cohesiveness of the group. Conspicuously missing here—or, for that matter, elsewhere—is any mention of precepts governing the more private aspects of family life.

After the Silla unification of the Korean peninsula in 668, the civil aspects of rule were further emphasized. The Royal Confucian Academy, established in 682, furnished a more systematic education to aristocratic youths. Its curriculum included Confucian classics and history. In 788, the government instituted a state examination with which to recruit officials. Open only to the aristocracy, it was an attempt to experiment with meritocracy in a strict hereditary class society. Many students went to the cosmopolitan T'ang capital to study. As a consequence, the earlier interest in Confucianism, which seems

---

[3] In the case of Koguryŏ, we have no information on its bureaucratic structure.

to have had a rather technical focus, acquired a scholarly component. In the late Silla, there seems to have been a considerable number of people educated in Confucian political philosophy who tried to uphold the Confucian ideal of public service.

THE KORYŎ SOCIETY

In the Koryŏ (918-1392), from its inception, Confucianism played a significant role in the formation of political ideology and government structure. It is particularly notable that Wang Kŏn, the founder of the Koryŏ state, turned to the Confucian concept of the Mandate of Heaven to claim his legitimacy. The Mandate of Heaven was the Confucian political theory posited on the belief that Heaven gave the right to rule to the most virtuous person even if he was otherwise ordinary. The legitimacy of the ruler in Korean states had hitherto been based on divinity of birth, and Wang Kŏn's proclamation of legitimacy based on the Mandate of Heaven was epochal in the political theory of rulership in Korea. That Wang Kŏn, not of royal birth, did turn to this concept and that he used it to successfully fashion the legitimacy of the Wang house indicate that the Confucian political ethos already exerted considerable influence.

In the early years of Koryŏ, T'ang served as the model for Confucianization of the government. The civil service examination was adopted in 958 and a rigidly hierarchical bureaucracy consisting of civil and military officials, known as the *yangban*, was instituted. Though the bureaucratic class was a self-perpetuating group with almost exclusive access to education and official posts, status was now determined by government post. T'ang also provided the ideal image of man. The civil bureaucrats, who came to dominate, were a small, cohesive group, mostly descendants of Silla aristocrats, who lived in the capital city of Kaesŏng. They came to share certain distinct characteristics of the "Confucian literati" that one generally associates with T'ang culture. The civil elite cultivated an image of refinement and attempted to master the literary arts and acquire a discriminating taste in other arts. The Confucian view of history also seems to have gained currency to the extent that moral criteria were used as the organizing principle in evaluating history. One can see this in Kim Pusik's *Samguk sagi* (The Historical Records of the Three Kingdoms, 1145), the first extant history of Korea. As the early Koryŏ civil elite's "Confucianness" seems to have been mainly aesthetic and literary rather than philosophical or religious, Confucian influence seems to have been limited to public behavior and public discourse. They did not denounce such social customs counter to Confucian practice as endogamy, nor did they renounce the Buddhist faith. In their minds, as expressed by Ch'oe Sǔngno, a very influential tenth-century states-man, Confucianism had a specific place in the political realm, just as Buddhism did in the spiritual realm.[4]

The rise of the educational establishment paralleled this rise of the civil elite. At first the state established a National Academy and re-gional schools to train bureaucrats. Sometime in the mid to late elev-enth century, private schools run by prominent scholar-officials came into existence and began to attract students. Soon these private schools, which came to number twelve, functioned as centers of edu-cational activity while state-run schools fell into ruin. The twelve pri-vate schools, like the state schools before them, were open exclusively to the children of the civil elite, and eventually the civil service ex-amination came to be administered at these same schools. The close relationship between master and disciples and examiner and exam-inee at the civil service examination ensured the perpetuation of this elite group.

The military coup of 1170 disrupted the supremacy of this civil elite and its milieu. The newly established regime, which resembled the military governments that ruled Japan from 1185 to 1867, lasted until the Mongols arrived in 1258, and its dominant ethos was nation-alistic and Buddhist. Confucian influence was definitely on the wane. This period, however, is usually described as a time of fluid social mobility, although not much is known about this presumed social mo-bility. The military needed administrative expertise, and it employed persons with some literary training who were not necessarily from elite families. The former civil elite, now in refuge, may have taken in students, thereby spreading Confucianism beyond the capital city, beyond the confines of the small, cohesive, group that had enjoyed dominance. Soon, however, a new elite, perhaps incorporating ele-ments of the old elite, seems to have asserted its dominance. The twelve private schools continued to operate during this period, pre-sumably fulfilling much the same function as before.

Ironically, it was during the Mongol domination of Koryǒ, which lasted from 1258 to 1356, that Neo-Confucianism took root in Korea. When the Yüan dynasty resumed the civil service examination in 1314, the Koryǒ examination came to serve as the provincial exami-nation for the Yüan empire. Three people who passed the Koryǒ ex-amination were allowed to sit for the metropolitan examination in Peking. The Yüan examination was based on the Neo-Confucian

[4] Hi-woong Kang, "Development of the Korean Ruling Class from Late Silla to Early Koryǒ," Ph.D. diss. (The University of Washington, 1964), pp. 100–250.

texts—the Five Classics and the Four Books with the Chu Hsi commentaries—and the Koryŏ examination perforce adopted the same texts. But it was not only through the texts that Koreans came to be introduced to Neo-Confucianism. Since Korea had been made a part of the Mongol empire, Koreans now had easy access to China, and they frequented the Yüan capital (now conveniently located in north China) on an unprecedented scale. Many remained for prolonged stays, especially those who were in the service of retired Koryŏ kings. The Koryŏ royal house had not been eliminated, but incorporated into the Mongol imperial family. The future Koryŏ king was required to marry a Mongol princess and, until his accession, to reside in Peking. Born and raised in that cosmopolitan capital, many Koryŏ kings chose an early abdication and retired to Peking, bringing a large retinue of Korean officials. Often their residences served as meeting places for Korean and Chinese scholars. King Ch'ungsŏn, for instance, abdicated in favor of his son in 1313, and upon returning to Peking set up a study hall known as Man'gwondang to which he invited renowned Chinese Neo-Confucian scholars such as Yao Sui, Yen Fu, and Chao Meng-fu. This gave Korean scholars firsthand exposure to current scholarship.

The Korean Neo-Confucian establishment steadily grew, and by the time the Mongols lost their influence, it was a force to contend with. By the mid-1360s, the new breed of scholars had rehabilitated the Royal College complete with a Neo-Confucian curriculum, and a large number of students flocked there.[5] It was not long before this young generation of Neo-Confucian scholars rejected the limited role Confucianism had hitherto played in the Buddhist world. They wanted nothing less than a total transformation of Korea into a Confucian social order in conformance with their vision of a moral universe. But for this, a new polity was needed. The reformers went to work. Allying themselves with a powerful general, Yi Sŏnggye, they replaced Koryŏ with the Chosŏn dynasty and embarked on the task of creating a Confucian normative society.[6] In this sense, the founding of the Chosŏn dynasty can be described as a "Confucian revolution."[7]

[5] Yi Sŏngmu, "The Influence of Neo-Confucianism on Education and the Civil Service Examination System in Fourteenth- and Fifteenth-Century Korea," in *The Rise of Neo-Confucianism*, ed. de Bary and Haboush, p. 138.

[6] Martina Deuchler, "Neo-Confucianism: The Impulse for Social Action in Early Yi Korea," *The Journal of Korean Studies* 2:73–75.

[7] Han Yongu, *Chosŏn chŏn'gi sahoe kyŏngje yŏn'gu* (Seoul: Ŭryu munhwasa, 1983), pp. 11–50.

Toward a Confucian Normative Society: The Search for Models

The Chosŏn founders based their societal models on the classics—in particular, ritual texts such as the *Chou-li* (The Rites of Chou), the *Li-chi* (Book of Rites), and the *I-li* (Rituals and Ceremonials). While these texts remained the source of inspiration and the ultimate reference point, the writings of Sung Neo-Confucian scholars also were influential in shaping the Korean reformers' moral and social vision. Chu Hsi's *Chia-li* (K. *Karye*, Family Ritual), for instance, emerged as a more practical guide to redirecting Korean social norms.[8]

The early Chosŏn Korean attitude toward the contemporary Ming society was rather ambivalent. They were trying to create their own version of the ideal society of the classical period, the very ideal society of antiquity that the Sung Neo-Confucians had looked back to. They acknowledged that it was in China that this "civilization" had begun and been maintained, if not in ideal form. The Ming dynasty, which restored China to civilization from "barbarian" Mongol domination, was a legitimate heir to this tradition. The Koreans' acceptance of Ming China's status as a direct heir to Confucian civilization and their acknowledgment of China's maturity as a Confucian society were not accompanied by a sense that Confucian civilization was uniquely Chinese or that the Chinese manifestation of it was intrinsically superior. Korean Confucians, like Chinese Confucians, regarded Confucianism as universal truth applicable to all civilized societies. That Korea was a relatively late convert did not signify that the quality of its Confucian civilization should be inferior to Chinese civilization. In fact, the Ming, compromised and even corrupted by the forces of history, was a pale imitation of the ideal society that the Korean reformers, full of zealous optimism, were determined to create.[9]

Korean perceptions of contemporary China were colored by the fact that Korea and China were political entities. The early Chosŏn relationship to the Ming was quite tense, and so diplomatic and other contacts were quite limited. The Ming, as the far more powerful and dominant of the two, must have seemed demanding and threatening during periods of diplomatic strain, and at times Koreans seem to have been much more aware of political separateness than cultural affinity. Still, Ming China, where Confucian norms had long since

---

[8] See Chung Chai-sik, "Chŏng Tojon: 'Architect' of Yi Dynasty Government and Ideology," in *The Rise of Neo-Confucianism*, ed. de Bary and Haboush, pp. 67–71. Also see Deuchler, "Neo-Confucianism," p. 84.

[9] Haboush, *A Heritage of Kings*, pp. 21–23.

evolved, was an obvious place to look toward in the Korean search for direction and guidance, and there was a certain amount of institutional mimicry of the Ming. Most notable was the verbatim adoption of the *Ta Ming lü* (Great Ming Statutes) as the Chosŏn criminal codes. It was as if, in searching for models for ritual and law as the two axes of the social order—ritual being a positive force expressing Confucian belief in man as a rational and self-regulatory agent and law as a corrective and punitive deterrent—Koreans were willing to accept the contemporary Ming version of the law with no compunctions. The Chosŏn reformers preferred to seek and define their own rituals, however, through consulting and examining other examples.

Much of the search for models in deciding upon the procedures and protocols of Chosŏn dynastic rituals was conducted by examining the practices of various Chinese dynasties, most notably those of the Sung court. Though Ming examples were consulted and investigated, they were more often than not passed over in favor of earlier practices. When it came to such crucial matters as the structure of the bureaucracy, education, and the reorganization of the family, this was even more true.

Education

The Neo-Confucian vision of the moral order was predicated upon a belief in man's perfectibility. Education—that is, moral education with the proper Neo-Confucian curriculum—was the means through which this was to be effected. This conviction in education as the central force in transforming society impelled Chosŏn founders to establish a nationwide public educational system. Highest priority in this endeavor was given to training bureaucrats inculcated with Neo-Confucian political ideology. Within a few decades, a comprehensive nationwide state-run school system emerged. The new Royal College was built in 1398, and four district schools were constructed in the capital by 1438. In 1406, a royal decree made a local school imperative in each district. Enrollment in the Royal College, a tertiary school, was limited to 200 students and was mainly reserved for licentiate degree holders who were preparing for the final *munkwa* degree. The four district schools of the capital, and local schools were primarily for students preparing for the licentiate degree. A maximum enrollment of one hundred students was authorized for each of the four district schools in the capital while an enrollment ranging from thirty to ninety students was permitted depending upon the administrative classification of the district.[10] These students were accorded certain privileges, including exemption from military service and the right to sit for the preliminary examinations upon the successful completion of coursework.

The curriculum at these schools typically consisted of the *Elementary Learning*, the *Classic of Filial Piety*, the *Four Books*, the *Five Classics*, philosophical and ritual texts by Sung Neo-Confucians, and various Korean and Chinese works of poetry and history. For several decades, meeting the need for textbooks was a serious challenge. The Ming court sent Korea some books, including new editions of the *Four Books* and the *Five Classics* with the Chu Hsi commentaries and other Sung philosophical works. The Korean envoys on their ambassadorial missions to China were routinely requested to look for, purchase, and bring back new books. The extensive use of movable type, starting in the early fifteenth century, facilitated the printing and distribution of these texts, soon ameliorating the shortage of textbooks. The state schools prospered, and by the end of the fifteenth century the number of students enrolled reached 15,550.[11]

Sometime in the first half of the sixteenth century, the scholarly establishment came into its own. Accomplished scholars appeared in large numbers. Yi T'oegye and Yi Yulgok, two of the greatest Neo-Confucian scholars Korea produced, were active during this period. The era of merely absorbing established wisdom was over; Koreans were embarking as contributors to scholarship. An institutional corollary to this was the growth of private academies. The state schools, staffed with colorless functionaries, lost their appeal. Many students did not want merely to study the Neo-Confucian texts, but wished to study with specific scholars of repute or at academies associated with distinct philosophical schools. The government encouraged the private academies, providing some of them with a charter, a tax-exempt status, and financial assistance. Private academies, which already had begun to appear as early as the mid-fifteenth century, multiplied rapidly, reaching more than 600 in number by the close of the seventeenth century. While academies still prepared students for the civil service examination, they also functioned as research centers for private scholars. As the educated population grew and education was no longer pursued purely as a means of attaining an official post, academies were increasingly looked upon as strongholds of intellectual and scholarly activity.

[10] Edward Wagner, *The Literati Purges* (Cambridge, Mass.: Harvard University Press, 1974), p. 20.

[11] Yi Sŏngmu, "The Influence of Neo-Confucianism," pp. 143–45.

A Neo-Confucian ideological underpinning also emerged in the civil service examinations. It was not just that the examination system was more comprehensive—it was now a three-tier system—or that it became the undisputed and principal channel to official status; the ideal performance of the successful candidate changed. Beauty of style in literary composition, which formerly had been held in highest esteem as the measure of a candidate's talent, now was placed second to knowledge of classics. Now moral knowledge was prized and it was believed to be best pursued through the study of the classics and other Neo-Confucian texts.[12] Thus, from the beginning of the Chosŏn dynasty, a classics licentiate degree holder came to be held in higher esteem than a literary licentiate degree holder, a complete break from Koryŏ practice.[13] How best to discern a candidate's moral understanding of the texts emerged as a major issue and it led to protracted and intense debates on the method of testing for the classics licentiate examination—whether it should be oral or written.[14]

The Confucianization of Government

From the very beginning, as one can infer from the dynastic founder's coronation edict, the mission of the new dynasty was the creation of a Confucian polity and society. Heading the list of most pressing tasks was a restructuring of the government and the establishment of a procedure to choose personnel to fill governmental posts. One could, in a way, view the evolution of the Chosŏn government as a successive, though not linear, series of phases for achieving this aim. What is noticeable is that changes in the government were not so much structural as functional. The Chosŏn government preserved much of the structure that it inherited from the Koryŏ. Of course, the Chosŏn government went through its share of institutional changes in its five-hundred-year dynastic span, but they were mostly variations within an acceptable framework. More meaningful changes, however, evolved through the function of the various offices and agencies, and the relationships among them and between them and the throne. This proceeded in the context of a rigid if ill-

[12] JaHyun Kim Haboush, "The Education of the Yi Crown Prince: A Study in Confucian Pedagogy," in *The Rise of Neo-Confucianism*, ed. de Bary and Haboush, pp. 191–94.

[13] In fact, the founder's coronation edict decreed the elimination of the literary licentiate examination from the preliminary examination, leaving only the classics licentiate examination. This decision was reversed and the literary licentiate examination was restored, but a literary licentiate degree did not regain the prestige that it had had previously. Yi Sŏngmu, "The Influence of Neo-Confucianism," pp. 148–49.

[14] Ibid, pp. 149–52.

defined class structure and a continuing rivalry between the throne and the bureaucracy, both of which characterized Korean government from the Silla period on.

Since the bureaucracy was relatively small and power was perpetuated to some extent within a rather small group, the throne was vulnerable to bureaucratic pressure exerted through ideological indoctrination. This pressure, however, was not always successfully applied or received. Depending on power groupings at the court, bureaucratic pressure on the throne was frequently either curtailed or circumvented. This suggests that for a century or so, despite bureaucratic efforts to gain ideological control of the throne, both the bureaucracy and the throne used Confucian ideology mainly as a mechanism of rule.

This relatively casual attitude toward Confucian ideology, however, did not last long. What had been viewed as the mechanism of rule soon emerged as a system of values to which the ruling elite submitted. This came neither suddenly nor without resistance. It involved many political upheavals, purges, and institutional changes. By the mid-sixteenth century, the political ethos of the Chosŏn court was predominantly Confucian. All decisions, large or small, had to be advanced, argued, and justified by Confucian rhetoric. The time-honored rivalry between the throne and the bureaucracy came to be expressed in a competition over who better understood and achieved Confucian virtue.[15]

This intensity of the Confucian ethos in political culture was institutionally represented by the Royal Lecture and the Censorate. The Classics Mat Lecture, on which the Chosŏn Royal Lecture was based, was a familiar institution in Confucian China. Yet the Royal Lecture at the Chosŏn court met thrice a day, compared to the Ming Classics Mat Lecture, which convened thrice a month. The frequency of the lecture and its gradual politicization rendered ample opportunity for bureaucratic counsel. Some of the early Yi kings canceled lectures with impunity, but by the early sixteenth century they did so at the expense of their image.[16]

The Censorate and the censorial voice, which had been subjected to the vicissitudes of time and fortune, also gained in stature and moral authority. In China, with the rise of imperial power, the function of the Censorate was increasingly reduced to surveillance of bu-

---

[15] Haboush, *A Heritage of Kings*, pp. 11–17.

[16] JaHyun Kim Haboush, "Confucian Rhetoric and Ritual as Technique of Political Dominance," *The Journal of Korean Studies* 5:39–50.

reaucrats.[17] In Korea, regarded as the conscience of the nation, the
censorial voice was as relentlessly sharp in its admonition of the
throne as in its censure of high-ranking ministers. The Censorate, in
effect, emerged as a full-fledged member along with the executive
branch and the throne in a tripartite power structure. Frequently the
censors, the best and the brightest of young bureaucrats equipped
with legal immunity when voicing criticism, contributed to the apparently moralistic tenor of the Chosŏn court.[18] Once accused, a bureaucrat could no longer function in his usual position until he was ex-
onerated of the charge either through due course or by the throne.
The king, when he came under attack, was also obliged to respond.
Thus, while it had no decision-making power, the Censorate played
an important role in the political processes of the Chosŏn court.[19]

This bureaucratic outspokenness, particularly among censors,
which seems to have become a characteristic of the Chosŏn court, was
related to the changing intellectual makeup of the bureaucracy. It
seems clear that those who entered the bureaucracy subscribed, if
only rhetorically, to the ideological underpinnings of Confucian of-
ficialdom. The combination of the recruitment of officials through
the civil service examination and the completely Confucian curriculum in educational establishments obviously exposed students and officials to the Confucian ideal of public service—a scholar should seek
office to fulfill his duty but he should take it only if he could dis-
charge this duty with no undue compromise. The prestige accorded
to the *sarim* scholars—the scholars of the woods—clearly expresses
the extent to which this ideal held sway at the time. This idea had
circulated widely among Confucians from the time of Confucius but
had fared differently at different periods in history. To understand
the appeal of this notion in Chosŏn political life from the sixteenth
century on, one must investigate the power groupings and the Korean political traditions in which this Confucian concept was politicized. While the relatively small ruling elite succeeded to a remarkable degree in perpetuating their power, they had no clear legal
sanction for their hereditary privileges, and they had to face increasing competition for office from both outside and within the group. It
seems that members of the ruling elite had to renew, individually,
their legitimation on the basis of ideological purity.

The decline of the public schools and the corresponding rise of the

[17] Charles O. Hucker, "Confucianism and the Chinese Censorial System," in *Confucianism in Action*, ed. David S. Nivison and Arthur F. Wright (Stanford: Stanford University Press, 1959), pp. 182–208.

[18] Wagner, *The Literati Purges*, pp. 122–23. Haboush, *A Heritage of Kings*, p. 19.

[19] See examples in Haboush, *A Heritage of Kings*, pp. 117–50.

private academies probably contributed to the relative ideological independence of scholar-officials. Most academies had a distinct identity expressed both by the philosophy they espoused and by the political camp or faction to which they adhered. Since the inclinations of the academies reflected those of their founders, they seemed to have split along regional lines. Kyŏngsang Province, the southwestern region, for instance, had about 300, by far the largest concentration in any one province,[20] and they mostly belonged to the Yŏngnam School. In their scholarship and in their political affiliations, the scholars of the Yŏngnam School were rivals of scholars of the Kiho School of the capital area, which continued to dominate power. It does not appear that the exclusion of the Yŏngnam scholars from power resulted in their developing a disaffection with the Confucian value system or the society. They considered themselves to be fully participating members in the community of Confucian scholars and certainly better guardians of scholarly orthodoxy and political principle than their rivals. The private academies, depending on their political and intellectual stance, had distinct relationships to the government and to the ruling elite. Collectively, they fostered the ideal of Confucian public service and played an important role in maintaining the supremacy of Confucian values in the educated population both in and out of power.[21]

Meritocracy and Heredity

Did the wider availability of education and the adoption of a comprehensive national examination system signify the rise of meritocracy during the Chosŏn dynasty? The founding ideologues did subscribe to the Confucian meritocratic ideal in their blueprints for the new state. The nationwide public school system and the examinations were devised to create a meritocratic hierarchy. It is unclear, however, whether there was a definite policy on the extent to which education and examinations should be open. The Kyŏngguk taejŏn (Great Statutes for the Governance of the State), the basic legal statutes of the Chosŏn state published in 1471, does not stipulate class qualifications to be a student or to sit for examinations. The indigenous class structure, however, soon asserted itself. Unlike in China, the examinations in Korea never came to function as a means through which power was widely dispersed. Yet, the meritocratic ideal intrin-

---

[20] Yi Ch'unhŭi, Yijo sŏwŏn mun'go ko (Seoul: Taehan min'guk kukhoe tosŏgwan, 1969), p. 17 and Appendix, pp. 1–35.

[21] Chŏng Sunmok, Han'guk sŏwŏn kyoyuk chedo yŏn'gu (Taegu: Yŏngnam taehakkyo ch'ulp'anbu, 1979), pp. 20–100.

sic to the examinations left some room for newcomers. An analysis of
14,600 who passed the *munkwa* during the Chosŏn dynasty reveals
that 750 lineages were represented among those who passed, but that
21 lineages produced 40 percent of the degree holders, while 560
lineages produced 10 percent.[22] This shows that, while power was
concentrated and perpetuated within a small elite, minor lineages
were not completely excluded.

The tension between class structure and the meritocratic ideal
seems to have been much more strongly felt during the later part of
the Chosŏn dynasty. During the eighteenth and nineteenth centuries,
the earlier societal model of a small ruling class governing a large
commoner and low-born population was gradually transformed.
With the changing economy, a larger and larger segment of the population, encouraged by government policy, aspired to and succeeded
in obtaining higher social status. Newcomers represented an increasing proportion of the candidates successful in the preliminary examinations. This upward social mobility did not challenge the concentration and perpetuation of power among the ruling group. What seems
to have happened is that the yangban class came to have more layers
and that the upwardly mobile groups came to constitute the lower
layers. Whatever its meaning, in some areas the changing demo-
graphics of social class reached absurd proportions. By sometime in
the nineteenth century, data from several districts in Kyŏngsang
Province show that more than half of the total population consisted
of yangban.[23] In a crucial sense, the traditional concept and structure
of class were seriously challenged. This seems to have been brought
about by a strange mixture that included a strong class-consciousness
and the Confucian meritocratic ideal. Class-consciousness fueled the
motivation for higher social status; this aspiration seems to have been
directed by the rhetoric of meritocracy and a certain degree of open-
ness into attempts to obtain yangban status and examination degrees.

The Confucianization of the Korean Family

In restructuring the family, the Chosŏn state faced its greatest challenge, and the family was the aspect of Korean society most markedly

[22] Edward Wagner, "The Ladder of Success in Yi Dynasty Korea," *Occasional Papers
on Korea* 1:4.

[23] Shikata Hiroshi, "Richō jinkō kansuru mibun kaikyubetsuteki kansatsu," in *Chōsen
keizai no kenkyū*, 3:368–482. Chŏng Sŏkchong, *Chosŏn hugi sahoe pyŏndong yŏn'gu*, pp.
248–51. Kim Yongsŏp, "Chosŏn hugi e issŏsŏ ŭi sinbunje ŭi tongyo wa nongi soyu," in
Chosŏn hugi nongŏpsa yŏn'gu, p. 427. Kim Sŏkhŭi and Pak Yongsuk, "18 segi nongch'on
ŭi sahoe kujo," *Pudae sahak*, 3:31–37.

transformed by the process of Confucianization. Unlike the government, the family system had been relatively untouched by Confucian influence. In order for society to make any claim to being successfully Confucianized, however, the family had to be restructured to meet the requirements of patrilineality and patriarchy. Both the classical and the Sung ritual texts, as well as Ming law, were predicated upon a social order organized patrilineally and practicing ancestral rites. As this structure was perceived as conforming to the moral order of the universe, such a reorganization was seen as an imperative. The magnitude of the task was enormous. Patricia Ebrey, in her chapter discussing the Confucianization of the Chinese family, remarks that the Neo-Confucian movement in Sung China harked back to the ancient patrilineal *tsung* (K. *chong*) system calling for an end to uxorilocal marriage, the adoption of no one but agnates, and the chastity of widows, who were to remain with their husbands' families. But she also makes it clear that those practices that Sung Neo-Confucians found objectionable were those that deviated from patrilineality and the patriarchal structure. The ancient *tsung* system may have suffered certain lapses, but the basic structure had not greatly changed.

On the contrary, Koreans had never lived under such a system. Of the distinguishing features of patrilineality and patriarchy that Ebrey lists, pre-Chosŏn Koreans practiced only one—namely, aristocratic families and many commoners had patrilineal surnames. During Silla, evidence suggests that, even among royal families, there was no strict rule regarding the use of paternal surnames and that succession, including the succession to the throne, was not limited to sons—it was also open to daughters, sons-in-law, and grandsons by both sons and daughters.[24] While royal succession was limited to sons during the Koryŏ period, the remainder of society, including the aristocratic-bureaucratic class, did not follow suit. In fact, most of the native customs and mores persisted throughout the Koryŏ period. Uxorilocal marriage was common, consanguineous marriage was practiced (though it became less common in the late Koryŏ), all children—including daughters—received an equal share of the inheritance, daughters or sons-in-law could participate in family affairs as fully as sons, men could have several wives of equal rank, and marriage alliances were easily formed and easily dissolved.[25]

An examination of a group of census registers dating from 1391, the very end of Koryŏ, reveals a society strongly divergent from Neo-

[24] Ch'oe Chaesŏk, *Han'guk kajok chedosa yŏn'gu* (Seoul: Ilchisa, 1983), pp. 99–206.

[25] Martina Deuchler, "The Tradition: Women during the Yi Dynasty," in *Virtues in Conflict*, ed. Sandra Mattielli (Seoul: The Royal Asiatic Society Korean Branch, 1977), pp. 7–10.

Confucian patrilineal norms, though certain Neo-Confucian reforms are already evident. These registers record a man and his wife, his four ancestors—father, grandfather, great grandfather, and maternal grandfather—his wife's four ancestors, and anyone living with the couple.[26] The registers depart from earlier Koryŏ practice, in which the wives of the four ancestors were also recorded.[27] These registers do not list widowed women as heads of households, but rather list the oldest surviving male member of the family as head. This contrasts with registers dating from 1333 and 1372, which list women as heads.[28] The 1391 method of recording became standard Chosŏn practice and was required by law.[29] The 1391 registers reveal that the coresidential family unit usually consisted of a couple and their children. In the case of married children, sons-in-law usually resided with their wives' families and remained until they reached about thirty years of age, at which time they moved out with their wives and children. An analysis of these records puts the marriage age at twenty for men and seventeen for women. This means that men usually spent about ten years with their wives' families. The oldest daughter, however, and her husband remained with her family. Remarriage is recorded for both men and women. Women as well as men, when widowed, kept their children. Women maintained ownership of property in marriage and took it with them in remarriage. Upon death, their children inherited their property, but when they had no children, it returned to their natal families.[30]

In matters concerning the dead, Koryŏ custom also differed from Confucian. With Buddhism the predominant religion, Buddhist funerary practices prevailed. The body was cremated within ten days of the time of death. The remains were then deposited in the custody of a temple for a period ranging from several weeks to several years, after which they were interred. Most often, a one-hundred-day mourning period was observed for parents. Though memorial services were offered on the anniversary date of the death at a temple before and after interment, no ancestor worship was practiced. These services were presided over by Buddhist priests and attended mainly by female relations of the deceased.[31] Toward the end of the Koryŏ,

[26] Hŏ Hŭngsik, "Kukpo hojŏk ŭiro pon Koryomal ui sahoe kujo," *Han'guksa yŏn'gu,* 16:75–78.

[27] Ch'oe Honggi, *"Han'guk hojŏk chedosa yŏn'gu* (Seoul: Seoul Taehakkyo ch'ulp'anbu, 1975), pp. 26–72.

[28] Hŏ Hŭngsik, "Kukpo hojŏk," p. 139.

[29] Ch'oe Honggi, *Han'guk hojŏk,* pp. 73–85.

[30] Hŏ Hŭngsik, "Kukpo hojŏk," pp. 97–105.

[31] Ch'oe Chaesŏk, *Han'guk kajok,* pp. 554–56.

Neo-Confucians began to observe certain Confucian rituals. Some scholars built family shrines for ancestral worship and observed three years of mourning (actually, twenty-five months) for their fathers. In 1391, a year before the founding of the Chosŏn dynasty, a three-year mourning period was officially adopted.[32] The new Chosŏn state engaged in systematic and thorough social engineering on a massive scale.

Funeral and Mourning Rites and Ancestor Worship

Funeral and mourning rites, together with ancestral sacrifices, when properly streamlined and defined, can be said to be the most characteristic features of Confucian patrilineage and patriarchy. As would often be the case, the Yi royal family led the way in practicing the proper Confucian rites. Meticulous attention was paid to the construction of royal ancestral shrines and to the protocols of sacrifices to be performed. When the first Chosŏn monarch died, the funeral and mourning procedures followed the prescriptions in Chu Hsi's *Family Rituals*. Royal example, however, was not the only means upon which the state relied; the Chosŏn government also used both moral suasion and the legal mechanism. Note that it seems the Confucian view of the law did not gain currency at first. During the early part of the Chosŏn dynasty, the state did not regard legal recourse as an undesirable last resort when all else failed, but rather as a positive force that complemented moral suasion. When it hesitated to resort to full use of legal recourse, it was more because of questionable efficacy than because of the Confucian bias against this procedure.[33] The way the state encouraged the adoption of Confucian funeral and mourning rites and the construction of family shrines illustrates this point.

The state repeatedly urged the yangban to set an example for the rest of the population. In 1401, Confucian funeral and mourning rites and ancestor worship were incorporated into the first of a series of codified laws. This produced little effect. The Censorate repeatedly memorialized the throne with requests that investigations be conducted and that violators be punished. In 1427, the Board of Rites set a time limit of several years; so few complied that the deadline had to be extended. This pattern was repeated several times. Even by the mid-fifteenth century, the old customs still held sway.

[32] Yi Sŏngmu, "The Influence of Neo-Confucianism," p. 136.

[33] William Shaw, *Legal Norms in a Confucian State* (Berkeley: University of California Press, 1981), pp. 19–20.

Sixty to seventy percent of the yangban still resorted to cremation.[34] The construction of family shrines was not widespread even within the capital.[35] It appears that the state was willing to use legislation, the first step in the legal mechanism, but hesitated to take the next step—investigating and prosecuting offenders—perhaps because there were too many violators. Once Confucian practice gained a firmer hold among the yangban population, however, its spread was probably accelerated by the use of the legal mechanism. The more Confucian norms gained popular acceptance, the more willing the government seems to have been to resort to stronger measures against violators. In 1474, the state decreed that not only would persons who cremated their parents be punished, but local officials and neighbors would be deemed responsible and punished as well. In 1555, a royal edict specifically ordered the arrest of those who failed to conform to Confucian norms for funerary, mourning, and ancestral rites.[36]

Confucian rites seem to have been gradually taking hold, and from the mid-fifteenth century on, this occurred at a somewhat faster pace. Once the ruling elite had turned to Confucian practices, momentum was built up, and the rest of the yangban followed. Not all Confucian rites were accepted at the same time, however, and even when they were accepted, some of them were superimposed upon Korean custom. By the late fifteenth century, mourning rites seem to have been faithfully observed among the ruling elite. *Drifting Across the Sea*, a Korean official's account of his shipwreck and subsequent landing in China in 1488, reveals an obsessive concern for the proper observance of mourning rites for his recently deceased father.[37] The book expresses a wholehearted acceptance of mourning rites by the official class, especially those rites concerning parents. Cremation also seems to have disappeared by the end of the fifteenth century. At any rate, few complaints about cremation are recorded.

Ancestor worship—the construction of a family shrine and the offering of sacrifices at designated times by members of the lineage—also seems to have taken hold between the mid-fifteenth and early sixteenth centuries. Interestingly, when ancestor worship took hold, Koreans did more than the law specified. The *Kyŏngguk taejŏn* stipulates that officials, depending on their rank, perform ancestral rites to either three or two generations; commoners, to one generation.[38]

---

[34] Ch'oe Chaesŏk, *Han'guk kajok*, pp. 565–66.

[35] Shaw, *Legal Norms*, p. 21.

[36] Ch'oe Chaesŏk, *Han'guk kajok*, p. 564.

[37] John Meskill, *Ch'oe Pu's Diary: A Record of Drifting Across the Sea* (Tucson: University of Arizona Press, 1965).

[38] *Kyŏngguk taejŏn*, 2 vols. (Seoul: Pŏpchech'ŏ, 1962), 1:261.

This conforms to the change the reformers proposed in 1390. But it was customary for the yangban to extend ancestral rites to four generations.[39]

Was this practice accompanied by changes in religious concepts concerning ancestors' souls? After all, the funeral and mourning rites revolve around assumptions concerning what happens to the soul of the deceased and the survivors' role in this process. The Buddhist conception of transmigration of the soul was consistent with the practice of cremation and a relatively short mourning period. Sometime, though it is impossible to say exactly when, ancestral rites came to be intimately related to a belief that the deceased ancestor continuously possessed a conscious soul, that this soul needed the continual support of its descendants, and that it had the power to bring blessing or, when displeased, calamity upon its descendants.[40]

It is quite probable that the practices of ancestor worship and religious belief in the soul began at different places and were conjoined later. The rites were insisted upon by the state, and once enough of the elite population practiced them, they must have become a symbol of prestige and thus acquired legitimacy. Belief in ancestors' souls, on the other hand, may have come through folk religion. Korean folk beliefs acknowledged the existence of supernatural beings, animistic spirits, and ghosts. Legendary founders and heroic leaders had been elevated to deities or guardian spirits, but it is not known how and when ancestral souls or spirits entered their ranks. The paraphernalia of ancestral worship, such as tablets and family shrines where ancestral spirits supposedly resided, may have played a role in spreading the belief. It is clear that ritual practice spread from the top down—from the ruling elite to the yangban population and down to commoners. Whether religious belief was transmitted in the same way is unknown; it is more likely that it spread in reverse fashion. It should also be pointed out that the Buddhist concept of transmigration of the soul did not completely disappear. In the realm of popular religion, a number of different beliefs and practices, some of them contradictory, coexisted.

Patrilineality and Patriarchy

Both ancestral and mourning rites involved a question of the ritual heir. Who should perform these rites? Who should be the chief

[39] Yi Sangbaek et al., Han'guksa, 8 vols. (Seoul: Ŭryu munhwasa, 1959–1962), 3:335–38.

[40] Roger Janelli and Dawnhee Yim Janelli, Ancestor Worship and Korean Society (Stanford: Stanford University Press, 1982).

mourner? What if there was no heir? Conformance to Neo-Confucian rites required not only that rituals be properly conducted, but also that they be offered by the heir who qualified by the standards of patrilineage and that, when there was no heir, one should be adopted from agnatic kin. This was clearly stipulated in the *Kyŏngguk taejŏn* which specified ritual heirs in descending order of preference: first came the first son born of the legal wife; next, younger sons born to the legal wife; then sons born to commoner concubines; followed by sons born to slave concubines. When no such heir was available, an agnatic male member was to be adopted and made the heir.[41] This patriarchal emphasis was very different from native Korean custom, which regarded daughters as full-fledged heirs. Did the adoption of Confucian rites by the elite mean that Korean family organization became patriarchal? Perhaps, but only very slowly. From the early Chosŏn even into the seventeenth century, the *Kyŏngguk taejŏn* notwithstanding, a daughter or a daughter's son could inherit the line and act as the ritual heir. Some families adopted the custom of requiring all children, including daughters, to share ritual duties equally on a rotating basis. Until the late sixteenth century, adoption was very rare; adopting a male agnate when the daughter's line existed was unheard of until the seventeenth century.[42] How then does one reconcile this apparent contradiction—that certain Confucian rituals were practiced while the family structure did not become fully patrilineal? The answer seems to be that, for a few centuries, the Korean elite adopted Confucian rituals but performed them within the rubric of existing family structure. That is, those rituals that were supposed to have been based on patrilineage were superimposed on nonpatrilineal structures.

One might conclude that it was easier to adopt Confucian rituals than to change the existing family structures. This is not surprising, considering that patrilineage or patriarchy fundamentally clashed with deep-rooted native concepts concerning women. The bone rank system of Silla had given equal importance to the rank of mother and father in determining a child's rank. Koryŏ women had an equal claim to family property and an independent social status. Even the *Kyŏngguk taejŏn* of 1474, which did not acknowledge the rights of daughters or their descendants to ritual heirship, upheld their rights to equal inheritance of property. The only person who was given more was the ritual heir, who received one and a half times the share

---

[41] *Kyŏngguk taejŏn*, 1:261.

[42] Mark Peterson, "Women without Sons: A Measure of Social Change in Yi Dynasty Korea," in *Korean Women*, ed. Laurel Kendall and Mark Peterson (New Haven: East Rock Press, 1983), pp. 37–43.

of other siblings.[43] Since the position women held and the role they played in family life were intimately related to all aspects of daily life, change came slowly and with difficulty. During the early Chosŏn, many practices antithetical to patrilineage persisted. One still finds women recorded as heads of households in the mid-fifteenth century.[44] Uxorilocal marriage remained common. Many fifteenth- and sixteenth-century officials not only started their married lives at the homes of their wives' parents, but retired to their wives' ancestral towns. It was not uncommon for men to be buried in the burial grounds of their wives' families.[45] Even new practices such as the compilation of genealogies reflected native inclinations. The two earliest extant genealogies of yangban families, one dating from 1476 and one from 1565, record sons and daughters in order of birth, unlike later genealogies, which record sons first and daughters last. Moreover, daughters' descendants, as well as sons', are continuously recorded.[46]

There is also evidence that yangban women remarried in the early Chosŏn. Both genealogies mentioned above record remarriage of daughters. The 1476 genealogy records them as a matter of fact, while the 1565 one includes remarks of disapproval. The remarriages recorded, however, had taken place in the early Chosŏn.[47] Even so, remarriage among upper-class women, not merely of widowed women but of divorced women as well, is quite revealing. From the beginning of the Chosŏn dynasty, the state made a considerable effort to prevent the remarriage of women: it encouraged chastity of widows, sent out periodic proclamations extolling the virtues of those who remained unmarried, and proffered them official recognition—for example, giving them red plaques to be hung at their gates. Before long, a legal sanction was applied to children of remarried women. The *Kyŏngguk taejŏn* of 1474 stipulates that the sons and grandsons of remarried women would not be permitted to serve in the bureaucracy or sit for the examination.[48] This legislation seems to reflect changing attitudes toward remarriage. One finds no case in which children of remarried women were discriminated against in

[43] *Kyŏngguk taejŏn*, 2:178–83.

[44] Hŏ Hŭngsik, "Kukpo hojŏk," pp. 138–44.

[45] For many examples, see Yi Sŭgon, *Yŏngnam sarimp'a ŭi hyŏngsŏng* (Kyŏngbuk: Yŏngnam Taehakkyo ch'ulp'anbu, 1979).

[46] Edward Wagner, "Two Early Genealogies and Women's Status in Early Yi Dynasty Korea," in *Korean Women*, ed. Kendall and Peterson, pp. 24–26.

[47] Ibid., pp. 28–32.

[48] *Kyŏngguk taejŏn*, 1:201.

the early fifteenth century, but in the early 1500s the appointment of the son of a remarried woman to office was criticized.[49]

There were other efforts by the state to force feminine behavior and mores to conform to Neo-Confucian norms. Most early injunctions were concerned with placing women in the domestic sphere. In 1392, the state proclaimed that yangban women were not allowed to associate with or to converse with men beyond a certain degree of kinship. In 1412, it was decreed that, if women were to go outside, their faces should not be exposed and their bodies should be as fully covered as possible. In 1462, the state forbade equestrian practice for women (this had been commonplace during the Koryŏ). After the Korean alphabet was devised in the mid-fifteenth century, the government began to publish morality books to popularize Confucian mores. Books written for women, emphasizing such Confucian virtues as wifely submission, devotion to parents-in-law, frugality, and diligence, appeared in the late fifteenth century. While it is difficult to evaluate the effect of any one of these measures—either in terms of legal, moral, or social pressures—it is evident that Confucian influence was gathering force. Those practices that were particularly offensive to the Neo-Confucian sensibility, such as remarriage, seem to have for all practical purposes disappeared among upper-class women by the sixteenth century.

It seems that at some point in the late fifteenth or early sixteenth century, Confucian ancestral and mourning rites took root, while those practices that were considered blatantly un-Confucian were disappearing. What persisted longest were those customs that had to do with daughters' maintaining full claims to property and their ritual roles in their natal families. Were these customs also finally "Confucianized"? The answer is yes, but a word of caution is in order. Research on the topic is in a preliminary stage. Until recently those documents that would shed light on family practice had remained in private libraries. Only recently has a systematic effort to collect them begun, as well as research utilizing them. A comprehensive picture that incorporates familial, class, and regional differences awaits further investigation.

Preliminary findings indicate that the watershed for "Confucianization" was the seventeenth century. A collection of inheritance documents of an illustrious lineage, the Kims of Puan, has the following preface, dating from the early seventeenth century: "Our family, unlike other families, no longer allows a married daughter to participate in the ancestor ceremonies on a rotational basis. For this reason a

---

[49] Wagner, "Two Early Genealogies," p. 29.

daughter will be given only one third of a share." Another set of documents concerns legal disputes between the Chins, the descendants of a daughter, and the Mas, a collateral branch of a patrilineal line, over inheritance of property and ritual headship. They reveal that the claims of daughters and their descendants were losing ground. First they lost ritual rights and then property rights in the fifty-year span from the late seventeenth century to the mid-eighteenth century.[50]

In fact, at some point in the mid-seventeenth century, patriarchy and patrilineality began to exert a meaningful grip on Korean society, and by the mid-eighteenth century they were undisputedly established. Uxorilocal marriage became rare and a rigid exogamy took hold. The adoption of an agnatic kin, even when there was a daughter, became commonplace at about this time.[51] It was not enough that a son should inherit the line, however. Primogeniture became so important that the line came to be continued through the oldest son even when he was adopted of distant agnatic kin. It is during this period that more and more families published genealogies[52] and that the method of recording changed. After the mid-eighteenth century, for instance, most genealogies recorded sons first and then daughters, and by the nineteenth century daughters' descendants are completely left out. The use of a character designating a generation in a two-character given name in a lineage came to be much more inclusive. During the fifteenth and sixteenth centuries only brothers or first cousins were given the same character in their names, but in the seventeenth century many families used the same character as widely as second cousins, and in the nineteenth century the character was often shared by the entire lineage.[53]

The formation of patrilineage in Korea was a long and complicated affair. It proceeded in disparate phases. First, formal rituals were adopted, probably under intense pressure from the state. Once the beliefs and ideologies associated with these rituals were accepted, structure and practice eventually changed to conform to these beliefs. Such practices as the publication of genealogies on a large scale, the decline in importance of the daughter's role in her natal family and the corresponding rise in the importance of the oldest son, and the widespread practice of sharing the same character in given names among the members of one generation in a lineage express the

[50] Peterson. "Women without Sons," pp. 39–41.

[51] Ibid, pp. 33–34.

[52] Song Chunho, "Han'guk e issŏsŏ ŭi kagye kirok ŭi yŏksa wa kŭ haesŏk," *Yŏksa hakpo*, 87:99–143.

[53] Ch'oe Chaesŏk, *Han'guk kajok*, pp. 700–706.

Korean willingness to accept patriarchal practice with a deepening commitment.

But can the "Confucianization" of the Korean family structure be described only in sequential phases? Did Korean native customs leave no mark? The wedding ceremony provides an example in which Neo-Confucian ritual had to be altered to accommodate Korean custom. Despite the concerted efforts of the state to introduce the wedding ceremony as it was prescribed in the *Family Rituals*, Koreans did not completely accept this procedure. The groom's personal abduction of the bride followed by a ceremony at his parents' house was deemed too abrupt for the bride. Instead, the ceremony took place at the bride's home, and she went to live with his family only after several return visits by the groom spanning anywhere from several months to several years. It was not unusual that, by the time she went to his house to live, she had given birth to a child.[54] It was also customary for women to return to their natal homes to give birth.[55] These customs appear to be the remnants of uxorilocal marriage.

If certain customs and habits persisted, did the native Korean perception of woman survive patrilineality in some form? This is noticeable only in that a woman's status continued to influence that of her descendants. Contrary to the Neo-Confucian norm—which required that all sons, even those by concubines, should precede agnate adoption—in the late Chosŏn, when there was no son by a legal wife, the heirship did not fall to a son by a concubine but rather passed to an adopted agnate. This practice was given legal sanction in the eighteenth–century law code.[56] Children by concubines, even those fathered by the most illustrious of men, were greatly discriminated against not only in their familial rights but also in their public careers and their status. They were prohibited from sitting for the final civil service examination, making it impossible for them to serve in the bureaucracy in any meaningful capacity. In fact, the plight of these people was one of the most hotly debated social issues of the Chosŏn dynasty.[57] One could say that the Korean conception of women influenced the particular shape of patrilineage, but it was subsumed into the patriarchal system. A woman was an agent, as much as her husband was, through which her children inherited status, but she lost all claims of inheritance to her natal line. But not all sons by the legal

[54] Deuchler, "The Tradition," p. 20.

[55] This custom seems to have been quite pervasive among the upper class. Hyegyŏng-gung Hong Ssi, *Hanjungnok*, ed. Kim Tonguk (Seoul: Minjung sŏgwan, 1961), p. 5.

[56] *Sok taejŏn* (Seoul: Pŏpchech'ŏ, 1965), p. 154.

[57] Haboush, *A Heritage of Kings*, pp. 94–95.

wife had equal rights. Korea practiced a modified primogeniture, and the first son by the legal wife inherited ritual heirship and a greater proportion of the property. Younger sons participated in the ancestral rites but did not preside over them, and their financial obligation was minimized, reflecting the smaller share of property they received, usually at the time of their marriage.[58]

LATE CHOSŎN SOCIETY

I have discussed the Confucianization of the yangban class. The question remains whether Confucian values and mores penetrated into the lower reaches of the society, and if so, to what extent and by what mechanism. One forms the impression that by the close of the eighteenth century, Confucian ethics and mores had spread to lower strata of society. There are many telltale signs, among them the fact that the educational establishment increased at all levels. The number of private academies, some of which accepted commoners, increased rapidly, reaching a point where the state chose to apply sanctions against the founding of private academies without permission. In addition, all sorts of primary schools sprang up, making education readily available to the lower strata. Since the curriculum at all levels in all educational institutions consisted of Confucian texts, those who received any education at all were exposed to Confucian ethics and values.

The diffusion of Confucian ethics, however, did not have to rely exclusively on literacy in classical Chinese. The Korean alphabet, which was devised nominally to educate the populace in Confucian mores, was also utilized. In subsequent centuries, printing was developed and the state published numerous moral tracts in the Korean alphabet, illustrating and encouraging Confucian virtues. Dissemination of these morality works helped to popularize Confucian ethics among the general population.

The spread of education also meant that a greater proportion of the educated population had no hope of attaining a government post. Patrilineage became much more significant in this context. Descendants of yangban who had no hopes for an official career zealously recorded genealogy and practiced ancestral rites as a means of maintaining a claim to social status.[59] Local yangban were also active in community affairs, often involved in the organization and enforce-

---

[58] Janelli and Janelli, *Ancestor Worship.*

[59] Fujiya Kawashima, "The Local Gentry Association of Mid-Yi Dynasty Korea: A Preliminary Study in the Ch'angnyŏng Hyangan," *The Journal of Korean Studies* 2:113–37.

ment of community compacts. This enhanced their local leadership roles, but also helped to spread Confucian mores. Community compacts were self-regulatory organizations. In many, all villagers, including slaves, were members. They met regularly, and the compacts' regulations—usually, Confucian social relations made applicable to each village—were read aloud. Difficult points were explained in a manner accessible to the illiterate and uneducated. Ledgers of good and bad deeds of all villagers were kept, increasing social pressure.[60] Through these procedures, all residents of villages were made aware of the elements of Confucian behavior. This was probably reinforced by such state efforts as the publication of moral tracts.

Such organizations and activities also provided opportunities for associations between persons of different classes and strata, and they probably made it possible for the manners and mores of the upper class to trickle down to the lower strata. Confucian rituals practiced by the upper class were avidly emulated by commoners. Commoners were permitted to practice ancestral worship for their parents and to mourn them for three years, but the material accoutrements of mourning that they were permitted to use were rather modest. However, when commoners could afford to use what the upper class used, they apparently did. In 1709 the court, alarmed at what it considered to be the lavish accoutrements that commoners were using for funerals and mourning rites, attempted to regulate these practices. Of course not everyone could practice ancestral and mourning rites in the same manner as the upper class; this was costly, and the mourning period lengthy. Still, in the later Chosŏn period, some form of ancestral and mourning rites was practiced by nearly all strata of society. Patrilineality and patriarchy also became the norm, though they assumed somewhat different forms depending on the social and economic status of the family. Admittedly, there were certain sectors of the society that remained rather resistant to the pressures of Confucianism. There were also religious practices, both Buddhist and folk, that differed markedly from Confucian precepts. Nevertheless, measured by any reasonable criteria, late Chosŏn Korea must be described as a society transformed into a normative Confucian society.

[60] Sakai Tadao, "Yi Yulgok and the Community Compact," in *The Rise of Neo-Confucianism*, ed. de Bary and Haboush, pp. 327–35.

Chapter 3

THE LEGACY OF CONFUCIANISM IN JAPAN

Martin Collcutt

In seeking to explain the startling recent economic successes of the countries on the Asian edge of the Pacific rim, many commentators have looked for historical and cultural commonalities among them that may have contributed to such rapid growth. Some have pointed to the importance of a shared Confucian heritage and suggested that this common Confucian tradition—defined in terms of an emphasis on such values as a secular, this-worldly orientation, personal discipline, diligence, ordered family life, respect for hierarchy and authority, social harmony, and an emphasis on education—may have played a significant role in the dramatic growth of Japan, South Korea, Taiwan, Hong Kong, and Singapore. This point of view contrasts sharply with earlier views, which have tended to see Confucianism as a retarding factor, one that was inimical to equality, freedom, democracy, and the rights of women and young people and thus something to be sloughed off in the process of modernization, rather than a positive contributor to democratic development, social equality, intellectual vitality, and industrial dynamism.[1]

In the case of Japan, the argument that Confucianism has contributed positively to the country's modern development and is still very much alive has been made by a number of scholars. Edwin O. Reischauer, for example, writes:

> Contemporary Japanese obviously are not Confucianists in the sense that their Tokugawa ancestors were, but they are still permeated with Con-

[1] For positive assessments of the Confucian contribution see Roy Hofheinz Jr. and Kent E. Calder, *The Eastasia Edge* (New York: Basic Books, 1982). The major criticisms of Confucianism are that it has tended to be extremely conservative, to support ruling elites and the status quo, to provide theoretical justification for authoritarianism, to justify inequality between sexes and age groups, and to obstruct the development of equality, freedom, democracy, and individualism. Criticism has been sharpest with regard to the role of Confucianism in the modern history of China, but it has also been voiced in relation to Confucianism in Japan, Korea, and more recently Taiwan, Singapore, and Vietnam. For a negative evaluation of Confucianism in Japan's recent economic "success" see Michio Morishima, *Why Has Japan "Suceeded"? : Western Technology and the Japanese Ethos* (Cambridge, England: Cambridge University Press, 1982).

fucian ethical values. Confucianism probably has more influence on them than does any other of the traditional religions or philosophies. . . . Behind the wholehearted Japanese acceptance of modern science, modern concepts of progress and growth, universalistic principles of ethics, and democratic ideals and values, strong Confucian traits still lurk beneath the surface, such as the belief in the moral basis of government, the emphasis on interpersonal relationships and loyalties, and the faith in education and hard work. Almost no one considers himself a Confucianist today, but in a sense almost all Japanese are.[2]

In *British Factory, Japanese Factory*, Ronald Dore suggests that Confucianism may have brought a more human face to industrial development in Japan than in the West and contributed to a beneficial sense of common enterprise in labor-management relations: "The modified Confucian world-view meant that those in positions of authority . . . have been rather less disposed than their Western counterparts to see their subordinates as donkeys responsive to sticks and carrots and more disposed to see them as human beings responsive to moral agents."[3]

Thomas Rohlen, who expresses some ambivalence about the advantages of the Confucian legacy in modern Japan, finds Confucian attitudes still embedded in Japanese education in the persistence of ritualized tradition and formality. He finds, for instance, significant differences in the attitudes toward school events in Japan and the United States:

Although schools in both cultures have formulas for events, less depends on convention in the United States. School events and ceremonies are readily changed, and most are abandoned if student support lags. Japanese school events, on the other hand, appear uniform and constant. They depend on tradition and teachers. The Confucian appreciation of formality in ritual as expressive of the moral order lingers in Japan, just as our democratic and Protestant heritage inclines us to events with a grass roots spontaneity that is informal and emotionally expressive.[4]

Rohlen describes the Japanese high school as a kind of Confucian moral community in which teachers and principal try to inculcate order and discipline by moral example. He gives the example of a prin-

[2] Edwin O. Reischauer, *The Japanese* (Cambridge, Mass.: Harvard University Press, 1977), p. 214.

[3] Ronald Dore, *British Factory, Japanese Factory: The Origins of National Diversity in Industrial Relations* (Berkeley and Los Angeles: University of California Press, 1973), pp. 401–2.

[4] Thomas P. Rohlen, *Japan's High Schools* (Berkeley and Los Angeles: University of California Press, 1983), p. 167.

cipal who went around his school quietly and humbly scraping chewing gum from chairs with a knife:

> No rules banning gum from the school are announced, nor are punishments set out for sticking it under the seats; only moral example and group sentiment are relied upon to solve the problem. Confucius would have approved. Otani [High School] is obviously quite a distance from attaining this ideal but the path forward is neither bureaucratic nor democratic nor socialist so much as it is Japanese and Confucian.[5]

But even while stressing the persistent influence of Confucianism in Japanese education, Rohlen also serves warning against putting too much emphasis on Confucianism in the shaping of contemporary Japanese values:

> Postwar Japan is rich in examples of the art of making meaning from an eclectic assemblage of insights. Modern science, anecdotal aspects of Western thought, democracy, socialism, watered down Confucian insights, popular Shinto ideas, and even Christian doctrines have found their way into various institutional efforts to shape an explanation for moral conduct that suits the Japanese without appearing tainted by the excesses of prewar nationalism.[6]

Are all Japanese "Confucianists at heart" as Edwin Reischauer suggests? If so, what does it mean to be a "Confucianist"? If they are not now, have they ever been? Has there been a time, for instance the Tokugawa period (1600–1867), when Confucianism enjoyed intellectual, ideological, and moral hegemony in Japan, when Japan might be said to have been "Confucianized"? If modern Japanese labor-management relations have a very human face, as Dore argues, is it really due simply to a Confucian heritage? And how could an originally foreign teaching associated with the Tokugawa feudal power structure and a rigidly stratified society survive in modern Japan? This chapter will explore the Confucian legacy to modern Japan by looking at continuity and change in the contribution made by Confucianism to Japanese intellectual life, political ideology, and moral values.

THE ANCIENT PERIOD: THE INTRODUCTION OF CONFUCIAN VALUES

For many Western intellectual historians of Japan, and for some Japanese scholars, Confucianism does not loom as a significant influence

---

[5] Ibid., p. 200

[6] Ibid., p. 264.

until the growth of the Neo-Confucian and Ancient Learning schools of thought in the seventeenth century under the Tokugawa shogunate. Earlier Confucian influences are frequently shrugged off with the statement that prior to Hayashi Razan and the emergence of the Neo-Confucian school, Confucianism was subordinated to Buddhism, being used by Zen monks to justify the supremacy of Buddhism. This point of view does less than justice to the long history of Confucianism in Japan prior to the Tokugawa period.

Admittedly, for much of that period Confucian ideas may not have spread far beyond the orbit of the literate elite. At the same time, certain structural relationships among Confucianism, Taoism, Buddhism, and Shinto were established in these earlier centuries that were to persist into modern times. We see, for instance, efforts to use Confucianism as one component of a political ideology of state underlying aristocratic, imperial, and warrior authority, we see attempts to inculcate and diffuse Confucian values among rulers and ruled, and, most important, we see the early development of an interactive, multipolar system of political thought and moral values in which the Unity—or, better, the constant interaction—of Buddhism, Shinto, Confucianism, and Taoism becomes the decisive model of ideological, intellectual, and ethical action. In many ways what Rohlen describes as the "art of making meaning from an eclectic assemblage of insights" was already operative in Japan in the sixth century and has continued to function without break to this day. Other possibilities—Christianity, socialism, Marxism, individualism, democracy, etc.—have been added to the available mix but have not changed the underlying eclectic tendency that was established long before the seventeenth century.

None of the components have ever achieved exclusive hegemony. In the long course of Japanese history there were times when Buddhism, or Buddhism and Shinto, or a Buddho-Shinto synthesis, seemed dominant within the multipolar system. At other times Buddhism was pushed aside and Confucianism, or Confucianism and Shinto, or Confucianized Shinto, came to the fore. At no time did Confucianism have the field to itself. On the other hand there has been no time since its introduction when Confucianism has not been an active player in the shaping of Japanese politics, intellect, and behavior.

Failure to recognize the inescapable, ongoing multipolarity of Japanese thought has led many intellectual historians into difficulties in trying to establish a Neo-Confucian orthodoxy as a de novo phenomenon in the seventeenth century. Any view that looks only sideways to China or Korea for intellectual influences and not *also* back at Japan's prior intellectual and ethical development is doomed to failure. Discussing seventeenth-century intellectual history or political ideology solely in terms of a Japanese development of Chinese or Korean Neo-Confucian scholarship is as limited as viewing early Meiji intellectual history simply in terms of a flow of "civilization and enlightenment" from the West.

Throughout the ancient period, especially during the Nara and early Heian periods, 710–c. 900, Japan was subjected to a stream of continental influences, including that of Confucianism from China and Korea. Until 894, when official missions to China were abandoned, Japan was in close contact with the continent. For petty rulers in the Japanese islands, many of whom had continental ancestry, China and Korea remained the great centers of civilization (*bun*), sources of Buddhism, Confucianism, and Taoism. Civilization, centralization, order, bureaucratic government, learning, literacy, art, agriculture, metal technology, all came from the continent. Embassies and travelers came and went. Many of these travelers had imbibed Confucian ideas in Korea or China and brought Confucian texts with them to Japan. The *Nihon shoki* mentions Korean scholars bringing Confucian teachings, including a copy of the *Analects*, from Paekche during the reigns of Emperor Ōjin and Keitai, probably sometime during the fifth century.[7] What can only have been a trickle at that time quickly became a flood.

Confucian values for loyal officals were embodied in the *Seventeen Article Constitution* attributed to Prince Shōtoku (573–621) and included in the *Nihon shoki*, compiled in the early eighth century.[8] The first article stresses loyalty to rulers and fathers and opens with a quotation from the *Analects* of Confucius: "Harmony is to be valued." The third article stresses obedience within a political hierarchy that mirrors a larger cosmic order: "The lord is Heaven, the vassal is Earth. Heaven overspreads, and Earth upbears." Article 4 expresses the Confucian ideal of mastering self and ruling others through the cultivation of the virtue of decorum (*li*): "The ministers and functionaries should make decorous behavior their leading principle, for the leading principle of the government of the people consists in decorous behavior." Articles 6 and 16 appeal to the classics as a source, thus opening the way to secularized notions of authority.

The *Seventeen Article Constitution* is always seen as a high-water mark for Confucian influence in ancient Japanese society. It emphasized the divine origin of the sovereign, advocated loyalty to rulers and an-

---

[7] W. G. Aston, trans., *Nihongi* (rept., Rutland, Vt.: Tuttle, 1972), pp. 261–62.

[8] Aston, *Nihongi*, pp. 128–33.

cestors, stressed harmony in social relations, and enshrined a set of moral precepts for an elite that was still in the process of formation. The emphasis on harmony (*wa*) with its strong Confucian moral component persisted as a recurrent theme in Japanese culture. Medieval Zen monks such as Musō Soseki stressed harmony in spiritual life and human relations, warrior chieftains advocated harmony among their vassals, and corporate leaders still emphasize the virtue today.[9]

However, alongside Confucianism, Buddhism and Legalism were also called into play in the interests of establishing social harmony and political order. The second article stresses the importance of reverence for the three treasures of Buddhism: "Few men are utterly bad. . . . But if they do not betake themselves to the three treasures, wherewithal shall their crookedness be made straight?" And the eleventh article emphasizes the Legalist principle of rigorous rewards and punishments: "Give clear appreciation to merit and demerit, and deal out to each its sure reward and punishment."[10]

Confucian influences were very much in evidence in the establishment of the centralized *ritsuryō* system during the Nara period, 710–784. The *Nihon shoki* and the other early histories were written under Confucian influence with the ideal of elevating a Chinese-style sovereign as the head of a centralized state on the T'ang model. The *ritsuryō* codes in their regulation of public and family life advocated Confucian social arrangements. Unlike China, Japan did not adopt a centralized examination system. However, the government college for the training of officials, the *daigakuryō*, and the provincial school system were created on a Confucian model and used Confucian texts. In family relations the codes called for children to show filial respect for parents and ancestors and for wives to be dutiful to their husbands. The *handen* system of equal land distribution invoked an earlier Chinese Confucian ideal of equal fields.

With such an influx, was Japan Confucianized in the ancient period? Or, putting the question another way, to what extent did the Japanese in the ancient period come to share a common set of values that contained a very strong Confucian component? Paucity of information about Japanese social organization and family life in the Nara and Heian periods makes it difficult to be very categorical. The best

[9] Thomas P. Rohlen, *For Harmony and Strength: Japanese White Collar Organization in Anthropological Perspective* (Berkeley and Los Angeles: University of California Press, 1974) discusses the importance of "harmony" in contemporary Japanese corporate thinking and looks for its premodern roots in Prince Shōtoku's Seventeen Article Constitution.

[10] Quotations from Ryūsaku Tsunoda *et al.*, ed., *Sources of Japanese Tradition* (New York: Columbia University Press, 1958), pp. 48–51.

we can do to try to gauge the extent of Confucianization of values in the Nara and Heian periods is to look at education and family relations, two areas in which Confucian influences were probably most strongly felt.

In the sphere of education, the Japanese reformers of the *ritsuryō* period made a real effort to establish a state-sponsored education system modeled on Chinese lines and incorporating Confucian ideals. The aim of this education system was to produce the central and local officials who would staff the new bureaucratic institutions of the centralized state and train them on the basis of Confucian texts. A college, the *daigakuryō*, was established in the capital around 670.[11] Instructors were Korean scholars and later Japanese who had been to T'ang China. With the establishment of Heijō as the new capital in 710, the *daigakuryō* was expanded as a department of the Ministry of Rituals. Instruction was provided by a Doctor of the Classics and several assistants. Four hundred students were admitted for the main course of Confucian studies. The students were largely drawn from the fifth court rank or above. Members of lower ranks, sixth to eighth, and graduates of the provincial schools could be admitted upon petition. The curriculum was devoted to the Confucian classics and followed the T'ang model. All students were required to study the *Analects* and the *Classic of Filial Piety*. In addition, students elected to study other Han and post–Han dynasty texts and commentaries. The Confucian character of the *daigakuryō* was heightened by the performance every spring and autumn of a *sekiten* ceremony in honor of Confucius. This Chinese ceremony, which involved animal sacrifices and vegetable offerings, became the main public manifestation of Confucianism in Japan and one index of Confucian influence in later periods.[12]

Outside the capital, provincial colleges were prescribed for each province. These were smaller versions of the *daigakuryō*. Students numbered from 20 to 50 and were drawn from the families of provincial officials or, if recruitment from this source was insufficient, from commoner families. The curriculum resembled that of the uni-

[11] Hisaki Yukio, *Daigakuryō to kodai jukyō, Nihon kodai kyōiku shi kenkyū* (Tokyo: Simul, 1968), pp. 5–22.

[12] Ibid. The *sekiten* ceremony in honor of Confucius was performed in the *daigakuryō* on those days known as *hinoto* in the second and eighth months. The ceremony died out at the time of the Onin War, 1467–77, but, as the Zen monk Keian Genju records in his diary, it had by this time been adopted by some provincial warrior families such as the Kikuchi of Saga in Kyushu. In the Edo period it was revived by the Confucian scholar Hayashi Razan and conducted at the Shōheikō and in domain schools. It is still performed today at the Yushima Confucian Hall and at the Confucian Sages Hall in Takushi, Saga Prefecture.

versity. Graduates could proceed to the university for further study
or take the state examinations in the Ministry of Ceremonial. As in
China, these examinations tested knowledge of the Confucian classics
and commentaries. They offered to those who did well the possibility
of access to government office.[13]

The century and a half following the establishment of the new
Heian capital in 794 was a period of relative stability and prosperity
for the state education system. The Confucian curriculum was expanded. Most provinces seem to have had a college. Through these
formal educational institutions, Confucian notions of harmony, order, filiality, ritual, and benevolence became widely known in elite
circles. It is impossible to know how widely they spread at lower levels
of society. In the eighth century the court did try to promote ideals
of filial children and dutiful wives among the people, but given the
miserable circumstances of daily life of the peasantry, the limited access to education, and the very low general level of literacy, it is unlikely that these values penetrated far beyond the formal school system. To the extent that these notions did filter downward to the
peasantry they were almost certainly mixed with folk ideas of devotion to local or ancestral deities, magical beliefs, and simplified ideas
of Buddhist *karma*.[14]

By the tenth century even the formal state-sponsored institutions
of education were clearly under strain. From the beginning there had
been severe obstacles to the success of these institutions of Chinese
Confucian learning. Although some emphasis was placed on reward-
ing merit in the recruitment of the new bureaucracy, the pool from
which that talent was drawn was very small. Educational opportunity
was offered only to court nobles and the provincial elite. Even then,
it was a long time before the *daigaku* and provincial colleges reached
anything like full strength. Further, in Japan the hereditary principle
proved stronger than claims of merit. Although they drew heavily on
China for ideas and institutions in the Nara and Heian periods, the
Japanese did not commit themselves to a Chinese-style examination
system. However well the child of a lower-ranking noble might do in
college or the examinations, he was always likely to be displaced by a
less talented but higher-ranking noble. Sons of families of the fifth
rank and above were automatically entitled to court ranks higher
than even the most brilliant and meritorious student could win
through examinations. Thus Confucian education did not become in

---

[13] Momo Hiroyuki, *Jōdai gakusei no kenkyū* (Tokyo: Meguro Shoten, 1947).

[14] Kyōko Nakamura, trans., *Miraculous Stories from the Japanese Buddhist Tradition: The
"Nihon Ryōiki" of the Monk Kyōkai* (Cambridge, Mass.: Harvard University Press, 1973).

ancient Japan, as it did in China, an important path to the highest offices of state. The *daigakuryō* functioned rather to train middle- and lower-ranking officials to whom birth normally denied high rank and office. The public, meritocratic ideal of Confucian education was also undermined by the growth within the *daigakuryō* of semiprivate halls of residence, such as the Kangakuin of the Fujiwara family, devoted to the scholarly interests of particular families, and the hereditary monopoly of academic offices began to appear within the college itself.[15] The influence of Confucian study within this limited educational framework was further undercut by the popularity of Chinese literature and the study of history. In 728 a Chinese literary studies course was established within the curriculum of the *daigaku*. This proved enormously popular with Heian nobles and it, and history, grew at the expense of the more narrowly Confucian curriculum.[16]

Confucian influence in every area of life was also circumscribed by the competing influence of Buddhism and devotion to the native *kami*. Although Japan's early sovereigns are frequently presented in the *Nihon shoki* as benevolent Confucian rulers, the source of their legitimacy was not a transferable Confucian or Chinese mandate to rule but divine—and unassailable—descent from the Sun Goddess. Shinto ritualists held a central position in the court hierarchy. The major rituals conducted within the imperial court and the residences of noble families reflected less a Confucian influence than devotion to ancestral *kami* or the performance of ceremonies having to do with fertility and the seasonal rice cycle.

But perhaps even more powerful than the *kami* as a competitor to Confucian hegemony was Buddhism. The energy devoted to temple-building, to the making of statues and sutras, and to the fostering of the *sangha* throughout the ancient period is an index of the strong emotional hold that Buddhism had attained within the imperial court and the more powerful central and provincial families. The Nara government under Emperor Shōmu looked mainly to Buddhism for ideological support, as the emperor invoked comparisons with the Cosmic Buddha Vairochana to enhance Shinto and Confucian trappings of authority. Even officials of the nominally Confucian *daigakuryō* seem to have embraced Buddhism as their private faith.[17] The influence of Buddhist clerics in the political and social life of the court was weakened as a result of the Dōkyō affair, in which an empress infatuated with the Buddhist cleric Dōkyō tried to set him on

[15] Hisaki, *Daigakuryō to kodai jukyō*, pp. 133–82.
[16] Ibid.
[17] Ibid., pp. 300–310.

the imperial throne, and the subsequent shift of the capital to Heian. Even so, emperors of the Heian period, taking their example from Kammu, generally sponsored the various Ways of Confucius, the Buddha, Lao Tzu, and the native *kami* without giving exclusive allegiance to any one of them.

This syncretic attitude was echoed by the Buddhist monk Kūkai in his *Indications of the Goals of the Three Teachings*. Kūkai argues that while Confucian moral principles may seem to be the accepted norm of aristocratic behavior, the Confucian path is not the only one available. Such virtues as filial piety were not the exclusive preserve of the Way of Confucius:

> My relatives and teachers opposed my entering the priesthood, saying that by doing so I would be unable to fulfill the Five Cardinal Virtues or to accomplish the duties of loyalty or of filial piety. I thought then: living things are not the same nature—there are birds which fly high in the sky and fish which sink low in the water. To guide different kinds of people there are three teachings: Buddhism, Taoism, and Confucianism. Although their profoundness varies, they are still the teachings of the sages. If an individual chooses one, he does not necessarily repudiate loyalty and filial piety in doing so.[18]

By the beginning of the tenth century the general decay of the *ritsuryō* system was well advanced. Confucian studies, still not very deeply rooted in Japan and cut off from fresh stimuli from China after 894, declined into an arcane and formalized pursuit. University posts were monopolized by a few noble families. Confucian scholarship became the private possession of select families who passed on their lore in secret transmissions. From the mid-Heian period Shingon and Amidist Buddhism appealed powerfully to the aristocracy and Buddhism even penetrated the curriculum of the *daigakuryō*. Examination standards declined as answers were formalized and passed on to candidates. Government weakness undercut the financial position of the university. Provincial colleges vanish from records by the eleventh century. In 1177 the university burned down and was not rebuilt.[19] Confucian studies survived, but only as the preserve of a few noble families.

If the role of Confucianism in formal state-sponsored education turns out to have been limited, was Confucianism any more successful in shaping family life and values in ancient Japan? How far did

---

[18] Yoshito S. Hakeda, trans., *Kūkai, Major Works* (New York: Columbia University Press, 1972), p. 102.

[19] Ibid., pp. 207–17.

the Japanese reformers of the *ritsuryō* period go in adopting new Chinese ways that might be described as Confucian in ideal or practice? The *ritsuryō* codes and the six national histories sought to record and promote political and moral order. They advocated rewards for such Confucian conduct as exemplary filial piety or chastity, deference to elder brothers, devotion to husbands and respect for wives, and respect for senior members of the family. They prescribed punishments for unfilial conduct. It is hard to know how widely the prescriptions in the codes were put into practice. The admonitions to filiality and wifely subordination remained the officially sanctioned family and social virtues. But if, as some scholars suggest, marriage in this period was heavily uxorilocal—that is, based on the wife's residence and on visits to the woman—then Chinese and Confucian values based on a patriarchal order in which wife and children lived in the father's or paternal grandfather's home are unlikely to have fit very easily.[20]

Some of these officially sanctioned values are reflected in an early collection of Buddhist morality fables, the *Nihon ryōiki*, in which Buddhist karmic effects are linked to such Confucian virtues as filial regard for aged parents:

> In an old capital there lived a wicked woman whose name is unknown. She had no sense of filial piety and never loved her mother.
>
> On one fasting day her mother did not cook rice and visited her daughter for the ceremonial meal. Her daughter said, "My husband and I are going to have our meal. We have nothing else to offer you."
>
> Carrying her young child with her, the mother went home and lay down. Looking outside, she saw a package of boiled rice left by the roadside. She filled her empty stomach with that and fell asleep exhausted. Late that night someone knocked at the door, saying, "Your daughter is screaming that she has a nail stuck in her chest. She is about to die. You must go and see her!" The mother, however, was sleeping so soundly from exhaustion that she could not go and help bring her daughter back to life. The daughter finally died without seeing her mother. It is better for us to give our portion to our mother and starve to death than to die without serving her.[21]

The evidence of the *Nihon ryōiki* suggests that around the year 800 Confucian notions of filial piety were mingling with Buddhist ideas

---

[20] On the fundamental incompatibility of Confucian morality and Japanese family life in the Nara period see Takeda Sachiko, "Ritsuryō kokka ni yoru jukyōteki kazoku dōtoku kihan no kōnyū," in *Kodai tennōsei to shakai kōzō*, ed. Takeuchi Rizō (Tokyo: Kōsō Shoin, 1980), pp. 27–45.

[21] Nakamura, *Miraculous Stores*, p. 136.

of karmic cause and effect, Taoist ideas of miraculous sages, and Shinto belief in powerful *kami* as part of the stock in trade of Japanese popular morality.

Within the *ritsuryō* legal codes Confucian practices were advocated, but concessions were also made to prevailing Japanese attitudes and practices. A Confucian mourning system was introduced, but it was less stringent than that advocated in China. The Confucian scholar and rector of the *daigakuryō*, Miyoshi Kiyotsura (848–919), for instance, urged Emperor Daigo in 914 to reorder Japan's national priorities, demoting Buddhism and promoting Confucianism. One of his requests was that Confucian mourning and ritual practices be more strictly enforced:

> Also there must be established regulations concerning memorial services and funeral expenses, consistent with the ranks held by the people. The regulations must be made applicable alike to ministers and functionaries of the court down to the common people. Nowadays those families in mourning go through seventy-seven days of lecture series [conducted by Buddhist priests] and Buddhist ceremonies at anniversary dates. The people squander their fortunes to give lavish offerings to the dead. The food on one table is spread over ten square feet, and fees collected by a monk can exceed one thousand gold pieces. To pay for these, some people have to rent out the houses in which they live and others have to sell their houses. Filial sons become fugitives from unpaid debts, and the young children unwittingly become victims of hunger and starvation.[22]

Clearly, the attraction of Buddhist funeral and memorial rituals was felt to be undercutting proper Confucian standards. In general, Japan continued to take its funeral and mourning practices from Buddhism rather than from Confucianism.

It is difficult to establish a clear picture of marriage and social relations in ancient Japanese society. However, in this and later periods, Japan seems to have preserved many practices that did not fit into, or yield easily to, a Chinese or Korean Confucian model. If patrilineality and patriarchality are characteristic of Confucian social relations, these seem to have been less emphasized in Japan. There are suggestions that matriarchal patterns were stronger in Japan than in China. The emphasis on a Confucian agnatic principle of male descent was less strong in ancient Japan than it was in China. Women, at least in aristocratic society, maintained personal property rights. Uxorilocal marriage was common in court society.[23] Marriage within

[22] David Lu, trans., *Sources of Japanese History* (New York: McGraw-Hill, 1974), p. 63.

[23] On Heian marriage practices see William McCullough, "Japanese Marriage Institutions of the Heian Period," *Harvard Journal of Asiatic Studies* 27 (1967): 103–67.

the clan was less frowned upon than it was in Confucian theory or practice. There was a greater tendency toward unigeniture, a single-heir system, in contrast to the equal fraternal inheritance advocated as ideal by many Chinese Confucians.

The Heian period closes with the weakening of the *ritsuryō* state along with its state-sponsored, Confucian-influenced institutions and the ideals on which they were based, and with the growing ascendancy of Buddhism over Confucianism and Shinto as the dominant worldview. Confucianism was not rejected, but the balance of influence among the available "Ways" shifted decisively in favor of the "Way of the Buddha." Buddhist ascendancy was felt in the grip of Shingon and Pure Land Buddhism within the Heian court, among provincial warriors, and in rural society. It strengthened in the twelfth and thirteenth centuries with the spread of ideas of *mappō*, the revival of the older schools of Buddhism, and the popularization of the teachings of the Pure Land, Nichiren, and Zen. Popular Buddhist preachers were less concerned with this-worldly morality and social relations than with individual salvation in a heavenly paradise or in the achievement of a personal enlightenment that transcended, or ignored, filial piety and other mundane values.

Taking stock of the position of Confucianism in the late Heian period, it is clear that much had been achieved. Confucianism had established a substantial place for itself in Japanese society and intellectual life. The ideal of a stable, this-worldly, secular moral order had been introduced and counterposed against both the basic world-denying outlook of Buddhism premised on notions of constant flux and the mythical, pre-moral, ritualized vision of early Shinto. In the realm of education, the central and provincial nobility in Japanese society had been introduced to Confucian ethical concepts and the ideals of the Confucian sage and loyal official. Confucian texts were used in the government academies and provided ideals of virtue and decorum as a basis for loyal bureaucratic service for officials. The *Analects, Classic of Filial Piety,* and other texts were part of the reading of every courtier. Confucian rituals were practiced within the court. Confucian ideas of hierarchy under heaven were used with Shinto and Buddhism to buttress imperial authority. The Confucian emphasis on man as a social being and on morality as fundamentally social and hierarchical, expressed in observance of the five cardinal relationships (ruler-subject, father-son, husband-wife, elder and younger brother, and friends), had been introduced. So too had the Confucian emphasis on duties to superiors and society and the disregard for assertions of "rights." Some efforts had been made to impose Confucian values from above in the area of kinship and family life.

Values of filiality, loyalty, and ordered hierarchy important to Confucians had come to influence the family life of the nobility. These influences persisted and, as suggested by the *Nihon ryōiki*, probably trickled down slowly to other strata of society. But at the same time, recognizing the interplay of complementary currents of thought, it is difficult to conclude that Japan was Confucianized in this period, or even that the nobility was influenced exclusively by Confucianism. Confucian values were advocated most vigorously in the Nara and early Heian periods. Thereafter, they tended to be diluted, as Buddhism and the amalgam of Buddhism and Shinto known as *honji suijaku* thought gained greater sway.

THE MEDIEVAL PERIOD: CONFUCIANISM AND THE "UNITY OF THE THREE CREEDS"

Confucian influences persisted in medieval Japan—the Kamakura and Muromachi eras—but they were weaker than they had been in the ancient period and were contained more in the realm of intellectual life than in that of ritual or family values. With the decline of the state-sponsored *daigakuryō* and the provincial colleges, study of Confucianism was restricted to a few families among the lesser nobility. They tended to reiterate ancient interpretations and were generally indifferent to the intellectual revival of Confucianism spearheaded in Sung China by Chu Hsi and other scholars. Thus, in the thirteenth and fourteenth centuries aristocratic family academies were replaced by Zen Buddhist monasteries as the principal centers for the transmission of Confucian ideas, as Chinese and Japanese Zen monks who were well versed in the Sung dynasty Neo-Confucian synthesis of Chu Hsi brought these interpretations to Japan. Ben'en Enni, the founder of the Zen monastery of Tōfukuji in Kyoto, is known to have brought back to Japan Confucian as well as Buddhist texts and commentaries in the early thirteenth century and to have lectured on them at court. In the fourteenth century the Zen monks Chūgan Engetsu and Gidō Shūshin were well known for their knowledge of Sung Confucianism. Gidō, for instance, lectured on the classic *Golden Mean* and other texts to Shogun Ashikaga Yoshimitsu and members of the imperial court.

Zen monks, however, were interested mainly in the promotion of Zen Buddhism. Introducing Confucian ideas to their warrior or courtly patrons was a means to that end. They presented Confucian ideas in such syncretic terms as the "Unity of Zen and Confucian Teachings" or "Unity of the Three Creeds," in which Confucianism was viewed as a valid Way, alongside Buddhism and Taoism, but one that was ultimately inferior to Buddhism, useful only in sustaining the superior insights of Zen. This theme of the Unity of the Three Creeds was frequently illustrated in ink paintings showing the Buddha, Confucius, and Lao Tzu as the "Three Sages of Tiger Valley" or the "Three Tasters of Vinegar."[24]

Sung Neo-Confucian ideas of ordered political hierarchy (taigi meibun), found their way into the political vocabulary of the age in such works as the Jinnō shōtōki and Taiheiki, which present the ideal of the virtuous ruler and discuss the values of loyalty, wisdom, and benevolence in Confucian terms. Confucian ideas could thus reinforce the ideals of valor, service, and family honor developing within Japanese warrior society.[25] But this Confucian-influenced historical view was paralleled in the medieval period by a Shinto-Buddhist-inspired view of historical development reflected in Jien's Gukanshō. "The Gukanshō is not written—as earlier histories all seem to have been—from a conviction concerning the desirability and power of cosmic harmony, Confucian virtue, or past models, but from belief in the way physical events are affected by unseen beings and divine truths."[26]

In medieval Japan there was no counterpart to the metropolitan college of the ancient period, and Confucian principles were no longer systematically inculcated. As the scholarly monk Jien commented, only a few of his contemporaries seemed to be studying Confucian texts:

> If we look back over the ages that have come and gone since ancient times, we will see that now—after a long period of precipitous deterioration—we have come to another time of improvement. . . . There remain a few who study Chinese historical and literary works and the Confucian classics. And it seems that a few are studying law.[27]

For the most part, education was provided by tutors within the families of the nobility or upper levels of warrior society, or by temples that took in lay students as well as Buddhist novices. Perhaps the most significant educational institution of the medieval age was the

[24] On the Unity of the Three Creeds as a theme in medieval Japanese art see John Rosenfield, "The Unity of the Three Creeds: A Theme in Japanese Ink Painting of the Fifteenth Century," in Japan in the Muromachi Age, ed. John W. Hall and Takeshi Toyoda (Berkeley: University of California Press, 1977), pp. 205–25.

[25] Ashikaga Enjutsu, Kamakura Muromachi jidai no jukyō (Tokyo: Nihon Koten Zenshū Kangōkai, 1932); Wajima Yoshio, Chūsei no jugaku (Tokyo: Yopshikawa Kōbunkan, 1965) and Nihon sōgaku shi no kenkyū (Tokyo: Yoshikawa Kōbunkan, 1962).

[26] Delmer M. Brown and Ishida Ichirō, trans., The Future and the Past (Berkeley: University of California Press, 1979), p. 12.

[27] Ibid., p. 224.

Ashikaga family school, which taught Confucian and Taoist texts, especially the *Book of Changes*, to Zen monks and a few warriors.[28]

One channel through which scattered Confucian values may have spread beyond monastic cloisters and the residences of a few scholarly nobles and *daimyō* in the medieval period was the copybooks known as *ōraimono*. These were collections of letters and responses to them gathered into one volume to serve as models of correct style and vocabulary. *Ōraimono* under seven different titles have survived from the Heian period and more than forty from the Kamakura and Muromachi periods. Some of them contained quotations from the Confucian classics and simple precepts for daily life. They were, however, unsystematic, and in view of the very limited literacy of the period could not have been widely used.

The civil wars of the late fifteenth and sixteenth century dispersed Zen monks and nobles to the provinces. Some found refuge with local *daimyō* who were interested in studying Confucianism as a source of political guidance. The Zen monk Keian Genju (1427–1508) introduced the *sekiten* service to the Kikuchi family and several other domains in western Japan. The *daimyō* Ouchi Yoshitaka of Suō Province imported Confucian books from Korea and had refugee nobles and monks come to Yamaguchi and lecture on Confucian texts. In Tosa, Minamimura Baiken taught a Zen-Confucian syncretism. As a result of such activity Confucian moral and ethical teachings became increasingly prominent in the house laws of sixteenth-century *daimyō*. In the "Seventeen Article Injunction" of Asakura Toshikage, c.1480, we find the influence of the Confucian *Analects* blended with that of Buddhism in the training of warriors:

A famous monk once said that a master of men must be like the two Buddhist deities Fudō and Aizen. Although Fudō carries a sword, and Aizen carries a bow and arrows, these weapons are not intended for slashing and shooting, but for the purpose of subjugating devils. In their hearts they are compassionate and circumspect. Like them, a master of samurai must first rectify his own way, and then reward his loyal subjects and soldiers and eliminate those who are disloyal and treacherous. If you can discern between reason and unreason and between good and evil and act accordingly, your system of rewards and punishments can be considered as compassionately administered. On the other hand, if your heart is prejudiced, no matter how much you know the words of the sages and study the texts they all come to naught. You may observe that the *Analects* [1.8] contains a passage saying that "A gentleman who lacks steadfastness cannot command respect." Do not consider that the term

[28] Yūki Rikuro, *Kanazawa bunko to Ashikaga gakkō* (Tokyo: Shibundō, 1959).

"steadfastness" represents only heavy-handedness. It is essential that you conduct yourself in such a way that both heavy-handedness and leniency can be applied flexibly as the occasion demands.[29]

From this quotation it is clear that Confucian values were advocated as a moral code for warriors in the medieval period, but this passage also suggests that they were presented unsystematically, and within a syncretic framework including Buddhist, Shinto, Legalist, and popular folk ideas. In contrast with China, where Confucian ideas and values were spread widely throughout the provinces via the examination system and family rituals, Confucianism in medieval Japan was largely restricted to a few noble families, to learned Zen monks and their shogunal patrons, and to some provincial warrior families.

In the mid-sixteenth century Jesuit missionaries reached Japan. They made converts among samurai and commoners and patrons among the *daimyō*, including Oda Nobunaga, who was to begin the process of political reunification that culminated in the establishment of the Tokugawa shogunate after 1600. For a century or so Christianity entered the multipolar configuration of intellectual and ethical possibilities open to the Japanese. Advocates of Buddhism and Shinto feared that they would be deprived of influence and sought to turn *daimyō* and feudal leaders against the alien creed from the West. But while Nobunaga and many *daimyō* were toying with Christianity and Southern Barbarian culture they were also showing renewed interest in Chinese Confucian teachings. Screen paintings and stories from the sixteenth century frequently illustrate the twenty-four models of filial piety from the Chinese classics.

Oda Nobunaga's great castle at Azuchi is a fitting symbol of the ongoing eclecticism of Japanese thought in which Chinese and Japanese, Buddhist, Confucian, Taoist, and Shinto themes were all harnessed to the enhancement of power and authority. In spite of Nobunaga's well-known antipathy toward Buddhism, Azuchi castle is believed to have had a Buddhist chapel on the sixth floor and a Confucian chamber on the seventh, the very topmost floor of the castle. Decorated by Kanō Eitoku with paintings of Chinese sage kings, Taoist immortals, and culture heroes, the chamber also included paintings of King Wen, one of Confucius' models of benevolence and virtue, who seized the Mandate of Heaven to overthrow the Shang dynasty and establish the Chou dynasty. Eitoku also painted the Duke of Chou, another of Confucius' ideal rulers, Confucius himself, and

[29] Satō Shinichi *et al.*, eds. *Chūsei hōsei shiryōshū* (Tokyo: Iwanami Shoten, 1959), vol. 3, pp. 335–43.

his ten disciples.[30] We do not know how actively Nobunaga may have been involved in the decorative agenda for Azuchi, but such heavy use of Confucian symbolism of legitimate and benevolent rule by a warrior who was bent on seizing the realm (*tenka*) was not accidental. It is a clear use of Confucianism as a central element in a warrior ideology of power well before the establishment of the Tokugawa *bakufu* and the Tokugawa patronage of Neo-Confucianism. But it is important to note that in Azuchi, too, Confucianism was used in conjunction with Buddhism, Taoism, and Shinto to help legitimate political authority and prescribe a moral and historical basis for Nobunaga's rule.

THE EDO PERIOD: THE DIFFUSION OF CONFUCIAN VALUES

After the attenuation of Confucian influence and its subjection to Buddhism through much of the medieval centuries, the fortunes of Confucianism revived in the Edo period. Confucian studies flourished and gained in vitality as never before. Confucian political ideas were used to support the Tokugawa power structure. There was a powerful Confucian influence on the lives and thinking of samurai and on commoners as literacy, schooling, and access to books and teachers increased. Buddhists were forced to defend their beliefs against Confucian critics.[31] Advocates of Shinto were also forced to reckon with, and learn from, Confucianism. In the shifting multipolar system of Japanese thought and moral values, Confucianism was certainly the dominant pole in the seventeenth and eighteenth centuries. Did its dominance amount to a hegemony—to what we might call a Confucianization of Japanese society in the Edo period?

Some commentators have argued a full-scale Confucianization thesis for the Edo period. This finds expression in the widely accepted view that it was Tokugawa Confucianism, especially the synthesis derived from Chu Hsi known as Neo-Confucianism, that provided the first really strong system of social ethics that the Japanese had known; that neither early Shinto nor Buddhism had provided precepts whereby the relations between ruler and ruled, father and son, hus-

[30] On the decoration of Azuchi Castle see Carolyn Wheelwright, "A Visualization of Eitoku's Lost Paintings at Azuchi Castle," in *Warlords, Artists, and Commoners: Japan in the Sixteenth Century*, ed. George Elison and Bardwell L. Smith (Honoulu: University of Hawaii Press, 1981), pp. 87–112.

[31] For one Buddhist priest's accommodation with Neo-Confucianism in the Edo period see Paul B. Watt, "Jiun Sonja (1718–1804): A Response to Confucianism within the Context of Buddhist Reform," in *Confucianism and Tokugawa Culture*, ed. Peter Nosco (Princeton: Princeton University Press, 1984), pp. 188–214.

band and wife, and elder and younger siblings should be regulated; that these Confucian ideals took root in samurai society and were quickly and thoroughly disseminated by precept and example throughout the society. It is also argued that the attacks on Buddhism by Nobunaga and Hideyoshi in the late sixteenth century and the eradication of Christianity in the early seventeenth century by the Tokugawa shoguns cut down intellectual competitors and opened the way for a rapid "takeover" of intellectual and ethical discourse by Neo-Confucianism, which was deliberately chosen as intellectual orthodoxy and political ideology by the early Tokugawa shoguns.

Without denying the importance or strength of the Confucian intellectual surge in the Edo period, we should bear in mind that at least some of these ethical principles had been introduced in earlier waves of Chinese and Confucian cultural influence. They had gained some foothold in the court, in Zen monasteries, and in the more literate sectors of warrior society and were accepted as part of the proper order of society. Moreover, as we have seen, medieval warriors injected Confucian ideals into their house codes, and Nobunaga seems to have made a more conscious and far-reaching ideological use of Confucianism to legitimize his conquests. Confucian values, therefore, were not a new arrival in the Edo period. What was new was their release from a Zen Buddhist intellectual environment, their greater systematization, and their more widespread diffusion. Also striking in the Edo period was the importance that came to be attached to scholarly pursuits by samurai, most of whom, prior to the seventeenth century, had little time or inclination for such activities. It is samurai and townsmen, rather than nobles or Buddhist monks, who become the intellectuals and specialists in Chinese studies (*kangakusha*) in the Edo period.

While recognizing a growing acceptance of Confucianism in Tokugawa society we should be wary of notions of total displacement of other rival, or complementary, value systems. Christianity was eradicated as a potential rival for reasons of *bakufu* policy, but Buddhism and Shinto remained influential, folk practices flourished, and there was a considerable degree of intertwining of value systems. From the eighteenth century a surging National Learning movement was challenging Chinese and Confucian studies, and some intellectuals were drawn to Dutch and Western studies. Confucianism itself was anything but monolithic.[32] Neo-Confucian followers of Hayashi Razan

[32] Tetsuo Najita has written: "What impresses me most about Tokugawa political thought is that it was constantly undergoing change. The once fashionable view popularized by the cultural leaders of early Meiji that Japan's normal evolution toward enlightenment was stymied by a monolithic ideology is, of course, a myth, a mere con-

claimed intellectual orthodoxy for their school, but that orthodoxy was not recognized unequivocally by the Tokugawa *bakufu*, by domain governments, or by other Confucian schools. Scholars of various Confucian allegiances debated fiercely, some in the name of Chu Hsi, others such as Itō Jinsai and Ogyū Sorai returning to earlier Confucian classics, and still others mixing their Confucianism with doses of Shinto or Legalism. Japanese Confucianists were placed in a particular predicament by the Sino-centric character of Chinese Confucian thought. As Kate Nakai has shown, Japanese Confucianists adopted varying stances toward the naturalization of Chinese Confucianism and worked out a fiction of Japanese centrality through the rhetoric of naturalization.[33] Still other scholars adopted an eclectic position or rejected Confucianism in favor of National Learning or Dutch studies. If we are thinking of the whole society, and not just of the samurai elite, it is probably more accurate to view Edo intellectual life and moral values as the product of the interplay of a variety of influences than to try to view them solely in terms of Confucian dominance. Even in samurai society, where Confucianism took deep hold, there was considerable intellectual diversity and change over time.

It used to be commonly believed that the Neo-Confucian school of Hayashi Razan was established as the orthodox source of *bakufu* "ideology" by Tokugawa Ieyasu in the seventeenth century. It was argued that Neo-Confucian ideas of a permanent natural and social order provided a useful intellectual buttress for preserving existing relationships between rulers and ruled and thus for keeping Tokugawa society orderly and justifying the Tokugawa shoguns' exercise of power. Ishida Ichirō, for instance, has described Neo-Confucianism as "a theology (*shingaku*) sustaining the *baku-han* structure."[34] Maruyama Masao argued that a Neo-Confucian ideology established in the early seventeenth century dissolved late in the century to be replaced by the teachings of Ogyū Sorai and the Ancient Learning school. For Maruyama, Sorai's thought made a revolutionary transformation in political theory in shifting from viewing state and society as "natural" and immutable to viewing them as a "creation" or artifice that could

---

venience with which to contrast traditional with modern. . . . It is an unassailable fact that 'Tokugawa Confucianism' was not an undifferentiated and unchanging ideology." "The Conceptual Portrayal of Tokugawa Intellectual History," in *Japanese Thought in the Tokugawa Period*, ed. Tetsuo Najita and Irwin Scheiner (Chicago: University of Chicago Press, 1978), p. 19.

[33] Kate Wildman Nakai, "The Naturalization of Confucianism in Tokugawa Japan: The Problem of Sino-Centrism, "in *Harvard Journal of Asiatic Studies* 40, no. 1 (June 1980): pp. 157–99.

[34] Ishida Ichirō, "Tokugawa hōken shakai to shushigaku ha no shisō," *Tōhoku Daigaku Bungakubu Kenkyū Nenpō*, no. 13 (1963).

be changed and were therefore subject to reform.[35] Sorai remains a central figure, but Bitō Masahide and other scholars have also pointed to the creative contributions of the Shinto-Confucian Yamasaki Ansai and the townsman-scholar Itō Jinsai. Tetsuo Najita, recognizing that the Tokugawa *bakufu* did not insist on a single political orthodoxy, suggests that Confucian ideas, especially those drawn from the rival teachings of Yamazaki Ansai and Ogyū Sorai, were "extracted and made to blend and converge into a functional 'ideology' which, through much of the Tokugawa period, was used to legitimate the *baku-han* system."[36] Elsewhere he has written of an "instrumentalist ideology," emerging in the "moral crisis" of the eighteenth century, derived from Sorai and Dazai Shundai and carried to merchant society by Kaihō Seiryō (1755–1817):

> This instrumentalism, generated out of Tokugawa ideology, is etched into my perception of the moral crisis of the eighteenth century. It makes that era particularly decisive in the metamorphosis of Tokugawa thought, which transformed itself into new forms of criticism and explanation that rejected as obsolete much of the earlier vision of political and social well being.[37]

Recently, the accepted notion of the establishment of Neo-Confucian orthodoxy in the seventeenth century and the Neo-Confucian tone to *bakufu* ideology have come into question.[38] Herman Ooms argues that early Tokugawa ideology was far from being exclusively Neo-Confucian. The *bakufu*, he argues, was veiled in a complex ideology made up of Neo-Confucian, Buddhist, Shinto, and folk elements. Far from Ieyasu patronizing Razan, it was Razan's followers who created the fiction of exclusive Tokugawa patronage to enhance their status among the Confucian schools.[39] This is not to say that

---

[35] In the Author's preface to the English Edition, *Studies in the Intellectual History of Tokugawa Japan*, trans. Mikiso Hane (Princeton: Princeton University Press, 1974), Maruyama modifies his view of Neo-Confucianism orthodoxy in the seventeenth century to suggest that Neo-Confucianism did not take strong hold until late in the century and that the Ancient Learning reaction against it was contemporaneous rather than sequential. See page xxxiv.

[36] Tetsuo Najita, *Japan: The Intellectual Foundations of Modern Japanese Politics* (Chicago: University of Chicago Press, 1974), p. 30.

[37] Tetsuo Najita, "The Conceptual Portrayal of Tokugawa Intellectual History," in Najita and Scheiner, *Japanese Thought in the Tokugawa Period*, p. 22.

[38] Watanabe Hiroshi, *Kinsei Nihon shakai to sōgaku* (Tokyo: Tokyo Daigaku Shuppankai, 1985).

[39] The limited role played by Razan and Neo-Confucianism within early Tokugawa ideology is discussed by Herman Ooms in *Tokugawa Ideology: Early Constructs, 1570–1680* (Princeton: Princeton University Press), 1985.

Neo-Confucianism was not gaining ground in the seventeenth century. It was. But it was not doing so as an exclusive intellectual orthodoxy, nor was it doing so to the exclusion of Buddhism or Shinto,[40] or at the expense of other currents of Confucianism. Official patronage of Confucianism of various schools increased under the third, fifth, and eighth shoguns and reached a high point in the Kansei reforms of 1787–93, and it is sometimes suggested that Matsudaira Sadanobu reinforced a Neo-Confucian orthodoxy in his ban on heterodox studies as part of the Kansei Reform effort. In practice, however, this did not confirm a Neo-Confucian "orthodoxy."[41] Moreover, by this time, Chinese and Confucian intellectual dominance was being challenged by a powerful nativist current known as National Learning, which rejected "Chineseness" (*karagokoro*) and employed a conscious archaism to reformulate the understanding of Japanese reality.[42]

Many *daimyō* followed the shogunal lead in patronizing Confucian scholars and Confucian studies. Domains such as Okayama under Ikeda Mitsumasa (1609–82) and Aizu under Hoshina Masayuki (1611–72) were particularly supportive of Confucian ideals. They set an example for other domains in patronizing Confucian scholars or building domain schools. Although many *daimyō* and samurai were enthusiastic students of Confucian learning and advocates of the Confucian virtues of righteousness, humanity, filiality, and loyalty for themselves and for commoners, no domain imposed anything that might be described as a policy of full-scale Confucianization in which the kinds of Confucian family rituals common in China or Korea were enforced.

Edo period samurai, who because of peace were increasingly assuming the role of civilian bureaucrats, found a moral and political *raison d'être* in the example of the Confucian scholar-official. Many *daimyō* and ordinary samurai were drawn to scholarship and were attracted by the rationality, humanism, sense of history, and intellectual and moral discipline they found in Confucianism. They were encouraged to study literary arts (*bun*) as well as the martial traditions (*bu*).

[40] Royall Tyler, "The Tokugawa Peace and Popular Religion: Suzuki Shōsan, Kakugyō Tōbutsu, and Jikigyō Miroku," in Nosco, *Confucianism and Tokugawa Culture*, pp. 92–119.

[41] Robert L. Backus, "The Relationship of Confucianism to the Tokugawa Bakufu as Revealed in the Kansei Educational Reform," *Harvard Journal of Asiatic Studies* 34 (1974): 97–162; and "The Kansei Prohibition of Heterodoxy and Its Effects on Education," *Harvard Journal of Asiatic Studies* 39 (1979): 55–106.

[42] H.D. Harootunian, "The Consciousness of Archaic Form in the New Realism of Kokugaku," in Najita and Scheiner, *Japanese Thought in the Tokugawa Period*, pp. 63–104.

Confucian influence is evident in the reformulation of martial values, the code of *bushidō*. Japanese warriors in the medieval period had been encouraged to internalize the virtue of loyalty. Loyalty to feudal lord was set above loyalty to family. However, in the warfare in the fourteenth, fifteenth, and sixteenth centuries that loyalty had usually been given reciprocally in return for spoils or protection. During the Edo period the samurai ethic was reshaped by shogunal precept and such works as the *Hagakure*, with their Confucian emphasis on loyalty, ordered relationships, and filial piety, into the cult of *bushidō*, in which loyalty was expressed as much in self-denying peacetime administrative service as in performance of martial arts or military service.[43]

The quintessential samurai virtue of loyalty to feudal overlord and the more explicitly Confucian virtue of filiality to parents could at times come into conflict. When they did, how was the conflict resolved? James McMullen has found a wide range of reactions to this dilemma in contemporary writings by or about samurai.[44] In Chinese Confucian thought the choice between them was generally left to the individual, with a tendency to favor filial piety. In samurai-dominated Japan, even among ardent advocates of the samurai tradition, there were several who did *not* put loyalty before filial piety in the early Edo period. However, there was, McMullen suggests, an "eventual ideological ascendancy of loyalty over filial piety in Tokugawa Japan."[45] This he attributes both to the great dependency of samurai on their feudal overlords in Tokugawa status hierarchy and to the fact that "the military character of Japan's ruling class from the twelfth century also created a predisposition to the attenuation of even primary kinship ties and the acknowledgement of loyalties transcending the family."

Of four Confucian samurai thinkers who discussed this problem McMullen finds that Hayashi Razan "tended to promote filial piety above loyalty except in certain well-defined contexts" and "he appears to have made little sustained or consistent attempt to relate Chinese Confucian ideas to the priorities of the Japanese samurai tradition."[46] Kumazawa Banzan, 1619–91, who condemned the policy of separating samurai from the soil, wanted a "decentralized society with samurai in extended families enjoying considerable autonomy

---

[43] Martin Collcutt, entry on "Bushidō" in *Encyclopedia of Japan* (Tokyo: Kodansha International, 1983), vol. 1, pp. 221–23.

[44] I. J. McMullen, "Rulers or Fathers? A Casuistical Problem in Early Modern Japanese Thought," *Past and Present* 116 (August 1987): 56–97.

[45] Ibid., p. 93.

[46] Ibid., p. 73.

and economic independence from their *daimyō*."[47] In such a rural society "filial piety would be the basis for the ideal social order."[48] Yamaga Sokō, 1622–85, an advisor on samurai ideals and military science to feudal rulers, tended to "exalt loyalty": Sokō acknowledged the genetic precedence of filial piety, or reiterated the Chinese Confucian view that loyalty and filial piety were incommensurable. This position, however, was constantly trimmed in favor of weightier emphasis on loyalty. For Sokō, the ruler-subject relationship was "the greatest" of the "great bonds of human relationships."[49] Asami Keisai, 1652–1711, a commoner and Confucian scholar who praised the samurai tradition as representative of the highest ideals in Japanese culture, showed a "distinct tendency to prefer loyalty over filial piety,"[50] especially loyalty to the imperial lineage. McMullen's research reminds us that for the Edo period samurai Confucian and feudal values were not always in perfect alignment and that many possible intellectual resolutions existed.

As in the ancient period, Confucian influences during the Edo period were most powerfully and broadly felt in the field of education and scholarship. Confucianism was the major current in Edo period institutions of learning, especially those for samurai. The strong Confucian current in the curriculum of domain schools has been clearly shown by Ronald Dore in his study, *Tokugawa Education*, and by Japanese scholars who have studied samurai education. Dore stresses that the overwhelming aim of Tokugawa writers on education was the inculcation of moral virtues. These moral virtues were to be attained by study of the Confucian classics and the realization in practice of such basic Confucian virtues as the five relationships: love and filiality in relations between parents and children, fairness and loyalty between master and servant, concern and deference in the relations between spouses, affection and respect in the relations between elder and younger brothers, and mutual trust between friends.[51] The ideal Way for samurai was to become a morally complete human being and an effective ruler of men: "The essentials of book learning (*bun*) are cultivating as a basis the Way of filial piety, respect for elders, loyalty

[47] Ibid., p. 78.
[48] Ibid., p. 78.
[49] Ibid., p. 79.
[50] Ibid., p. 85.
[51] Ronald P. Dore, *Education in Tokugawa Japan* (Berkeley: University of California Press, 1965), p. 34. Kasai Sukeharu, *Kinsei hankō no sōgoteki kenkyū* (Tokyo: Yoshikawa Kōbunkan, 1960), *Kinsei hankō ni okeru shuppansho no kenkyū* (Tokyo: Yoshikawa Kōbunkan, 1962), and *Kinsei hankō ni okeru gakutō gakuha no kenkyū*, 2 vols. (Tokyo: Yoshikawa Kōbunkan, 1969–70).

and trust, to clarify the principles whereby nations are governed and the people made content, and so to strive to be useful in the public service."[52]

Under Confucian instructors, *han* schools were centers for the study of the classics, the inculcation of Confucian moral ideals, and devotion to Confucius. A number of schools had special halls honoring Confucius, and the *sekiten* service was observed at least once annually in 110 schools and twice annually in 86. *Han* schools were important in introducing samurai youths to Confucian teachings, but it is worth pointing out that of the more than 200 *han* schools established in the Edo period, relatively few were founded in the seventeenth century, and fewer than 30 by 1750. The real spurt came after the mid-eighteenth century, with about 180 domain schools being established between 1751 and 1867. Further, although Confucian studies were an important part of the curriculum, Dutch studies, astronomy and military studies, and Japanese classical studies, *kokugaku*, were also included.

A few domains admitted commoners together with samurai children to the domain school. Some domains provided separate education facilities or sponsored lectures for the non-samurai population. Some samurai attended private academies, *shijuku*, run by Confucian scholars. Very often all classes were given by a single scholar who emphasized particular Confucian or other texts and interpretations. By 1872 there were some 1,400 such private schools in Japan, of which more than 600 concentrated on Chinese studies or a mixture of Chinese and Japanese studies.[53]

The diffusion of Confucianism in Edo period Japan was no longer dependent on nobles or Buddhist monks, as it had been in the ancient and medieval periods. The Edo period saw the emergence of Confucian teachers (*jusha*), professional scholar-educators, many of samurai origin, who made their living by studying and teaching the Confucian classics. The greater spread of Confucian ideas and values in the Edo period was largely the result of the activities of this growing body of professional Confucians. Some of these *jusha* were used as advisors and instructors by the Edo *bakufu*, others by *daimyō*. Many Confucian-minded *daimyō* employed *jusha* as advisors on questions of ritual and as tutors for their families. Some scholars set themselves up as private educators. Recent research by Watanabe Hiroshi, based on dates of death of identifiable scholars of the Chinese classics,

---

[52] Dore, *Education in Tokugawa Japan*, p. 43.

[53] Richard Rubinger, *Private Academies of Tokugawa Japan* (Princeton: Princeton University Press, 1982), p. 13. Ishikawa Matsutarō, *Hankō to terakoya* (Tokyo: Kyōikusha, 1978), p. 29.

shows that their number was quite small in the seventeenth century but grew steadily through the eighteenth and nineteenth. For the decade 1650–59 Watanabe identifies deaths of eighteen *kanbungaku-sha* (Confucian scholars), for the period 1700–1709 he gives a figure of forty, for 1750–59 one hundred and one, for 1800–1809 two hundred, and for the Bakumatsu decade 1860–69 two hundred ninety-two.[54] The status of these men varied; rarely high, it tended to fall as the period progressed. Most domain Confucian scholars were samurai of middle to lower status.[55]

Confucian values were also spread by Confucian books in a society in which literacy was improving and a publishing industry developing. Many Confucian books were imported from China and Korea; others were printed in Edo, Osaka, and Kyoto. The shogunal college and many domain schools also published Confucian texts. During the Edo period some 1,394 Confucian titles and a further 763 Chinese historical works were published in this way. Confucian books were bought and read by literate commoners as well as by samurai scholars.[56]

Confucian rituals were performed at the *bakufu*-sponsored Yu-shima Seidō and at other Confucian halls. A few *daimyō* seem to have adopted Confucian funeral rituals. Some scholars affected Chinese-style robes. It is not easy, however, to determine to what extent samurai households, or those of other social groups, may have practiced what we might describe as Confucian rites. The Buddhas and the *kami* were at least as important as the Confucian sages in the validation of family rituals surrounding birth, coming of age, betrothal, childbirth, and death in most samurai families. It seems likely that Japanese samurai commitment to Confucianism diverged most sharply from Chinese or Korean practice in this area of personal and family observances.

The reception of Confucianism within the merchant and artisan sectors of Tokugawa society is less studied than that for samurai society, but is obviously vital to any understanding of the degree of Confucianization of the society. By the mid-eighteenth century there

[54] Watanabe Hiroshi, *Kinsei Nihon shakai to sōgaku*, p. 22.

[55] John W. Hall, "The Confucian Teacher in Tokugawa Japan," in *Confucianism in Action*, ed. David S. Nivison and Arthur F. Wright (Princeton: Princeton University Press, 1959).

[56] See Kobayashi Zenpachi, *Nihon shuppan bunkashi* (Tokyo: Seishōdō, 1978); Konta Yōzō, "Genroku Kyōhō ki ni okeru shuppan shihon keisei to sono rekishiteki igi ni tsuite," *Historia* 19, and idem, *Edo no honya-san* (Tokyo: Nihon Hōsō Shuppan Kyōkai, 1977); Suzuki Toshio, *Edo no honya*, vols. 1 and 2 (Tokyo: Chūōkōronsha, 1980); and Munemasa Isoo, *Kinsei Kyoto shuppan bunka no kenkyū* (Kyoto: Dōmeisha, 1982).

were a growing number of schools open to merchants and their families. Some of these were established by Confucian scholars, others by groups of merchants or *han* officials. Rural and urban schools established by *han* authorities in the late Edo and early Meiji period are known as *gōkō*. They were the forerunners of early Meiji elementary schools. Some were set up as extensions of *han* schools for samurai children; others aimed at providing education for commoners. In contrast to private academies (*shijuku*) and "temple schools" (*terakoya*), which were privately managed, *gōkō* were generally run by domain officials or by groups of samurai under *han* supervision. Some were managed jointly by *han* officials and commoners, or by urban or rural commoner groups. Under official sponsorship, teachers were sent from the *han* schools, school lands were exempted from taxes, part of the teaching expenses were paid, and textbooks were provided.

The earliest *gōkō* was in Okayama *han*, followed by the Gansuidō in Setsu, 1717, the Kaihodō in Edo, and the Kaitokudō in Osaka. In the Tengakukan (Mimasaka) and the Keigyōkan (Bitchū), the *Analects* and *Mencius* were used as texts. In the Enpō Gakkō (Mito) and the Uedamachi school in Saga, samurai children studied the Chinese classics while children of commoners worked at copybooks (*ōraimono*). At the Isezaki school, which was managed jointly by *han* officials and commoners, teachers from the *han* school were sent to give regular lectures three times a month. They taught reading to children and lectured on the Confucian classics to adults. Textbooks included the *Lesser Learning*, *Four Books*, and *Five Classics*. Like most other such schools, age of entry and length of study were not strictly regulated. In urban schools some lectures were directed at the cultivation of merchant values such as obligation (*giri*), for instance, as well as discussion of such Confucian ideas as Heaven (*ten*), principle (*ri*), and material force (*ki*). In rural areas the virtues of frugality, cooperation, and thrift—considered essential to village life and farming—were stressed. This was rather different from the more academic, textually based classical education of the *han* schools.[57]

There were a number of private academies (*shijuku*) that offered a Confucian-based education to commoners. These were generally established by scholars, performers, or samurai in their homes to teach the Chinese classics, letters, performing arts, or martial arts. Those that were established by Confucian scholars under *bakufu* or *han* auspices to teach samurai children are known as *kajuku*. These had close ties with *han* schools. Many schools, private academies in the full sense of the word, were not officially sponsored. Among the famous

[57] Ishikawa Ken, *Kinsei no gakkō* (Tokyo: Kōryōsha, 1957).

shijuku of the early and mid-Edo period were Nakae Tōjū's Tōjū Shoin, Matsunaga Sekigo's Kōshūdō in Kyoto—which was said to have had 5,000 students, among them Kinoshita Jun'an and Kaibara Ekken, and taught the *Four Books* and *Five Classics*—Yamazaki Ansai's *juku*, and Itō Jinsai's Horikawa *juku*. These ranked alongside the family *juku* of the Hayashi family as training centers for many scholars of the Edo period who were active in education, politics, and culture. Many of these *juku* were open to townsmen—for instance, Itō Jinsai's influential Horikawa *juku* in Kyoto.[58]

From the mid-Edo period, with the proliferation of *han* schools and *gōkō* and the growing use of the Hayashi Shōheizaka Gakumonjo as a training center for Confucian scholars for the various *han*, the influence of the private *juku* declined. Even so, many continued to flourish. From this period, in addition to Confucian-oriented *juku*, scholars of National Learning such as Motoori Norinaga also established private academies. Shingaku lecture halls, although not strictly private *juku*, also flourished as centers for popular education in urban and rural areas. From the early nineteenth century there was an upsurge in the establishment of *shijuku*. It is hard to find reliable figures, but estimates suggest that there were probably several thousand throughout the country. Many of these catered to townspeople and had Confucian elements as part of the curriculum.

What were the reasons for the upsurge in commoner education? Undoubtedly, growing prosperity and productivity in urban and rural society led to greater interest in reading, writing, and the abacus. Many commoners enrolled in *shijuku*. Some of the smaller reading and writing *juku* are hard to distinguish from *terakoya*; most, however, offered a higher level of education than *terakoya*. Also, some of these private academies offered new scholarly directions, in contrast to Confucian schools. Some were devoted to Dutch studies and Western learning—for instance, those run by Siebold, Otsuki Gentaku, and Fukuzawa Yukichi. National Learning (*kokugaku*) academies also increased with growing interest in the Japanese classics. In the Bakumatsu period some *juku*, like that of Yoshida Shoin, devoted themselves to the moral and political training of young samurai who were to play a major role in the Meiji Restoration.[59]

Several schools for commoners, *gōgaku* and *shijuku*, have been intensively studied. Among them are Itō Jinsai's Horikawa *juku* in Kyoto, the Kaitokudō and Gansuidō in Osaka and Settsu, and the

---

[58] Rubinger, in *Private Academies of Tokugawa Japan*, discusses the various kinds of Shijuku.

[59] See Umehara Tōru, *Kinsei shijuku no kenkyū* (Tokyo: Shibunkaku, 1983). Also Rubinger, *Private Academies of Tokugawa Japan*.

Kaihodō in Edo. In all of these schools, townspeople could acquire a Confucian education directed to moral and practical values. The Horikawa Gaku-ha was established by Itō Jinsai and Tōgai at Hori-kawa in Kyoto. Jinsai was an advocate of a variant of the Ancient Learning school and advocated a rejection of metaphysical Neo-Confucian interpretations in favor of a return to Confucius and Mencius. The emphasis was on experiential learning. The school was at its peak in the early eighteenth century and townsmen were actively involved.[60]

The Kaitokudō was a private academy for Osaka townsmen. It was established in 1724 by and for townsmen under the sponsorship of Tokugawa Yoshimune. Although nominally Neo-Confucian, the curriculum was fairly free, and lecturers were drawn from different schools of Confucian thought. It was not aimed at the education of Confucian scholars. The first head was Miyake Sekian, 1665–1730, who studied Wang Yang-ming and Neo-Confucian thought. Nakai Chikuzan, 1730–1804, was fourth head of school. Most students were commoners. They included Tominaga Nakamoto, 1715–46, a soy sauce merchant, whose father helped set up the school. Tominaga's intellectual interests shifted from Confucianism to Buddhism, then to kami-devotion and the way of sincerity (makoto); he later became interested in astronomy, Dutch learning, and rationalism. He influenced Motoori Norinaga and Hirata Atsutane. Yamagata Bantō, 1748–1821, was another famous Osaka townsman-scholar.[61]

Like the Kaitokudō, the Gansuidō in Settsu has been well studied, and its documentary sources collected and edited. It was established by seven influential local families in Settsu under guidance from founders of the Kaitokudō. The curriculum offered an eclectic mix of Wang Yang-ming, Ancient Learning, and Neo-Confucian teaching. Teachers included Miwa Shūsai (1669–1744) and Itō Tōgai. In addition to its educational role, the school also provided relief to victims of famine.[62] In Edo the Kaihodō school was established in 1723

---

[60] Ishida Ichirō, Itō Jinsai (Tokyo: Yoshikawa Kōbunkan, 1960); Yoshikawa Kōjirō, ed., Itō Jinsai, Itō Tōgai (Tokyo: Iwanami Shoten, 1971). John Joseph Spae, "Itō Jinsai, A Philoshopher, Educator and Sinologist of the Tokugawa Period," Monumenta Serica Monograph 12 (1948; rept., 1967).

[61] There is a fine recent study of the Kaitokudō and Osaka merchant values by Tetsuo Najita, Visions of Virtue in Tokugawa Japan: The Kaitokudō Merchant Academy of Osaka (Chicago: University of Chicago Press, 1987). In Japanese see Miyamoto Mataji, Chōnin shakai no gakugei to Kaitokudō (Tokyo: Bunnan Shuppan, 1982).

[62] Osaka Daigaku Fuzoku Toshokan, ed., Gansuidō bunko mokuroku (Osaka: Osaka Daigaku, 1972); Umetani Noboru and Wakita Osamu, eds., Hirano Gansuidō shiryō (Osaka: Seibundō, 1973); Tsuda Hideo, Kinsei minshū kyōiku undō no tenkai (Tokyo: Ochanomizu Shobō, 1978); Takeshita Kikuo, "Gansuidō setsuritsu no zente," in Otani

by a *rōnin* Confucian scholar, Sugano Kenzan. The *bakufu* granted him 30 *ryō* and a site in Fukkawa. The Kaihodō was open to samurai and commoners. It taught the essentials of the *Lesser Learning* and the *Four Books*. The school was sponsored by the *bakufu* as part of Yoshimune's plan for the encouragement of learning. It was run by the Sugano family until taken over in1845 by the Hayashi family.[63]

It is hard to know what access women might have had to *shijuku* and *gōkō*. Some would have had family tutors. Many would have had access to the growing number of *terakoya* and Shingaku halls in the late Edo period. There was a genre of instructional and moral literature for women advocating devotion to ancestors, father, and husband.[64] There was also a vogue for such edificational collections of biographies as the *Kinsei kijin den*. Some edificational books, such as the *Kyōgiroku*, distributed to *terakoya* by the *bakufu* to encourage filiality, were printed and distributed as "charity books." These would have been read by men as well as women and in villages as well as towns.

Merchant-house codes (*kakun*) and wills are a fruitful source for the definition of merchant values and of the Confucian component within them. Although merchants nominally occupied a lowly place in the traditional Confucian world order, they were not indifferent or immune to the influence of Confucian ideas of respect for seniors, orderly family and social hierarchy, and loyalty. These were blended with notions of thrift, industriousness, frugality, discipline, and the house (*ie*) as an ongoing institution, to make a vigorous merchant ethic.[65] Confucian ideas were also incorporated into the literature and popular culture of urban Japan. Chikamatsu's extremely popular dramas for the puppet and Kabuki theaters made skillful dramatic use of the conflict between duty (*giri*) and human feelings (*ninjō*):

> Confucian sentiments, in diluted or distinctively Japanese adaptations, are found in many varieties of Tokugawa literature. Perhaps the most

---

Joshi Tanki Daigaku Kiyō 12, and "Gansuido no keiei," in *Otani Joshi Tanki Daigaku Kiyō* 13.

[63] Monbushō Sōmukyoku, ed., *Nihon kyōiku shi shiryō* (Tokyo: Monbushō, 1890–92); and Ishikawa, *Kinsei no gakkō*.

[64] In addition to Kaibara Ekken's *Onna daigaku*, there were such titles as *Onna imashime, Onna rongo*, and *Hime kagami*. The number of these books published increased markedly in the late eighteenth and early nineteenth centuries.

[65] For an introduction to these, see Sakudō Yōtarō, *Edo jidai no kamigata chōnin* (Tokyo: Kyōikusha, 1978). On the broader question of *chōnin* thought and attitudes in general, see the many works on Osaka townsmen written by Miyamoto Mataji in *Miyamoto Mataji chosakushū*, 10 vols. (Tokyo: Kōdansha, 1978). Also see Ishida Ichirō, *Chōnin bunka* (Tokyo: Shibundō, 1961).

striking examples are in the plays of Chikamatsu, which have often been described in terms of the principles of *giri* (duty) and *ninjō* (human feelings) which they are said to embody. These terms, though borrowed from Chinese and considered to be essential elements of Confucian teachings, acquired strongly Japanese meanings.[66]

There was also in Edo literature a strong strain of didacticism and moralizing that encouraged Confucian virtues and warned against vice (*kanzen chōaku*). This note was sounded in the novels of Bakin and many other writers. But, as Donald Keene points out, Confucian virtues were also parodied by late Edo writers such as Tsuruya Nanboku, whose Kabuki dramas "are a reflection of the general decline of morals and ideals" in late Edo society.[67]

In rural society some of the possible sources of Confucian values already mentioned were available to wealthier villagers in less remote parts of the country. There was growing diffusion of the printed word, some access to *gōkō* or *shijuku*, some contacts with traveling scholars, men of letters, and performers. From the mid-Edo period three institutions that must have played increasingly important roles in shaping the values of people in villages as well as towns were the reading and writing schools known as *terakoya*, the moral instruction centers where Shingaku advocates lectured on the virtues of hard work and thrift, and the mutual self-help societies advocated by agriculturalists *nōseika* like Ninomiya Sontoku.

Scholars who have studied the reading and writing schools known as *terakoya* estimate that more than ten thousand were established in the Edo period. In the seventeenth century the average rate of foundation was less than one a year. By the end of the eighteenth century it had risen to twenty or so a year. In the 1820s it was fifty a year, in the 1830s one hundred and thirty, and in the 1850s and early 1860s over three hundred a year. Some of these schools probably failed after a year or two, but most were more enduring. Thus by the close of the Edo period very basic instruction in reading, writing, and the abacus was going on all over the country. *Terakoya* offered only a low level of education and literacy. Even so, the copybooks that were used advocated Confucian virtues, especially filial piety, some of which probably had an effect on the minds and behavior of the students. The *bakufu* actively encouraged this instructional and moralizing ef-

---

[66] Donald Keene, "Confucianism in Tokugawa Literature," in Nosco, *Confucianism and Tokugawa Culture*, p. 122. Minamoto Ryōen distinguishes two types of *giri*. The natural sense of obligation for another person's kindness might be thought of as a warm *giri*. There was, however, a colder *giri*, motivated by fear of criticism rather than natural emotions. Minamoto Ryōen, *Giri to ninjō* (Tokyo: Chuō Koronsha, 1969), p. 49.

[67] Keene, "Confucianism in Tokugawa Literature," p. 136.

fort. On one occasion, the *bakufu* minister Mizuno Tadakuni called together the teachers of sixty-two schools and rewarded them for their services. A number of *han* governments (for instance, Akita and Tsugaru) actively encouraged the establishment of *terakoya*. Most *terakoya*, however, were probably established under private or local initiative. It has been estimated that by 1868 some 43 percent of boys and 10 percent of girls attended some form of school. All of them would have been exposed to at least the main Confucian ethical concepts.[68]

Shingaku began as an urban phenomenon, appealing to merchants and artisans, but in time it spread into rural areas and became a source of popular moral instruction. Ishida Baigan and his followers drew freely on Confucianism, Buddhism, Shinto, and Taoism in shaping their teaching that the heart (*shin* or *kokoro*) was the basis of knowledge, experience, and morality and that a personal and social morality could be forged from the thoughtful performance of everyday activities. Among Confucian writings, Baigan studied Mencius and the Sung Neo-Confucian scholars, and lectured on the *Four Books*, the *Classic of Filial Piety*, and the *Lesser Learning*. Shingaku teachers stressed the public value of such mercantile virtues as industriousness, diligence, thrift, trust, and honesty. Baigan's teachings were further developed by Teshima Toan (1718–86), Nakazawa Dōni (1725–1803), and Shibata Kyūō (1783–1839). These Shingaku advocates wandered the country as lecturers. Nakazawa is said to have visited twenty provinces and opened twenty-one lecture halls. Uekawa Kisui, a disciple of Teshima Toan, was a scholar of Chinese learning who introduced a strong Neo-Confucian intellectual streak into Shingaku. Kamata Ryūō advocated unity of the Three Creeds: Buddhism, Confucianism, and Taoism. Their teachings also filtered through *terakoya*. They were also active in organizing relief from famines and epidemics.[69]

Ninomiya Sontoku and his many followers established village self-help associations (*hōtokusha*); by early Meiji there were more than 1,000 of them in villages throughout the country. Their aims were

[68] Ishikawa Matsutarō, *Hankō to terakoya* (Tokyo: Kyōikusha, 1978), p. 147. See also Ishikawa Ken, *Terakoya* (Tokyo: Shibundō, 1960), *Nihon shomin kyōiku shi* (Tokyo: Tōkō Shoin, 1929), and *Kinsei Nihon shakai kyōiku shi no kenkyū* (Tokyo: Gōdō Shuppan, 1976).

[69] On the Shingaku movement see Robert N. Bellah, *Tokugawa Religion: The Values of Pre-industrial Japan* (Boston: Beacon Press, 1957). Also the same author's "Baigan and Sorai: Continuities and Discontinuities in Eighteenth Century Thought," in Najita and Scheiner, *Japanese Thought in the Tokugawa Period*, pp. 137–52. In Japanese see Ishikawa Ken, *Sekimon shingaku shi no kenkyū* (Tokyo: Iwanami Shoten, 1947), *Shingaku—Edo no shomin tetsugaku* (Tokyo: Nihon Keisai Shinbusha, 1964), and *Shingaku kyōka no honshitsu narabi ni hattatsu* (Tokyo: Gōdō Shuppan, 1982).

rural improvement and village self-sufficiency. They offered guidance in better farming practice, provided interest-free or low-interest loans for fertilizer, seeds, or farm implements, organized road and dyke building, and engaged in communal land-reclamation projects. Ninomiya's thought was eclectic but included Confucian strands. He juxtaposed a Human Way (*jindō*) against a Heavenly Way (*tendō*). While the *tendō* was natural and immutable, *jindō* was a human artifice and therefore subject to change, and improvement. The influence of this movement continued to be felt in the Meiji period.[70] Ohara Yūgaku (1797–1858) was active in agrarian reform movements and leadership in the Kantō region. He pressed for improvements in technology, inter-village cooperation, rationalization of village fields, and rural relief. Behind his practical suggestions for local improvement lay reading in Confucianism and the *Book of Changes*. At the core of his thought was the idea of *sei* (nature) as the expression of Heavenly Will (*tenmei*), The fulfillment of *sei* was the Way, composed of loyalty and filial piety.[71]

Life for all classes in Tokugawa Japan could be harsh, especially for the peasantry, who made up the bulk of the population and whose labor produced the tax rice that went into *bakufu* or domain granaries to provide stipends for samurai. Encouraged by the authorities to be frugal, hardworking, loyal, and filial, there were times of famine and brutality when the peasants could endure no more and rose in revolt. Irwin Scheiner has pointed out that for most of the Tokugawa period peasants, too, were moved by Confucian ideals of benevolent government and proper authority (*taigi meibun*). None of the many Tokugawa peasant rebellions challenged the basic assumption that "righteous lords should dispense justice." Most of these revolts called not for an overthrow of the feudal system but for a rectification of the benevolence and grace due to them from the lord. Toward the end of the Edo period, however, revolts calling for "world renewal" (*yonaoshi*) rejected Confucian notions of "benevolence" or "redress of grievances" and turned to millennial belief in world-restoring compassion of the popular deity Miroku (Maitreya) or virtuous rebels such as Ōshio Heihachirō.

Even from the above very superficial sketch of developments in Tokugawa society, it should be clear that there was a considerable degree of Confucianization. Although it is hard to find evidence for

[70] Naramoto Tatsuya, *Ninomiya Sontoku* (Tokyo: Iwanami Shoten, 1959); Kodama Kota, *Ninomiya Sontoku* (Tokyo: Chuo Kōronsha, 1970); Morita Shirō, *Ninomiya Sontoku* (Tokyo: Asahi Shinbunsha, 1975).

[71] Naramoto Tatsuya and Nakai Nobuniko, *Ninomiya Sontoku—Ohara Yūgaku* (Tokyo: Iwanami Shoten, 1973).

extensive use of Confucian rituals in daily life, it is clear that through scholarly exchange, schools, literacy, moral exhortation, and popular literature Confucian moral values were presented to people of all social levels in all parts of the country. This became particularly evident in the nineteenth century.

At the same time, Confucian values were not always presented in a "pure" form. Once we move away from the debates of the various Confucian schools, the presentation seems much more eclectic. We see Confucian moral values mixed with notions from Buddhism, Shinto, Taoism, and folk religion. Moreover, proponents of National Learning (*kokugaku*) and Buddhism, while overtly resisting or rejecting Confucianism, incorporated Confucian attitudes toward scholarship and history or inculcated Confucian moral virtues as part of their own message of material reward in this life for those who do good deeds. Likewise, the urban virtues revealed in the literature of Saikaku and Chikamatsu drew their inspiration from a variety of intellectual sources.

In the political arena perhaps the most powerful force in late Edo thought was Mitogaku, which blended Chinese Confucian historicism and ethical teachings with Shinto myth into a new and explosive political synthesis that began by buttressing the *bakufu* and ended by dissolving the political rationale for Tokugawa control. Later Mito scholars, striving to reconcile Chinese historical principles with the reality of the Japanese political tradition of divine descent and the sacrosanct character of the Japanese emperor, eventually denied the shogun the "name" of king, leaving him only the effective reality of authority, and eventually shifted effective authority so that it too was focused on the emperor. Concern for proper hierarchy thus brought about a reordering of the political hierarchy in which the shogun was downgraded and the emperor reinstituted as sovereign in "name" and "substance."[72] The late Edo period scholar Aizawa Seishisai, author of the *New Theses*, argued vehemently that Japan, not China, was the true "Middle Kingdom" or "Divine Realm." To protect this Middle Kingdom, as Bob T. Wakabayashi points out, "Aizawa would affirm Chinese moral culture, infuse it with elements of *Kokugaku* myth, and seek to reinforce it with superior Western techniques."[73]

Ultimately the "intermingled" quality that we have seen in so much of Japanese thought and values in the Edo period makes it very difficult to apply a notion of Confucianization. We find, rather, the re-

[72] Kate Wildman Nakai, "Tokugawa Confucian Historiography: The Hayashi, Early Mito School and Arai Hakuseki," in Nosco, *Confucianism and Tokugawa Culture*, p. 91.

[73] Bob T. Wakabayashi, *Anti-Foreignism and Western Learning in Early Modern Japan: The "New Theses" of 1825* (Cambridge, Mass.: Harvard University Press, 1986), p. 56.

iteration of values that may well have arisen at some point from a Chinese Confucian source but had, in the course of time and the process of diffusion, become divorced from an unambiguously perceived connection with a specific intellectual tradition to become part of the general, and constantly shifting, stock of Japanese ideas and values.

We see this very clearly in the teachings of the Fujikō, a popular religious movement advocating devotion to the divinities associated with Mt. Fuji. This movement was extremely popular in Edo and the whole Kantō region from the seventeenth century, and sent tens of thousands of pilgrims to climb Mt. Fuji annually. Jikigyō Miroku, the leader of the Fujikō, advocated three principles essential to success in life:

1. Good works bring their own reward. Evil acts bring misfortune.
2. Hard work brings wealth, health, and long life.
3. Laziness ends in poverty, sickness, and a short life.[74]

The ideal of Jikigyō Miroku and many other popular religious leaders in the Tokugawa period was the attainment of a stable and harmonious social order. In the process, ideas of orderly relations, respect for elders, diligence, and self-development, which were traditionally seen as being within the sphere of Confucian values, were detached and applied within a different intellectual framework to the problems of daily life. In the case of Fujikō the ideal of thrift, social harmony, and success through hard work and cooperation probably owed less to overt Confucian teaching than to Jikigyō Miroku's personal experience as a merchant who had made a success of his own life by the exercise of those very values.[75]

Moreover, there were other impediments to full-scale Confucianization in the Edo period. Compared with Buddhism, which was integrated into the Tokugawa control system and received powerful official patronage, and even compared with Shinto, Confucianism was institutionally weak. The *bakufu* did not use an examination system to recruit its officials and never accorded Neo-Confucianism, or any other form of Confucianism, exclusive institutional support. The number of professional *jusha* was not large; they had little institu-

---

[74] Quoted in Miyata Noboru, "Chōnin no shūkyō," in *Edo Chōnin no shinkō*, ed. Nishiyama Matsunosuke (Tokyo: Yoshikawa Kōbunkan, 1973), p. 241.

[75] On Fujikō see Royall Tyler, "The Tokugawa Peace and Popular Religion: Suzuki Shōsan, Kakugyō Tōbutsu, and Jikigyō Miroku," in Nosco, *Confucianism and Tokugawa Culture*, pp. 92–119, and Martin Collcutt, "Mt. Fuji as the Realm of Miroku: The Transformation of Maitreya in the Cult of Mt. Fuji in Early Modern Japan," in *Maitreya the Future Buddha*, ed. Alan Sponberg and Helen Hardacre (Cambridge, England: Cambridge University Press, 1988), pp. 248–69.

tional cohesion and, in most cases, little social clout. Except for a very limited number of *daimyō* families, religious practices in the home remained Buddhist or Shinto or incorporated folk elements and popular gods (*hayarigami*). And for much of the Edo period Buddhist books continued to be published in greater numbers than Confucian texts.

In the sphere of education, where Confucianism had the greatest impact, there was considerable diffusion of Confucianism, but also limits to Confucian influence. Even in the domain schools, Confucian studies did not monopolize the curriculum, and standards of Confucian learning among most samurai were probably not very high. Although there was undoubtedly some civilizing of samurai through Confucian learning and education, samurai did not entirely abandon their martial traditions or values. Loyalty as an ethical principle was probably more heavily emphasized in samurai society than filial piety. Of course it can be argued that loyalty in an Edo period context had been thoroughly transformed under the Confucian insistence on proper relationships between superior and inferior. Even allowing for this, there were aspects of *bushidō* and the warrior tradition of loyalty that had as much to do with birth, family honor, feudal obligation, and local loyalty as they had to do with Confucian teaching. Frequent reference was made in Tokugawa ruling circles to the promotion of merit (*jinzai*). Meritorious individuals were expected to show Confucian virtues. At the same time, the prevailing principle for officeholding in Edo Japan remained heredity rather than merit. As in the ancient period, Confucian learning was respected but did not necessarily lead to high office. Confucian ethical ideals may well have tinged family values in the Edo period. They probably enhanced the patriarchal authority of males. They also affected the role of women and attitudes toward them in the middle and upper levels of society. They were reflected in the training of children. There is no indication, however, that they transformed the basic patterns of kinship or family ritual or that they displaced popular religious practices in the home.

THE MODERN LEGACY OF CONFUCIANISM

The Meiji Restoration and the rapid nation-building that followed affected the fortunes of Confucianism as they touched every segment of Japanese society and intellectual life. The Charter Oath issued by the new government in 1868 included the statement, "Knowledge shall be sought throughout the world so as to strengthen the foundations of imperial rule." As Western influence began to pour into

Japan from the 1860s, it looked for a time as if Confucianism and Confucian values would be swept aside as remnants of a discredited feudal past. The emphasis seemed to have shifted from traditional moral education to practical knowledge and Western models useful to a nation trying to strengthen itself. Fukuzawa Yukichi and other proponents of "civilization and enlightenment" from the West were critical of the role Confucianism had played in supporting the feudal edifice. In *Onna daigaku hyōron*, for instance, Fukuzawa launched a bitter attack on Kaibara Ekken's *Onna daigaku* for its hierarchical attitude toward women.

However, after a brief eclipse in the 1870s, Confucianism found new respectability and a place for itself among the mix of influences shaping the development of modern Japan. Although scholarship of the kind that had been so actively practiced by Edo period samurai scholars dwindled, the ethical and social influence of Confucianism on the mass of society was at least as profound in the late nineteenth and early twentieth centuries as it had been in the late Edo period. This influence was exerted both as part of a self-conscious Confucian revival by scholars around the throne, as part of an effort to shape an appropriate constitutional form for Japan, and in a more general revival of "indigenous" moral principles expressing a distinctive Japanese national essence (*kokutai*). These ideas were enshrined in government-controlled school textbooks, which offset Western values and civil ethics with larger and larger doses of imperial adulation and such traditional values as filial piety and loyalty.

In the first flush of the Meiji Restoration, its samurai leaders sought to create an imperial state on the model of the Confucian-inspired Nara *ritsuryō* system. This was set aside very quickly, however, as the leadership after 1872 began to adopt a variety of Western institutions. With the abolition of the old Tokugawa regime the *bakufu*- and *han*-sponsored schools were abolished or reorganized on Western lines. In 1872 the Ministry of Education moved away from the teaching of Confucian ethics in courses on moral training (*shūshin*) to an emphasis on utilitarian skills and Western examples. School textbooks based on Confucian ethics were replaced by translations of American and French readers. Some of the best intellects of the day had already turned to Western learning. The enthusiasm among intellectuals for *bunmei kaika* ("civilization and enlightenment") superseded and outdated interest in Confucianism or Chinese studies. Some advocates of Western learning derided Confucianism as outmoded and irrelevant in the new age in which Japan must fight for survival in a world dominated by powerful nation-states.

This, however, was a temporary and rather superficial phenomenon. Even while the advocates of "civilization and enlightenment" derived from the West were deriding Confucianism as outmoded, leaders of the Meiji Restoration and the new Meiji government remained convinced of the validity of Confucian values. Kido Takayoshi, like many other members of the Iwakura Embassy to America and Europe in 1872–73 was astonished at Western males' excessive deference to women and their disregard for the basic virtue of filial piety. He clearly worried about the potentially corrosive influence of Western values. He told his friend Kume Kunitake about an exchange he had had with an an elderly American scholar:

> "The person whom you love most in your house is your wife, isn't that so." I said, "No, it is my parents more than my wife." The old codger assumed, "Of course, there is intimacy between parent and child, but it cannot equal the love of husband and wife. For example, when you return to your country after your trip to Europe, you will undoubtedly rejoice first of all with your wife, won't you?" Again, I said, "No. In Japan no matter how much I may love my wife I must first ask about the welfare of my parents and greet them. Then I speak to my wife. That is the proper etiquette." When I explained this, the old scholar was surprised and thought for a while with a dubious expression on his face. He finally murmured, "In a country with a teaching like that, a parent will be idle and not work." It seems his chief worry was that parents would develop the bad habit of relying on their children and not earn money. If I am to draw inferences from the man's talk, the path of loyalty and piety will be imperiled by *bunmei kaika*.[76]

Within a decade of the Meiji Restoration, Confucianism was making a comeback among intellectuals and in government circles. Even some of those who were most active in the introduction of Western ideas and values found a place for Confucian values in the rapidly changing society. Nakae Chōmin, for instance, was active in the introduction of American and European political theory and the development of a theory of popular rights. In 1887 he ran afoul of the government's Peace Preservation Law aimed at the Freedom and People's Rights movement and was forced to leave Tokyo for Osaka, where he worked to reconstruct the Liberal party. Chōmin's ideas of freedom and equality, expressed in his concept of *rigi* ("principle and justice") were shaped not only by Western thinkers but by the moral philosophy of Mencius, as interpreted by Itō Jinsai.[77]

---

[76] Cited, and translated, by Marlene J. Mayo in "The Western Education of Kume Kunitake," *Monumenta Nipponica* 28, no. 1 (Spring 1973): 3–67.

[77] Sannosuke Matsumoto, "Nakae Chōmin and Confucianism," in Nosco, *Confucianism and Tokugawa Culture*, pp. 251–66.

Thus a role was found for Confucian moral principles within a mixed ideology of nationhood. It found influential spokesmen in Nishimura Shigeki, Egi Kazuyuki, Inoue Kowashi, and Motoda Eifu. Nishimura was a Ministry of Education official and philosopher who sought to synthesize Confucian ethics with Western thought. Egi was an influential Ministry of Education official. Inoue Kowashi, who played a major role in drafting the Meiji Constitution and the Imperial Rescript on Education, has been described as a "Neo-Confucian idealist" who tempered the German constitutional theories of Johann Kasper Bluntschli, Hermann Schultz, and Hermann Roessler with Confucian ideas of a Way based on law or principle (*ri*).[78] Motoda Eifu was lecturer to the Meiji emperor, and was instrumental in devising ways to elevate the status of the emperor within the political structure of the Meiji Constitution. The emperor was presented as a benevolent sovereign, father of his people and moral preceptor of the nation. Loyalty and filial piety were designated cardinal virtues, and Confucian moral principles prescribed as the basis of education for the nation. The emperor was hedged about with Chinese rituals and buttressed with a peerage borrowing its titles from the Chou dynasty. Motoda, like other of his contemporaries who were looking for a traditional moral basis for Japanese values, was also active in trying to bring Confucian ethical principles (*shūshin*) back into prominence in the education system. He criticized the overly Western technical education that young Japanese were receiving in the 1870s and 1880s:

> Outstanding in imagination and technical accomplishments, they are deficient in the spirit and soul of our country, their foundation in morals and in courage for righteous causes is shallow and one would try in vain to make pillars of the nation out of them. . . . Efforts are being made to convert Japanese into facsimiles of Europeans and Americans. All this is due to a confusion between the root of education and its branches.[79]

For Motoda, as for Inoue, the "root" should be Confucian ethics blended into political and moral behavior to stiffen the national spirit (*kokutai*). With Inoue and Nishimura, Motoda drafted the Imperial Rescript on Education in 1890, which blended notions of the divine ancestry of the imperial line with Confucian notions of the duties of subjects. The Rescript accepted the value of acquiring knowledge and skills but highlighted the importance of moral values:

[78] Yukichi Sakai, "The Constitutionalism of Inoue Kowashi," in Najita and Scheiner, *Japanese Thought in the Tokugawa Period*, pp. 161–80.

[79] Donald H. Shively, "Motoda Eifu, Confucian Lecturer to the Meiji Emperor," in Nivison and Wright, *Confucianism in Action*, p. 327.

Know ye, Our subjects:

Our Imperial Ancestors have founded Our Empire on a basis broad and everlasting, and have deeply and firmly implanted virtue; Our subjects ever united in loyalty (*chū*) and filial piety (*kō*) have from generation to generation illustrated the beauty thereof. This is the glory of the fundamental character of Our Empire, and herein also lies the source of Our education. Ye, Our subjects, be filial to your parents, affectionate to your brothers and sisters; as husbands and wives be harmonious, as friends true; bear yourselves in modesty and moderation; extend your benevolence to all; pursue learning and cultivate arts, and thereby develop intellectual faculties and perfect moral powers; furthermore, advance public good and promote common interests . . .

Memorized by millions of teachers and schoolchildren and read aloud in every schoolroom, the Rescript was both the product of an intense debate over the balance between utilitarian (Western) and moral (Japanese) values in education and a powerful document in shaping political, social, and educational attitudes in subsequent decades. Confucian ethics, especially loyalty and filiality, were returned to the elementary school curriculum and directed to the enhancement of a national solidarity that would contribute to strengthening and modernizing the country without the loss of its traditional virtues. In the process, Confucianism was realigned with Shinto notions of the divine origins of the imperial line and reinterpreted in the service of national objectives, which soon came to include the acquisition of a colonial empire.

However, values such as loyalty (*chū*) and filial piety (*kō*), which were emphasized in the Rescript, were not always seen as Confucian. For many people they had become part of the accepted traditional value system of Japan. Indeed, there were statesmen, officials, and journalists who supported the thrust of the Rescript without accepting it as a symbol of Confucian revival. Although Confucian moral principles were unmistakably written into the Rescript, there was what Carol Gluck has described as a "disavowal" of its Confucianism, even by some of its most ardent supporters. On the one hand some proponents of Confucian values in the Rescript such as Nishimura Shigeki warned against the use of the word "Confucian" (*jukyōteki*) as sounding feudal and arousing negative associations. On the other hand some opponents of Confucianism argued that the moral virtues referred to in the Rescript were by no means the special preserve of any unique Confucian Way but were either an immemorial Japanese morality or merely a Japanese version of universal pedagogical principles.[80]

Elementary school textbooks in the Meiji and Taishō eras illustrate a similar shift in the direction of greater state control and enhancement of the imperial system and unique Japanese polity (*kokutai*) through injection of traditional "Confucian" values into school texts. Irokawa Daikichi, in discussing the regeneration of the emperor system (*tennōsei*) as spiritual structure in these decades, has pointed to the tightening of government control over textbooks and the promulgation of traditional values:

> Once the People's Rights movement was suppressed, the government took the offensive in education. It revised the School Act, issued the Rescript on Education, and instituted controls on anti-establishment education. The authorities launched a thoroughgoing systematization of the curriculum including the textbooks. But even in this period, which lasted through the nineties, the textbook inspection system allowed some variety to reach the schools. Mixed in with the number of sycophantic texts centered on loyalty, filiality, and *kokutai* were works aimed at modern civic education. The best of these were Tsubouchi Shōyō's *Japanese Readers* (*Kokugo tokuhon*) . . .

Irokawa goes on to show how in succeeding decades the Tsubouchi textbooks were forced to include more and more chapters inculcating nationalistic and imperial values at the expense of egalitarian and pacifist principles.[81]

The rehabilitation of values and practices that had always been associated with Confucianism in Meiji and Taisho period Japan was not confined to the arena of education and political thought. The *Analects* and other Confucian texts continued to be published and widely read. Writers, newspaper columnists, and philosophers such as Inoue Tetsujirō (1855–1944), who worried about Japan losing its identity in a headlong rush for Westernization, turned to Confucian ethics as a source of harmony and cohesion. The old Confucian shrine, the Shōheikō in Tokyo, was revived after 1907 and *sekiten* services again conducted. A Confucian Association, the Shibunkai, was reestablished in 1918. Its aims were to combat what was seen as the materialist spirit of the West, social unrest, and the decline of public morals.

---

[80] Carol Gluck, *Japan's Modern Myths: Ideology in the Late Meiji Period* (Princeton: Princeton University Press, 1985), p. 126.

[81] Irokawa Daikichi, *The Culture of the Meiji Period* (Princeton: Princeton University Press, 1985), pp. 301ff.

It endeavored to influence education by promoting the study of Chinese and, particularly, Confucian texts.[82]

Since Confucianists such as Motoda and bureaucrats such as Inoue Kowashi had deliberately sought to revive Confucian ethics and align them with the goals of the modernizing state, it is not surprising that traditional values associated with Confucianism should have been sucked into the vortex of domestic and continental ultranationalism in the 1930s as one strand in the ideological justification of Japan's superior mission. Although the word Confucianism was not always used, after 1933 active promotion of Confucian virtues became government policy. At home this was reflected in the nationalist tract *Fundamental Principles of the National Essence of Japan (Kokutai no hongi)* (1937), which blended Shinto myth with the image of a Confucian-style ruler and a loyal, filial, harmonious population in which each individual diligently performed his or her appointed function. On the continent an attempt was made to use Confucianism to take some of the edge off Japanese colonial aggression. In Korea, Manchūkuo, and China the Japanese actively promoted Confucianism and presented themselves as the restorers of a Confucian cultural tradition.

Confucianism's association with prewar nationalism tainted it in the postwar period. There was again a disavowal of Confucianism and the traditional values it was thought to represent. The Occupation reforms in education, the new Constitution, democratization, and the push for economic recovery and high-level economic growth all seemed to leave little place for Confucian values or the Way of the Sages. At the same time, the generalized values of respect for parents and seniors, loyalty to one's employer, acceptance of hierarchy, strong emphasis on education, and positive evaluation of thrift, diligence, and hard work all clearly continued to thrive and helped fuel Japanese postwar economic recovery.

In more recent years, however, there has been a modest revival of interest in Confucianism itself. In part this interest is cultural and scholarly: the reading of the *Analects* and other Chinese classics as part of Japan's cultural heritage. In part it springs from a sometimes controversial desire on the part of some politicians and commentators to see more emphasis on "moral" values in the school curriculum and in the home. In part, too, it now seems to relate to a conscious recognition by some observers that the rapid rates of economic growth being shown by newly industrialized East Asian countries

---

[82] Warren W. Smith, Jr., *Confucianism in Modern Japan: A Study of Conservatism in Japanese Intellectual History* (Tokyo: Hokuseido Press, 1959).

from Korea to Singapore may be at least partially explicable in terms of a shared Confucian heritage.

Probably very few Japanese would attribute their recent economic success to Confucianism; they would more likely disavow any significant role for Confucianism in modern Japan. If, however, the question were phrased without explicit reference to Confucianism, but rather in terms of such qualities as stability and order in family relationships, harmony and hierarchy in the workplace, loyalty to employers and superiors, and the importance of education, diligence, and self-cultivation, many would be willing to concede that these qualities have played some role. It is difficult, however, to determine the extent of that role and to decide conclusively whether these qualities really came from a definable Confucian source at any particular point. All that can be done with any confidence is to suggest that some of the values that were encouraged and spread as part of the diffusion of Confucianism proved surprisingly durable and found acceptance within the ethical fabric of modern Japan. In spite of repeated disavowals of Confucianism itself, these values have continued to exert influence in twentieth-century Japan. It is perhaps in this very limited sense that Edwin Reischauer could say that although no one considers himself a Confucianist in Japan today, almost all Japanese are.

Winston B. Davis, who has written perceptively on the role of religion and values in modern Japanese development, sums it up very well: "It is possible that Confucianism (in its diffuse form) has had something to do with the diligence, sincerity, and frugality of 'post-Confucian' East Asia—or, at least, with the articulation of these virtues. It is possible that the Confucian examination system paved the way for the development of the meritocracies and 'diploma societies' of the present. It is not impossible that the moral tutelage of the Confucians prepared the Far East for the 'preceptorial systems' that later would guide its economies—from the 'massive unilateral persuasion' of the People's Republic of China to the 'administrative guidance' of capitalist Japan. . . . It is also possible that the kind of consensual system of decision making and responsibility sharing one finds in Japan today had its origin (at least in part) in the kind of 'discussions' commended by the Confucianism of the Seventeen Article Constitution. I think it is likely that the spirit of cooperative, ethical reciprocity one finds in Japanese industrial paternalism goes back to the moralism of Confucius. (I also think that this 'spirit' is largely an ex post facto beautification of industrial relations. While resonating in a positive way with popular tradition, I do not think it was 'the cause' of the industrialization of Japan and the Far East.)"[83] Davis is right to remind us of the difficulty of assessing the weight of such interlinked historical variables as Confucianism, Buddhism, and Shinto. We cannot, ultimately, attribute Japan's striking economic development simply to the persistence or resuscitation of Confucian values. At the same time, we must recognize that those values have contributed to the course and character of Japan's modern development and have at times been harnessed to provide a convenient rationale for modes of behavior—such as the emphasis on "harmony"—that may have derived from very diverse sources.

[83] Winston B. Davis, "Religion and Development: Weber and the East Asian Experience," in *Understanding Political Development*, ed. Myron Weiner and Samuel P. Huntingdon (Boston: Little, Brown and Co., 1987), pp. 221–80.

PART II

The Modern Transition
De-Confucianization or
Re-Confucianization?

Chapter 4

COMPARISONS OF MODERN CONFUCIAN VALUES IN CHINA AND JAPAN

GILBERT ROZMAN

A CURIOUS situation exists in the literature on China and Japan dating back through most of the past century. Writings on China repeatedly attribute backwardness in modern development to Confucian beliefs and practices, while studies of Japan usually credit Confucian values with paving the way for rapid development. What accounts for this discrepancy? To what extent is it being resolved in recent interpretations? Through a review of how Confucianism has been viewed from within the two countries and how it has endured in the social relations of each, we can draw attention to what is common to the Confucian tradition and how it interacts with modernization and with diverse social systems. In this way, we can try to distinguish the tradition itself from the debates about it.

The long-prevailing interpretation of China points to this country as an extreme instance of the obsolete past standing in the way of the emergent future. China, perhaps as much as any other prominent country, came to represent the tradition-bound society, and its Confucian traditions epitomized an inward-looking view incapable of pragmatic borrowing and of an open-door mentality toward the achievements of modernization. According to this image—still widely accepted in the 1980s—China's reformers are battling not only with Stalinist dogmatism, but also with a rigid and xenophobic Chinese worldview. Formed by Confucian teachings, the Chinese personality, as it existed to at least the year of revolutionary victory in 1949, was thought to be embedded in family-centered loyalties (especially filial piety and female subordination), in backward-looking rote learning of outdated classics, and in hierarchical political traditions that drained the initiative from individuals. Confucianism represented the antithesis of modern, individualistic, scientifically oriented, democratically guided human behavior. This negative approach to the past has been used to justify all major political movements of the twentieth century, from the 1911 and 1949 revolutions to the May Fourth Movement and the Cultural Revolution and even to the reform program from 1978 for building "socialism with Chinese characteristics."

Each of the major intellectual and political traditions reasserted these negative interpretations of Chinese Confucianism in successive periods. The Marxist-Leninist-Stalinist tradition was perhaps the most negative. Drawing some of their inspiration from the writings of Marx, including his discussion of the virtually stagnant Asiatic Mode of Production, and from the negative treatment of "feudalism" by Lenin and Stalin, Chinese communists vigorously rejected the Confucian traditions of their society. Communist theorists found in the mainstream of Chinese history only negative examples; they focused on the evils lurking in the traditional forms of family, school, community, and government. China's Cultural Revolution carried to an extreme the repudiation of "old ideas, old culture, old customs, and old habits" that is inherent in the Marxist-Leninist-Stalinist tradition.

Western conservative and liberal views of China beginning in the first half of the eighteenth century also long downplayed the Confucian tradition. They concentrated on what was missing, whether Christianity, individualism, or political pluralism. For example, Max Weber's *The Religion of China*, a study influential among social scientists, drew attention to aspects of the Confucian ethical tradition antagonistic to the endogeneous development of capitalism. Although Weber briefly suggested that the Chinese may be more capable than the Japanese of "assimilating capitalism,"[1] he did not explain what in the Confucian tradition would contribute to development as a latecomer to capitalism. For several decades after World War II the questions addressed by social scientists still presupposed historical weaknesses or missing links in China: Why was a communist revolution necessary to modernize China? Why had Japan modernized, but not China? Why was the Soviet model rejected as inapplicable to China's developmental needs? Those answering these questions, including some who sympathized with the new path chosen by China's leaders, often pointed an accusatory finger at the Confucian tradition. Even radical change could be justified in such unpromising circumstances.

Intellectual attitudes within China likewise turned sharply against the philosophical and ethical edifices of the old society. First came the gathering force of Western liberal thought that arrived in the nineteenth century and continued to spread in the twentieth. Second, and riding the crest of Westernization, came modern nationalism, which was driven forward by China's political fragmentation and anti-im-

---

[1] Max Weber, *The Religion of China* (New York: The Free Press, 1964), p. 248.

perialist anxieties. Finally, both of these forces were overwhelmed by the powerful wave of Marxist-Leninist-Stalinist thought, redefined in its Maoist variant, which had the advantage of becoming official orthodoxy in 1949. Each new current of thought confronted the Confucian heritage directly as an intellectual adversary and indirectly, mediated through changing social structures, as a way of life. Despite the presence of some who advocated combining elements of the Confucian past with each new current of thought, the predominant tendency was to reject China's past.

Similar negative views of Japanese Confucianism became pronounced in two periods, but lost ground at other times. In the 1870s Westernizing reforms inundated Japan, prompting a deprecatory assessment of past Confucian practices. Westernization entered Japan with a more sweeping assault on the past than the drawn-out struggle that continued into the twentieth century in China. Yet, in the 1880s and 1890s Japanese leaders succeeded in fusing traditional outlooks, including Confucian values, with nationalism. This fusion and the increased censorship after the early 1920s thwarted any large-scale reassessment of Japanese traditions until after the Second World War. With its traumatic "unconditional surrender" in 1945, Japan again faced a period of negative thinking about its historical values. In the 1870s Confucianism stood for stagnant thinking, restrictions on individual initiative, and impractical education. Seventy years later, narrow thinking and restricted individual choice became virtually universal targets again. Japanese equated the Confucian tradition with blind loyalty to superiors. Elimination of such "feudalism" promised to open the way for many more elements of society, including young people and women, to contribute more fully toward progress. Nonetheless, by the 1960s and especially the 1970s the Japanese had regained their confidence in the recent achievements of their country and in its earlier history. Worldwide fascination for the heritage that helps account for the "Japanese miracle" now reinforces native pride.

Except for a decade or two of rejection on two occasions, Confucian traditions have won considerable support for most of modern Japanese history. The label "Confucianism" was not at the forefront in the era of state Shintoism prior to 1945 and is even less so in the postwar growth era, but the selective approval of traditional or neo-traditional social relations has favored Confucian values. The cultural consensus reached in the 1890s focused on the links between family, community, and nation and placed great emphasis on moral education. The self-congratulatory Nihonjin-ron (how Japanese are distinct) literature of the 1970s and 1980s has turned again to the family, the community (especially the workplace), and the national bureaucracy. Its recitation of the values that guide Japanese and its enthusiasm for moral and demanding education are reminiscent of long-standing Confucian themes.

Outside of Japan one finds a mixture of responses to the idea that current achievements and the premodern legacy are linked. Some observers point to the ideological motives of nationalistic and conservative Japanese for judging their own traditions superior. Others look beyond the Confucian elements in the tradition to nativistic traditions or the samurai code of conduct. Both North and South Korea are not well liked in Japan, and preoccupation with socialism in China has also impeded a search for regional commonalities. Japanese emphasize their own uniqueness. Nevertheless, increasingly in response to high economic growth rates and other signs of advancement elsewhere in East Asia, attention is shifting to a regional image of Japan as one of a set of Confucian-based societies. The changing image of the past in Japan is in this way related to developments elsewhere in East Asia, especially in China. These connections can be traced more clearly by comparing China and Japan across five periods of transformation, from the second half of the nineteenth century to the present. Before doing so, however, we should make some distinctions among types of Confucianism.

TYPES OF CONFUCIANISM

Over a long time span and across three countries often not in close contact with each other, a tradition rich in intellectual abstractions could easily acquire diverse applications. There was no religious or secular authority that had a stake in reasserting a common regional interpretation. Moreover, even within a single society, especially given the absence over long periods of a unified central hierarchy of Confucianists, there was ample opportunity for social-class and regional differences in perceptions of Confucianism to develop. While Ch'ing China, with its single government and examination system coupled with strict censorship of ideas deemed heterodox, restricted the scope for the diversification of Confucianism, Tokugawa Japan produced fertile soil for just such diversification. The separate social classes each developed their own worldview, since the way of the samurai was recognized as an ideal only for the elite. Political decentralization meant that each domain recognized its own Confucian teachers and, increasingly, its own amalgam of intellectual traditions. It is necessary to differentiate types of Confucian thought, which, in retrospect, even if not originally considered to be separate from each other, had differing potential for influencing the modern adaptation of Confucianism.

Prior to discussing types of Confucianism in some detail, together with their consequences in the modern era, it will suffice to present our own identification of the types and locate them at various levels of the society. At the top level, we find *imperial Confucianism*, centering on the ideology and rituals supportive of the emperor's rights and the delegated authority of those who exercised power on his behalf down to the lowest rung of officials. Some observers have focused almost exclusively at this level, seeing Confucianism as a conservative system supporting existing governmental authority. The second level is *reform Confucianism*, which is a set of ideas and precedents favoring government renewal and intervention to improve society. However neglected these ideas might be in ordinary times, they could be invoked in times of trouble to help set a new course for the society. The third level is *elite Confucianism*. Although from one country to the next the character of the elite social class varied, in each country we can find a set of ideals and demands that the elite was taught to follow, in accord with Confucian education. Fourth is *merchant-house Confucianism*, which could be found in some business organizations and signified an extension of ideals of personal relations into the business world. In modern Korea we can even find the notion of the hero-merchant striving for the prosperity of his country. Finally, we must take note of *mass Confucianism*, as practiced by the ordinary population, including the vast numbers of peasants.

By pointing to variations of Confucianism in practice, despite a common core of concepts and assumed unity (as in the case of Christianity or socialism), we establish a basis for comparing countries and for tracing how some aspects of Confucianism disappear and others survive in the modern era. These types were present to various degrees in the East Asian countries and fit differently into the overall social context.

The Base from Which Change Began in the Nineteenth Century

Confucianism in late imperial China retained wide authority over the intellectual life of all educated people and, more simplistically or eclectically interpreted, of most people with little or no education as well. It provided an ethical system, a religion, a philosophy of history, an educational curriculum, and a political ideology. Its explicit pronouncements about human relations defined a way of life to be practiced in family, lineage, community, and the public arena. These pronouncements had become embodied in specific rituals and codes of conduct, some of which fulfilled the religious function of giving meaning to life-cycle events, especially marriage and death. Confucian teachings thoroughly guided the study of history and all manifestations of proto-social-science reasoning about how human institutions evolve and interact. These teachings became the essence of the educational system leading to the several levels of imperial examinations. They also permeated perceptions of the political system, from assumptions about the training and recruitment of officials to specifications about interactions between ruler and subject. Perhaps in no other society of comparable complexity and development (level of literacy, rate of urbanization, scale of commerce, size of bureaucracy, etc.) did a single intellectual framework establish such an all-encompassing hold over thinking about social behavior. Its hold remained intact into the second half of the nineteenth century.

In comparison with the post-Renaissance competition of ideas in all of the above-mentioned intellectual spheres across much of Western Europe, the mounting struggle between Westernization and Slavophilism in Russia, or even the more localized ferment of contending approaches to Confucian, syncretic, and nationalist thought in Tokugawa Japan, China maintained a monolithic intellectual tradition. A multitude of diverse, localized "little traditions" posed little challenge. Rather than facing new challenges from within and without, China's Confucian tradition in the course of its second millennium had become more deeply solidified and, in the orthodox teachings of Neo-Confucianism, more fully and narrowly articulated to the exclusion of alternative ways of thinking. Legalism and Buddhism had left an earlier imprint, which had largely been incorporated into the "Great Tradition," while more otherworldly elements of Buddhism and Taoism were left to operate as part of localized "little traditions" without much impact on the general worldview. Over the centuries there arose, of course, new interpretations of Confucian concepts and new applications of earlier schools of thought within the Confucian tradition, but the intellectual universe experienced relatively little tension or expansion.

By the nineteenth century the meaning of Confucianism was found largely in the institutions that it inspired. First, one finds the family characterized by a high degree of solidarity, ancestral reverence, patriarchal authority, filial piety, female subordination to specified males, and respect for the elderly. Second, one finds the educational system featuring long-term study, intensive rote learning, respect for the printed word and the teacher's authority, and expectations of both prestige and career opportunities from superior performance.

Third, China's Confucian traditions were reflected in lineage organizations at the community level and also by pseudo-kinship or common-local-origin ties carefully cultivated and based on introductions and go-betweens in the arenas of business and politics. Fourth, the examination system resulted in the existence of an educated elite, trained to seek a calling in service, whether in or out of government office. Fifth, there were traditions associated with imperial authority, bureaucratic administration, moral appeals by government, and the power of the state to overcome divisive and unworthy aggrandizement of power or wealth. Skim off the Confucian language (as occurred in the first half of this century), and the Confucian-based assumptions about these institutions remain deeply embedded in modes of daily life. Confucianism was more a way of life than a belief system. When it faded as a set of formal beliefs, it survived above all in the consciousness of intellectuals concerning their role in society.

As one might expect, in any given historical era there was inevitably considerable strain between the Confucian teachings and actual practices. Such strain seemed to be on the rise in the nineteenth century, especially after Westerners forcibly established their presence in China and after long periods of civil war and ineffectual administration heightened popular cynicism about the imperial government's capacity to rule China under new circumstances. In the 1860s and 1870s it seemed sufficient to seek a traditional remedy for this malady; officials pinned their hopes on a restoration of the dynasty through the improved application of Confucian teachings. They sought to reaffirm the virtuous nature of imperial rule by promoting moral officials, rooting out corruption, and giving visibility to the performance of state rituals that highlight the natural linkage between the properly ordered society and the cosmic order.[2] Nonetheless, the reform orientation in Chinese Confucianism remained weak. Whereas only one decade after Perry's warships arrived, the Japanese were debating ways to replace old institutions (and in the following decade actually accomplished a thorough revamping), the Chinese responded to more severe demonstrations of their country's inability to resist the West and of internal weakness with a half-century of indecision and procrastination in considering major institutional changes and in moving beyond meager efforts to utilize Western technology for self-strengthening. Only much later was the hold of Confucian thought severely challenged.

[2] Kwang-Ching Liu, "The Ch'ing Restoration," in *The Cambridge History of China*, vol. 10, part 1, *Late Ch'ing 1800–1911*, ed. John Fairbank (Cambridge, England: Cambridge University Press, 1978), pp. 410–12, 438–43.

In the mid-nineteenth century, Japanese Confucianism differed in important respects from Chinese Confucianism, although the classic texts and popular concepts were largely the same. Originating as a borrowed doctrine from a country that was no longer an awe-inspiring regional presence, Confucianism retained some imprint of foreignness and of being a means rather than an end. Because there was an awareness of a separate Japanese tradition and the country by this period deviated from some features deemed essential for Chinese Confucianism (for example, Japan had more rigid class divisions), Japanese had more flexibility in contemplating alternative ways of thinking. Also, the decentralization of the country into 260 domains increased the competition of ideas through local schools of thought.

The levels of intensity of the various types of Confucianism were not the same in Japan and China. By comparing each type in the two countries we can highlight some of the differences. Also, by looking at the balance among the various types, we can gain an impression of how the overall configuration of Confucianism had different meanings in Japan and China. Confucianism was more varied in Japan, and it was more pronounced at intermediate levels in the society.

The first type, *imperial Confucianism*, dates back over 1,000 years and centers on the role of the emperor, incorporating elements of what later came to be called state Shintoism. The imperial-centered interpretation of the doctrine was downplayed in the Tokugawa period, but it remained in the background and was invoked in the 1860s as respect and loyalty for the emperor and again in the 1880s and 1890s as loyalty to the imperial house and love for country. Whereas in China the discrediting of Manchu imperial rule and the highly ritualized existence of the imperial house as the political focus of the country cast in doubt the entire system of loyalty to the center, the emperor's detachment from the Tokugawa system of rule made it easier to link Confucian loyalty and modern nationalism. China's Mandate of Heaven could be lost and after 1911 was lost for good. Japan's hereditary "descent from heaven" remained sufficiently distant from political intrigue and decline that its symbolic and ideological value, whether perceived as Shinto or Confucianist, retained much force. Japan's imperial Confucianism was less central and more detachable from other parts of the tradition than was China's.

The second type, *reform Confucianism*, was found in Chinese attempts to give new moral authority to a dynasty seemingly in decline; however, it had not been taken seriously in late imperial China. A school stressing statecraft (*ching shih*) was advocating improved administrative skills, but it was able to make only minor inroads in the nineteenth century. In contrast, three times during the eighteenth century and the first half of the nineteenth century the government in Edo led a reform movement guided by Confucian principles. Among other objectives, each reform called for less concern with consumption, more attention to production, and increased moral education. The Meiji Restoration swept away much of the old order in a flurry of Westernization. It departed sharply from the earlier message in reform periods to resist ostentatious consumption unbefitting one's status, but there was something of the same moralistic reform tone, and this became pronounced by the 1890s. Reform Confucianism prepared the way for the radical reforms of Westernization. It was a more vital force in Japan than in China, in part because imperial Confucianism remained less articulated.

The third type of Confucianism, *elite Confucianism*, can in Japan be largely equated with the "way of the samurai," a set of ideas supportive of devoted service to one's lord and self-sacrifice and self-cleansing to purify one's ability to serve. Neo-Confucian interpretations passed on by Zen Buddhists spread among the samurai bands over several centuries and became national doctrines under Tokugawa sponsorship. This samurai Confucianism was more discipline-oriented and martial than Chinese elite practices. It retained a strong impact among the armed forces, the bureaucracy, and part of the intellectual elite in the Meiji era, who linked their own call to service with self-discipline and undivided pursuit of a goal. Indeed, through moral training and legal codes the Meiji leadership sought to spread the samurai (Confucian) values to all classes, directly linking imperial and samurai Confucianism. The corresponding values of China's scholar-official elite were closely bound to the study of classics and the preparation for examinations and imperial service; they lacked the independent articulation of samurai Confucianism.

Ch'ing China had only a small bureaucracy for its huge population; personalized networks developed through which one could gain influence with officials. Tokugawa Japan was intensely and locally administered by large bureaucracies, which operated, to a considerable degree, through impersonal hierarchies based on designated statuses, leaving little room for personal bonds formed through past interactions. China's scholar-officials or literati were widely dispersed and relied largely on informal connections with bureaucrats or their underlings. The Japanese samurai elite was concentrated and regimented, consistent with its military origins. China's prominent family and lineage associations reached up through connections that continually needed to be reestablished, giving rise to intense competition for scholarly credentials and to irregular financial payments as personal connections and factions were created. In Japan intermediate levels of the society were layered through more stable hierarchies, often reflecting bureaucratic regulation and intergenerational continuities in mutual obligations. Elite Confucianism acquired a more organized form centered on the collective pursuit of ideals.

The fourth type, *merchant-house Confucianism*, may seem to be a misnomer, for merchants were at the bottom of the ideal four-class hierarchy of samurai, peasant, artisan, and merchant. The pursuit of material gain through commerce in both China and Japan had negative overtones for the elite. Yet, large merchant houses, which had developed from family businesses by adding relatives and apprentices and by establishing branch offices, espoused Confucian morality. They too claimed to be serving political authority and the needs of society and downplayed their concern for short-run profits. Loyal service to an organization that modeled itself on the family and sought to create an atmosphere of unity and harmony was consistent with Confucian thinking. Authority was paternalistic, guided by an almost religious reverence for the traditions and uniqueness of the merchant house and by rituals to perpetuate obligations and a sense of indebtedness. Thomas P. Rohlen uses words such as gratitude, propriety, humility, hierarchy, moral leadership, and worship of ancestors to describe the traditions of the merchant houses.[3] The inability to gain samurai status fostered a long-term perspective, but even in China there were merchant houses that lasted for centuries and embraced many of these same values. In Japan some of these establishments, such as Mitsui, made the transition to modern business and, together with Confucian-inspired samurai, who transferred quickly into the business world after their stipends were withdrawn, helped to sustain a merchant-house brand of Confucianism. The fuller fusion of political administration and merchant organization as distinct but mutually supportive entities and the spillover of samurai principles as a model for townspeople left Japan with a solid foundation of merchant-house Confucianism.

The fifth and final type of Confucianism is that practiced by the ordinary population, especially the peasants. This *mass Confucianism*, as the three chapters of Part I point out, was more deeply rooted in the eighteenth and nineteenth centuries than earlier. While Confucian principles were often distant from the daily lives of the people, as literacy spread and as governments consciously inculcated values they became widely disseminated ideals. Because they were largely

[3] Thomas P. Rohlen, "Managerial Philosophy in a Confucian Setting: The Japanese Case and Its Implications for Western Management," unpublished manuscript.

concerned with micro-level institutions such as the family, they in-creasingly became a factor in the lives of the masses.

Mass Confucianism provided a similar base in China and Japan. To be sure, there were differences in family structure, educational orientation, and other conditions, which, I have argued elsewhere, gave Japan some advantage in modernization.[4] Yet I think that the similarities by world standards in family solidarity, educational aspirations, and other outlooks on life deserve emphasis. The other forms of Confucianism were represented in China as well, but for these types differences are more noteworthy. The great strength of the imperial, reform, and merchant-house types was unique to Japan. Its distinctive samurai type at the elite level adds to the impression that Japanese Confucianism, embedded in a different social-class system, offers a different foundation for change. Imperial Confucianism in the Ch'ing period developed in ways harmful to reform, elite, and merchant-house types of Confucianism, making Confucianism seem to be a more repressive force in China.

The values are largely the same, although Japanese tradition gave greater weight to some. From imperial and samurai Confucianism came a deeper commitment to unquestioned loyalty, from samurai Confucianism came greater concern for self-sacrifice and group orientation, from reform Confucianism came a greater inclination to adapt to new circumstances, and from merchant-house Confucianism came a more realistic long-term application of traditional values to the business world. Mass Confucianism was gaining in early nineteenth-century Japan and could be more easily redirected to modern ends through the presence of the other forms of Confucianism.

Having concentrated so far on differences between Japan and China, I think it is also important to keep in mind some similarities in the regional Confucian tradition. In Tokugawa and Ch'ing societies, as well as in Yi dynasty Korea, leaders had made conscious decisions to bolster their rule with Neo-Confucian teachings in the hope of establishing a stable polity and encouraging orderly behavior among the people. In turn, each state sought from its ideology support for loyalty to superiors. Yet, the Confucian doctrine did not make this an unquestioning, passive acceptance of authority. It called on people to be of service, to work locally and in a manner appropriate to their status to secure the goals of the state. For some, this was a call to official service—to conceive of it as a high calling and to aspire to it as a means to help realize the ethical precepts in the Con-

---

[4] Gilbert Rozman, ed., *The Modernization of China* (New York: The Free Press, 1981), Chap. 5.

fucian teachings. The doctrines made a reciprocal claim on the authorities: the emperor and state officials were asked to perform
rituals and conduct state affairs in a manner conducive to harmony
in the realm. The well-functioning state observed strict limits against
intervention in local life, although its responsibility for moral well-
being permitted extensive censorship and surveillance or suppression
of potentially heterodox groupings. The three East Asian polities developed their own clearly delineated hierarchies, but these did not
exclude merit. Above all, government service was perceived as a meritorious calling. This was especially true in China, where a series of
examinations were important in the recruitment of most officials. It
was also true in Korea, despite the restriction of government examinations to the *yangban* class, and to some extent in Japan, where there
was some disregard of samurai ranking in order to reward talented
samurai born to a lower rank.

The state in each country granted considerable autonomy to local
communities, preferring to work through community leaders than to
bypass them or to rely on some form of outside authority. Confucian
practices were conducted largely within the home and were reinforced by community associations. They centered on family cycle
events: birth, marriage, inheritance, and death. All of the countries
relied on mourning practices to reinforce a sense of household continuity that may, along with access to a commercial economy in land
and goods, have helped orient families toward long-term planning.
All stressed filial piety, which may have prepared individuals as adults
to transfer virtually unconditional loyalty to a single outside organization. All placed the newly married wife in the unquestionably subordinate role of daughter-in-law before a powerful patriarch and his
wife; women rarely had any choice but to strive for acceptance as
diligent mothers and homemakers.

Assumptions about human nature in East Asia stressed the potential for improvement through mental training—in family rituals, in
attitudes toward work, and in study habits. Family strategies could be
developed on this basis and usually on the expectation of a stable environment for gaining the fruits of one's labors. It is particularly
noteworthy that these societies channeled expectations toward
schooling. In Korea the yangban status was associated with education; it was widely sought and, once attained, led to higher aspirations
to pass exams. In Japan literacy rates climbed steeply during the two
and a half centuries of the Tokugawa period. In China the prestige
of scholar-officials continued to draw vast numbers to the district-
level examinations that might lead to higher-level examinations and
elite social standing. Education to serve one's family, to help it to rise

in status within one's community, and, for some, to earn government recognition and office was a powerful magnet for the ambitious.

By the nineteenth century, state-directed adherence to Neo-Confucian-inspired rituals had been largely replaced by spontaneous community and family activities. The rise of the private academies in Korea, the presence of countless private schools or tutorial arrangements in China, and the spread of new types of private schools located at temples and elsewhere in Japan were all broadly based developments. The national leadership's actions in past centuries had helped build popular support; even after the old governments fell in each country during the period 1868–1911, the people generally retained deeply held attitudes about family, education, work, and the state that could be sustained in a very different environment.

In each country the base for change in the second half of the nineteenth century included (1) careful controls (symbolized by blind weddings) and planning by family and lineage or community; (2) high educational aspirations and recognition of the hard work over a long time required for genuine achievement; (3) intense competition to earn money in order to buy land, invest in business, or collectively raise the standing of one's local area (on an area-wide level, seen as interdomain rivalry in Japan and as competition between commonplace-of-origin associations in China); and (4) the ideal of a unified state invested with moral authority and enlisting the efforts of energetic and educated officials (symbolized by the large-scale bureaucracies of premodern East Asia). In comparison with other premodern populations, to describe traditional East Asian families we would add —to the usual adjectives used—future-oriented, motivated, competitive, and accustomed to bureaucratic governance.

The Period of Rapid Decline of Confucianism

In China the process of decline became intense only in the 1890s, and it continued unabated into the 1920s. In Japan the decline occurred abruptly in the 1860s and 1870s, but already in the 1880s a counterreaction was limiting the negative trends. Confucianism in Japan declined earlier, faster, and under more controlled conditions.

One factor facilitating a speedy decline in Japan was the more limited physical presence of Confucian symbols. China was blanketed by physical manifestations of this belief system. Its bureaucracy made use of hundreds of temples of Confucius scattered in China's administrative centers; the yamen buildings set aside for the magistrate's rule in each district; and the examination halls divided into tiny cells in which candidates for local, provincial, or national degrees were locked for days to expound on the great books of the tradition. At the village level the lineage system practiced Confucian rituals in tens of thousands of ancestral halls. In Japan there were Shinto shrines, Buddhist temples, the castles of each domain, and other structures, but practically no buildings primarily associated with Confucian rituals.

The two countries also differed in the number of Confucian "practitioners" they counted. In neither country was there a clergy; that was not part of the tradition. In China the examination system produced a dense network of degree holders, some of whom had climbed to at least the lower rungs of the bureaucratic ladder through an outside posting and many more who benefited from the prestige of their public recognition by carrying out local functions. Virtually the entire well-educated population of China gained its community standing through the authority of its Confucian education, and brought an extraordinary uniformity of training in Confucian teachings to formal or informal leadership roles. In Japan there were many educated in Confucian ideas, but this did not earn them a special status. They were first of all samurai within a particular organization or townsmen using education for an occupation not centered in propagating Confucianism; a few were teachers. Yet, even in this capacity their status was usually defined more by their organizational ties than by the content of their teachings, and even the content was more varied than in China. China's social base for maintaining Confucianism was far larger.

As early as the beginning of the 1870s the Japanese government supplied the teachers with a new curriculum and with numerous employment prospects in a promised compulsory school system. The mainstay of education for some time to come remained language instruction, which did not require much retooling. In the transition years, bureaucrats were more concerned about the geographical origins and, for a time, hereditary status of central officials than about their Confucian training and beliefs. In Japan the social basis for Confucianism melted away.

In China the transition was much longer and more painful. Intellectuals exposed to foreign thinking led in the ferment. An important milestone, in some ways comparable to the humiliations felt by Japanese from Western intrusions and unequal treaties in the 1850s and early 1860s, was the Sino-Japanese War of 1894–95. Japan's success drew attention to the achievements of the Meiji Restoration in casting aside traditional ways. Chinese began to blame elements of the Confucian tradition for the inability of the state to rally the people. The spread of Western ideas made many people aware of an alternative to the existing order. The initial response, as exemplified by K'ang Yu-wei, the architect of the abortive Hundred Days Reform of 1898, was to locate in Confucian thought a basis for a "forward-looking reform-oriented strategy to achieve political cohesion and vigor."[5] The first serious reexamination of China's heritage centered on Confucianism as a political ideology that had endowed the emperor, known as the Son of Heaven, with absolute authority, supported by a bureaucratic elite but without popular participation. Reformers sought to somehow harness Confucian thought to the twin engines of democracy and nationalism, gradually unveiling plans for a constitutional monarchy and a more egalitarian political process in accord with immediate needs rather than cosmic design. Nonetheless, lacking a separate and untarnished tradition of imperial Confucianism and a widely appreciated tradition of reform Confucianism, the advocates of change from above failed. Japan's more decentralized political order made it easier to rally regional support against the discredited administration at the center, while the Ch'ing rulers in Beijing were harder to dislodge.

Following the dashed hopes that resulted from the Empress Dowager's palace coup against the reform-minded Kuang-hsu emperor in 1898 and the fiasco of the Boxer Uprising two years later which she had encouraged, the rethinking of Confucian political premises took a more radical turn. The imperial government's agreement, in principle, to reform opened the gates in 1901 to a tumultuous debate, which quickly outraced the Beijing government's limited concessions. To the extent that Confucianism had become equated with the imperial system of rule as practiced in the Ch'ing dynasty, it could not stand the test of time in an age of imperialism and modernization. It offered no alternative vision for China.

A similar debate in Russia at the same time also led to some updating of a political system that stifled aspirations for participation and responsible government. In both China and Russia, the Russo-Japanese War of 1904–5 intensified the demands for change, demonstrating to many the advantage constitutional government held over autocracy. A large number of Chinese students who went to Japan in the decade 1900–1910 contributed to the clamor for learning from the Japanese experience.[6] The outcome in China was quicker and less

---

[5] Hao Chang, "Intellectual Change and the Reform Movement, 1890–8," in *The Cambridge History of China*, vol. 11, part 2, *Late Ch'ing 1800–1911*, ed. John K. Fairbank and Kwang-ching Liu (Cambridge, England: Cambridge University Press, 1980), pp. 288 and 318–29.

[6] Marius B. Jansen, "Japan and the Chinese Revolution of 1911," in Fairbank and Liu, *Cambridge History of China*, vol. 11, part 2, pp. 348–61.

amenable to compromise than in Russia. The Confucian political ideology, as interpreted by the narrowly based Manchu rulers, was even more incongruous with modern political needs than was the system of tsarist rule in Russia. When two millennia of imperial rule ended in China, an enormous vacuum was created with little hint of the political system that should replace it. Only a brief debate before 1911 prepared Chinese to rethink the relevance, if any, of their Confucian heritage for the political system of the future. Under these circumstances, the complete collapse of the old system meant that traditional elements would not, as they did openly in Japan after 1868 and indirectly in Russia after 1917, quickly resurface as part of a stable new order. Instead they retained force at the local level and reemerged in subtle forms at the central level after a long interval of instability, repudiation, and piecemeal introduction of new forms.

While political reform was the first rallying cry for those who would reinterpret Confucianism, educational reform proved to be their first major accomplishment. Reformers agreed on the stultifying effects of the examination preparations, with their time-consuming memorization of outdated writings. In 1901 the eight-legged essay was dropped as the required form for writing test answers, and in 1905 the imperial examinations—the mechanism for upward mobility and socialization—were abolished.[7] Modern schools, albeit retaining for a time Confucian moral education writings, were soon established. Roughly a decade later, in the climate of the May Fourth Movement, which blamed many of China's troubles on the outdated language and literature in Confucian writings, the contents of the school curriculum became more Westernized. Unlike Japan, which had converted its traditional schooling directly into a base for mass education, a sharp discontinuity developed in China between the old and the new. Those with old training seemed irrelevant in the new era, while in the uncertain times, many with new learning faced a problematic future. Attendance rates were low, even while some excellent students in modern schools carried forward the traditional commitment to learning.

The educational transition in the first quarter of this century was accompanied by much disillusionment with traditions and with the intractability of China's problems. Intellectuals considered bureaucrats and warlords to be obstacles, contrasting their own virtue and nationalism with the unprincipled and even traitorous behavior of those holding power. Spurred by government complicity in accepting

[7] Chuzo Ichiko, "Political and Institutional Reform, 1901–11," in Fairbank and Liu, *Cambridge History of China*, vol. 11, part 2, pp. 377–80.

Japan's offensive Twenty-one Demands in 1915 and by the breakdown of central government, students turned their liberal education against manifestations of China's backwardness. Confucian thought bore the brunt of the assault.

It is not unlikely that a stable government that had captured some of the moral high ground could have retained a place for some aspects of the traditional teachings. Certain scholars, including some who had gained prominence as early reformers, tried to accomplish an intellectual synthesis of the new and the old; yet they were unable to rally support. The central government and largely autonomous regional governments were discredited. Forces out of power were more concerned with change than with stability. Modern schools from the start became known as opponents of tradition rather than being reincorporated into a system of support for the established order. We find a sharp contrast with the clearly defined moral teachings of Meiji schools in the 1880s barely a decade after the decline of traditional schooling.[8]

Many Chinese intellectuals blamed the Confucian tradition for their country's backwardness, for the inability to set a new course after the fall of dynastic rule, and for the unresponsiveness of the Chinese people, who were burdened by their "national psychology." They groped for a new philosophy of history, perhaps even substituting for the cosmological certainty of Confucianism a kind of religious faith in some approach to the science of human society. "Newness" became an appealing slogan, as in the "New Youth" and "New Culture" movements.

In a climate of boycotts and other anti-imperialist activities, it was insufficient to seek only to borrow from the West and Japan and to cast aside all that is Chinese. Neotraditionalists such as Liang Ch'ich'ao sought to draw on "unique Chinese norms of interpersonal relations and spiritual self-cultivation."[9] Others turned to Marxist critiques of Western values that resonated with traditional Chinese suspicions of individualism. They were more concerned about unity than competition, about moral authority than equality, about activism against unjust authority than reliance on freedom of speech. Sun Yat-sen fits into this mold. He called for democracy while worrying about

---

[8] Richard Rubinger, "Education: From One Room to One System," in *Japan in Transition: From Tokugawa to Meiji*, ed. Marius B. Jansen and Gilbert Rozman (Princeton: Princeton University Press, 1986), pp. 223–25.

[9] Charlotte Furth, "Intellectual Change: From the Reform Movement to the May Fourth Movement, 1895–1920," in *The Cambridge History of China*, vol. 12, part 1, *Republican China 1912–1949*, ed. John K. Fairbank (Cambridge, England; Cambridge University Press, 1983), pp. 362–64.

anarchy in a population that he described as "a sheet of loose sand." Sun wrote of the need for a period of tutelage before the people exercised full political rights and was attracted to Lenin's principle of democratic centralism.

The ethical system of Confucianism figured prominently in the reform literature of the May Fourth Movement. In place of obedience to superior, the May Fourth writers chose love as the symbol of the new morality.[10] The movement for women's liberation gathered force. For a time naive enthusiasm for what was new enabled Chinese to put off difficult choices. One could be in favor of both the self and the collective. In the 1920s Western values reached a peak in popularity. The critical task of choosing between rival outlooks such as capitalism and socialism and of finding a place for traditional values awaited resolution of the political crisis faced by China.

Japan had also experienced a period of unqualified Westernization and scorn for native traditions. These attitudes prevailed in the 1870s and for part of the 1880s, when the slogan "civilization and enlightenment" (bunmei kaika) meant to look to the West for progress. Donald T. Roden describes the unruliness of the swashbuckling 1870s.[11] Kenneth B. Pyle describes a time when Japanese were alienated from their own cultural heritage.[12] The new generation was cut adrift from old models. Similar to the May Fourth generation in China, they found their elders useless to society and gained confidence that their own superior Western learning would enable them to build a new order. Cultural disorientation occurred in Japan as well as China.

In both countries there were few advocates of Confucian doctrines left after the period of decline had continued for just two or three decades. The intellectual community, much of the urban populace, and some rural residents as well had been cut loose from certain age-old bonds and now associated Confucianism with backwardness. Why did such an abrupt decline take place? It was not because of ruthless suppression of the old system's practitioners and prominent adherents, as occurred in some countries where alien movements embarked on a battle to uproot existing religions or political traditions. Confucianism was poorly institutionalized for resistance because it lacked a clergy or hierarchy of religious structures. Outwardly it was easily vanquished.

---

[10] Leo Ou-Fan Lee, "Literary Trends I: The Quest for Modernity, 1845–1927," in Fairbank, Cambridge History of China, vol. 12, part 1, p. 477.

[11] Donald T. Roden, Schooldays in Imperial Japan: A Study in the Culture of a Student Elite (Berkeley: University of California Press, 1980).

[12] Kenneth B. Pyle, The New Generation in Meiji Japan: Problems of Cultural Identity, 1885–1895 (Stanford: Stanford University Press, 1969).

Formal expression of adherence was suddenly gone. The old system of belief in China and Japan yielded mostly to intellectual pressure. In China this pressure came largely from below, through reform movements. In Japan it came both from intellectual pressure and from the speedy replacement of the old system with a new opportunity structure.

Japan's decline was less disruptive for many reasons. It had more diversified Confucian approaches to utilize. There was less consciousness that all were packaged together in a single doctrine called Confucianism. Furthermore, non-Confucian traditions associated with Japanese nationalism were available. Above all, the process of decline was managed in Japan by a central government able to build a new structure as rapidly as the old one disintegrated. Indeed, it was also able to plan much of the disintegration itself, such as in the shift to a new educational system. As a result of its rapid and managed shift away from a widely encompassing Confucian order, negative views of the tradition did not gain as deep a hold as in China.

Mention should also be made of Japan's more vertical lines of social control beyond the family or lineage. Confucian forms of hierarchy had been grafted onto samurai feudal loyalties, and both had been reorganized to create a largely impersonal chain of bureaucratic command. Administration did not penetrate as deeply in China. It would take longer to reestablish social control and then to identify the new forms of authority with Confucian values.

Focusing on the level of the family may help us to contrast the transition of declining Confucianism in the two countries. Confucian values center on the family, while modern Western values center on the individual and communist values center on the state or the party. The Confucian tradition is concerned with constructing a harmonious society out of the building blocks of harmonious families. The obligation of the ruler is to set a good example through moral edicts and ritual deeds and also to establish a social structure in which families can pursue their material and spiritual goals with little interference. Of course, in practice the family was constrained by the state's own self-aggrandizement and by intermediate organizations whose collective goals were sometimes given precedence by the state over family goals. In Japan intermediate organizations, such as samurai retainer bands and community associations, served as a powerful counterweight to the family, but there too the Confucian family principles prevailed for most people on most occasions. In East Asia the corporate family—sanctified in moral teachings and in law and buttressed by rights over property and opportunities for advancement—reigned supreme.

Western teachings of the nineteenth and twentieth century did not deny family-oriented values. Brought to East Asia by missionaries, secular intellectuals, and businessmen and officials, these values conflicted with local traditions by pointing to other goals that could take priority over family goals or could provide an alternative route for realizing family goals. They challenged generational hierarchy by asserting that the younger, usually modern-educated generation could achieve family prosperity better than their elders. This appeal resonated with the long-standing Confucian approval of education as a means of leading youths out into the world to serve their families.

In Japan, even before modern education produced many subversive effects within the family, state and intermediate organizations were transformed. Here too the appeal was to serving one's group better under new circumstances. In the competitive atmosphere of Tokugawa society, and the earlier warring states, samurai bands had rallied behind their lords. Unconditional loyalty to lord, not unlike filial piety, was couched in the rhetoric of service to an organization striving for honor and gain. In the 1860s, justifying their commitment by the rationale that their organization and even their country needed a rededication along new lines, lower and middle samurai sidestepped the customary hierarchical lines to prod their organizations into concerted action.

The Japanese family remained well buffeted from the early tides of change. Before Western education or modernization of the economy had exerted much impact on the family, higher-level bodies had been stirred to reform. Already by the time the context of life was changing rapidly from the 1890s, Japanese leaders had glued a revised set of Confucian family values onto the superstructure of a modernizing country. Japanese society notably consisted of a threefold hierarchy—family, community or work organization, and state. In comparison with many Western modernized societies, the corporate family held a tight hold over the individual, hierarchical intermediate organizations including elite schools created strong bonds of solidarity, and the state, both in rhetoric and in policy, created a center-oriented focus that could sustain militarism as well as coordinated economic growth. Within this framework, the Confucian traditions of patriarchy, family loyalty, ancestor reverence, and generational and age hierarchy retained a good deal of their force.

The collective response to the fundamentally new circumstances of modern times occurred slowly in China. Whereas only fifteen years transpired from the jolt of Perry's arrival to the revolutionary impact of the Meiji Restoration, as many as seventy years passed before the train of events produced by the Opium War led to the downfall of the Ch'ing dynasty. Even then the organizations at regional and local levels, which had been too weak to galvanize into reform forces under the imperial system, remained fragmented. Until the virtual unification of China under the Kuomintang in 1927 and, in many respects, continuing through the decades of Japanese invasion and Civil War until 1949, there was no new framework in which family strains could be confined. Chinese leaders failed to combine the Confucian tradition with a centrally organized response to imperialism and modernization. The only attempt that had any chance of success was under the Kuomintang; opinions vary whether the force of external interference or the internal shortcomings of the Kuomintang strategy caused that short-lived attempt to fail on the Chinese mainland. After the Kuomintang strategy was redesigned on the previously Japanese-ruled island of Taiwan, it met with great success in modernization.

For over a century the combination of individual, family, intermediate organization, and state was in disequilibrium with China's needs to modernize and to reestablish national strength. China's late imperial overcentralized government and undermobilized society had much to do with this organizational incoherence. Central government became too preoccupied with surveillance and too encumbered by corruption to permit a revitalization of local government. Family strategies became divorced from national and community interests. After 1911, under the burden of overpopulation, poverty, and disorder, individuals slipped away from family bonds. In urban areas, others, faced with new opportunities and new ideologies, chafed under the restraint of family bonds. Rather than working through prior organizations, as disciplined samurai had done in the 1860s, China's urban discontents founded their own secret organizations or contributed to the intellectual turmoil with sharp critiques and calls for a radically different social order. When driven into rural and outlying areas, they found support in divided communities and Japanese-occupied areas with the help of nationalist and class-struggle slogans. The communists promised new organizations that would bring order and justice to Chinese society.

Highly organized Japan fostered loyalty to emperor, loyalty to family, and other Confucian values (under a mixed ideology of Shintoism and nationalism) as its modernization accelerated to the 1930s. Deeply disorganized China—under threat from regional warlordism and community instability—turned against Confucianism in favor of new ideologies. The emperor was gone after 1911; there were calls for a more democratic system of authority, but increasingly also for a centralized system that could stem anarchy. Unjust hierarchy and inequality came to be perceived as the legacy of Confucian "feudalism." In its place redistribution—especially of land—was required. The star of Marxism rose high as an alternative to the old, discredited social order.

THE PERIOD OF PARTIAL REVIVAL FOR CONFUCIANISM

One hears a lot about Islamic fundamentalism, Christian fundamentalism, and even a revival of Russian orthodoxy as a form of nationalism. The decline of a long venerated tradition in favor of liberal or Marxist values has in many parts of the world produced a sharp backlash. Yet, neither in Japan nor in China can we find much evidence of a fundamentalist movement. After the defeat in 1877 of the Satsuma Rebellion led by samurai and the failure in 1916 of Yüan Shih-k'ai's effort to have himself crowned emperor, calls for returning to the old society were no longer audible. Two reasons for this were the absence of any religious organization, which might have become a springboard for challenging secular authorities, and the ability of many in the old Confucian-trained elite to use their superior education for modern ends.

While fundamentalism did not pose a threat, the social base for rampant Westernization long remained fragile. The bourgeoisie, apart from small-scale traders embedded in traditional community relationships, was small and did not have much access to power. The emerging intelligentsia reacted ambivalently toward the Western powers, in part because of unequal treaties and other manifestations of imperialism but also because of unrelenting pride in some aspects of their own venerable civilization. Perhaps most important, the new military forces and state bureaucracies found it in their interest to reach a mass audience—to rally support among little-educated villagers who remained deeply influenced by mass Confucianism. It was necessary to build a spiritual rubric for claims to increased political control, consistent with the traditional appeal to moral suasion. The potentially disorderly ways of grass-roots democracy and balance-of-power politics did not win central backing.

The Japanese government moved swiftly on many fronts to combine Westernization with traditionalism. In the 1880s the government followed a massive wave of reforms with a cautious program of consolidation. It suppressed political opposition influenced by Western principles of political activism. At the same time, it justified its own claims for unity and loyalty on the dual basis of popular fears of social disintegration and recurrent moods of crisis about international relations, often related to Japan's dashed hopes for revising unequal treaties. As early as 1881 the Minister of Education developed a program for moral education in the schools. Responding to an earlier call by the Meiji emperor for a reemphasis on Confucian education, he sought to combine training in loyalty to the imperial house, love of country, filial piety, respect for superiors, and charity toward inferiors. The 1890 Imperial Rescript on Education made moral training the primary objective of schooling; it endured until 1945 as the foundation of a concerted effort to transmit moral values through the schools.

Moral training of future leaders was approached with no less urgency. Donald T. Roden observes that while elementary schools were asked to inculcate civic propriety, elite higher schools sought to graduate men with pure thoughts, above the lure of money or personal gain. In this way, the new elite would carry forward the tradition of the favored domain schools, which trained samurai as leaders dedicated to public service. The Confucian classic, known as *The Doctrine of the Mean*, had expressed faith in education as a socializing force for a select group of superior men who would run the government. In pursuit of similar aims, the new Meiji elite higher schools fostered school spirit and a close-knit community using Western techniques of athletics and masculine rites as well as combined traditional and Western methods of asceticism and obedience to elder students.[13] In comparison with China, which before the 1950s lacked a modern educational system for more than a small fraction of its youth and offered diverse training—including Western-run schools—for future leaders, Japan moved forward by the 1890s to both compulsory schooling and the clear articulation of an elite program within a centralized hierarchy of schools.

Entrance examinations play a central role in the Confucian tradition. They channel career aspirations, produce a meritocratic elite that can be further shaped through the sponsorship of the existing elite, lead to the dissemination of the national culture to local elites, set the standard for discipline and motivation, and bolster an ethic of fair competition. Such examinations were a key to China's premodern stability, but China failed to adapt them to changing educational needs. Even in the 1950s and again in the 1980s, Chinese leaders were ambivalent about the new products of educational elitism with whom they were reluctant to share power. Despite its own weak examination tradition, in the 1880s Japan quickly grasped the merits of rigorous entrance examinations and made this the cornerstone of its recruitment of officials and reshaping of sponsored social mobility.

[13] Donald T. Roden, *Schooldays in Imperial Japan*.

Confucianism is concerned with moral education to internalize and fulfill clearly defined social roles. Conformity is eased by clear definitions of one's identity, facilitated by hierarchy built into the language and by direct and predictable transitions from home to school to work. Self-realization becomes easy in a variety of roles. Despite confusion after 1868 and again after 1945, Japan has generally been successful in reinforcing this central feature of the Confucian tradition, while China has not.

Family instability also became an important concern of the Meiji government well before the end of the century. Under the influence of Western knowledge, youths began to challenge aspects of "family tyranny," as they would in increasing numbers in China by the 1920s. As part of a population still at least eighty percent rural, having few occupational outlets outside of the family farm or family business, most citizens could not easily embrace attacks on patriarchal authority or the subordination of women. Indeed, the more fluid social-class atmosphere of the Meiji era made it easier for the restrictive samurai standards regarding women to spread to other groups. Liberals were put on the defensive by leaders who turned to traditional morals as a means to forestall social disintegration. The family-centered principles of Confucianism, such as the authority of the male household head, were incorporated into the family code of 1898. As Japan modernized rapidly over the next half-century, this code grew more and more out of touch with reality. Nonetheless, it gave a powerful boost to Confucian values both as ideals and as legally enforceable provisions.

Understandably, it was not all clear sailing for traditional values in modernizing Japan. Foreign theories about social relations entered the country with particular intensity in the 1880s and again in the 1910s and 1920s. The first period saw the spread of classic Western liberalism combined with the popular contemporary evolutionary theories of Herbert Spencer. In contradiction to traditional assumptions about collectivity and hierarchy, this unbridled individualism favored the initiative of free citizens backed by legal rights against the restraining power of the state and other organizations. Several decades later, in the period of Taisho democracy, socialist ideas from the Soviet Union as well as social reform thought from the West spread widely among intellectuals and disadvantaged groups objecting to the unbalanced character of Japan's modernization. The new thinking placed faith in a reorganized state representing a mass constituency or in voluntary associations working to solve social problems through political participation. The centralized Japanese state preempted the appeal of individualism in the 1880s, taking some coercive actions against the People's Rights movement but relying largely on structural reforms supportive of parliamentary rule and moral education centered on Confucian and Shinto traditions. In the 1920s and 1930s it relied more on harsh repression, while also realizing some success in mobilizing public opinion to support aggressive foreign policies and domestic unity to facilitate them.

Victory over China in 1894–95 and again in the 1930s (although incomplete) served as proof that a centralized Japan acting in unison could restore national dignity. Japan's expansion across the region was justified as an effort to create an East Asian Co-Prosperity Sphere which would be guided by regional values superior to Western or Soviet ones. It was difficult for individual Japanese to quarrel with success. Even as their own lives were increasingly guided by personal interests (such as the urban-area love marriages without parental guidance in the choice of a partner), there was not much advocacy of individualism. The moral teachings of the schools and media and the laws of the country backed by restrictions on political activism kept rival values from being widely disseminated. Nonetheless, Taisho democracy had opened the door to public awareness of other values.

There is no denying that the Confucian tradition combined with "the way of the samurai" had played a role in the rise of Japanese militarism. Already in the Tokugawa era, the Chinese Confucian preference for loyalty to family and lineage had been qualified by the Japanese emphasis on loyalty to lord (among samurai) and community solidarity. Confucian teachers had found it easier to gain the ear of daimyō and the shogun by placing stress on the inculcation of loyalty and hierarchy. The grafting of imperial Confucianism onto nationalism and the persistence of samurai Confucianism helped lead Japan toward repression at home and militarism abroad. Leaders took advantage of mass Confucianism to counteract liberal tendencies. Some of the same Confucian qualities that facilitated Japan's rapid conversion into a major world power with an industrialized economy, a strong military, and a relatively educated and disciplined work force also made it possible for a militaristic government to isolate critics and rally popular support.

Japan's transition from 1868 to 1945 demonstrated that Confucian traditions, once modified, could become a platform for modernization, even if democratization lagged. They are compatible with a centralized, paternalistic approach to the rapid transformation from a premodern society to one largely modernized. The postwar experiences of Taiwan, South Korea, and Singapore (but not Hong Kong, which has been governed by Britain in a more decentralized manner) reaffirm this conclusion. What remained to be seen was whether the

Confucian tradition would prove, as the Stalinist form of socialism did, to be unable to support further rapid modernization of a country already largely developed or whether, after some sharp adjustments, it could also become the platform for catching up to the West and surpassing it on many indicators of modern development.

Was Japan more true to its Confucian traditions in the 1930s than it is in the 1980s? Although there are diverse elements in the tradition, which could lead to a different conclusion, our answer is no. Militarism accentuated aspects of samurai Confucianism and imperial Confucianism, while postwar development has drawn heavily on merchant-house Confucianism and reform Confucianism. Both are supported by mass Confucianism. Of course, as a society becomes more modernized it moves further and further away from specific forms found in its premodern traditions; in this sense, we can conclude that Japan is much further from Tokugawa Confucianism than it was a half-century ago. We would add that militarism is more consistent with the still not very modernized transitional elements in the Confucian tradition, while liberal values are more readily fused onto already highly modernized elements still consistent with the spirit of the tradition.

In China Confucianism also made a partial comeback in circumstances in which it too was directly connected with militarism. Eager to forge a strong nation, the Kuomintang sought to create institutions similar to those that had enabled Japan to become powerful. Gaining power through their military organization, the new leadership of China sought to establish a strong central authority supported by a population steeped in Confucian values passed on via moral education. Because the Kuomintang succeeded in modernizing Taiwan, some observers think that it could have succeeded throughout China. Yet, apart from the Japanese invasions that denied the Kuomintang the opportunity to consolidate control over China, there were other obstacles. Through comparisons with Japan we can identify at least three.

First, returning to our earlier discussion, we find less diverse traditions of Confucianism in China. The absence of samurai Confucianism meant that the military that came to power in the late 1920s was not the same loyal, disciplined, morally educated force that it was in Japan sixty years earlier. Second, the long interlude of decline left Confucianism more battered in China. Since imperial examinations had been abolished for more than two decades and the imperial system had ended in disrepute in 1911, it was not easy, especially in military circles on the periphery of what was largely a civilian tradition, to find continuities with the past. Third, the greater inroads of alternative systems of thought made agreement on a particular approach to tradition more difficult. Western liberalism had a substantial following among the urban educated, as did Marxism-Leninism, which could also appeal to mass discontent with imperialism and social injustice. When the Kuomintang fled to Taiwan in 1949, they were able to consolidate based on a much larger ratio of their own forces to the population, a much weaker presence of rival systems of thought, and a society shaped by Japanese occupiers. To some observers the case of Taiwan suggests what might have happened if the Kuomintang had gained power in China as soon as the Ch'ing dynasty had fallen, avoiding a disruptive transition in which some parts of the Confucian tradition were weakened. To others, Taiwan shows how the combination of Japanese and Chinese Confucianism can succeed better than Chinese Confucianism alone. Still others think that it was necessary only to sweep aside political fragmentation and avoid suppressing Confucian traditions in order for China and its offshoots to realize the full benefits of a heritage conducive to rapid modernization. The heritage of imperial Confucianism could be converted to state-guided development in which public service is prestigious and the populace is orderly. Merchant-house Confucianism, with more emphasis on family businesses than in Japan, creates a vast reservoir of entrepreneurship. In any case, mass Confucianism provides a population ready to study hard and work diligently. China was at a disadvantage with respect to Japan, and the mainland in the 1930s and 1940s was at a disadvantage with respect to Taiwan, but each had Confucian elements that could facilitate rapid modernization.

From 1927 to 1949 Confucianism was, along with liberalism and Marxism-Leninism-Stalinism, one of three intellectual frameworks that competed for the minds of the Chinese people. Liberals were reluctant to concede its value because of their own assumptions about the need to abandon traditions in order to develop and because Confucianism increasingly became linked to a corrupt form of militarism. Yet, as the invasion by Japan intensified, liberals had nowhere else to turn except to the communist movement in the outlying countryside. The liberals did not have a convincing answer to questions about political organization and social justice in conditions of invasion and rural poverty. The communists were more forceful in their denunciation of Confucianism. They had some advantage in rallying a populace aroused against the old order, which had let their country decline sharply and made it possible for Japan to occupy most settled areas. The narrow approach to Marxism, with its intolerant attitude toward moderate figures and tradition, although voiced by Mao Tse-tung in his Yenan writings early in the 1940s, did not become a major factor in the struggle for mass support. Just as it is incorrect to view Japan's wartime ideology as a full blossoming of Confucianism, it is wrong to view the success of the communists as a mass repudiation of Confucianism.

China's communists equated Confucianism with feudalism, which stood in the way of modern development. In their view, this way of thinking kept the masses backward, without modern knowledge and organizations to reflect their class interests. Traditional hierarchical relations kept poor peasants in a psychological state of dependency and left women and youth under patriarchal authority. There was no need to study the value of the old ways of thought for the future or even their interaction with communist thought, since the latter would fully replace the former. As Charlotte Furth notes, radical young Chinese "passed on to history their totalistic interpretation of the evil dragon, 'tradition,' slain once and for all in the streets of Peking in May 1919 . . . [and sought] to appropriate for themselves the precious symbolism of modernity."[14]

In this context, Confucian values were revived by the Kuomintang government. Chiang Kai-shek's New Life movement from 1934 was the most concerted step in this direction. Unlike the focus in Japan fifty years earlier on a series of social relations linking family to emperor, the Chinese emphasized universal principles that could be applied to many relationships. Much attention centered on the Confucian term "*li*" (social propriety). Seen as a means to secure loyalty, hierarchy, and discipline, "*li*" became an obvious device to increase political centralization. The New Life movement failed to win a widespread following. Lloyd E. Eastman refers to it as "a sloganized Confucianism, encapsulated for mass consumption in simple dicta regarding personal conduct and hygiene."[15]

In its new form taking shape in the 1930s, Confucianism was no longer a single all-encompassing system of thought. From a revival of Confucian thought, neotraditionalists anticipated a spiritual strength and unity that would overcome the divisiveness afflicting China. They proclaimed an ethical system that could give stability to family, community, and state. It stood for altruistic public-mindedness and unselfish responsibility to family. Distinct from Japan's experience,

[14] Charlotte Furth, "Culture and Politics in Modern Chinese Conservatism," in *The Limits of Change: Essays on Conservative Alternatives in Republican China*, ed. Charlotte Furth (Cambridge, Mass.: Harvard University Press, 1976), p. 22.

[15] Lloyd E. Eastman, "The Kuomintang in the 1930s," in Furth, *The Limits of Change*, p. 201.

this stability was to take shape before or in place of massive reforms rather than in their wake.

Despite their efforts, advocates of Confucian values were unable to convince many people that they stood for a humanistic and rational outlook on society. Conditions were not ripe for a reaffirmation of the moral vitality of Chinese customs as a basis for national unity and sustained economic growth. There was insufficient confidence that China had already overcome the elements in its past that had led to weakness and poverty. Increasingly, these views of tradition seemed irrelevant in the face of communist calls for wartime mobilization and land reform in order to eliminate the weakness of the old order.

However unpopular Confucianism had become among cosmopolitan intellectuals, its ethical principles and, to a considerable extent, its political ideology and philosophy of history remained firmly embedded in the lives of ordinary people. Even those who cooperated with the communist movement were more disturbed by the breakdown in the old order than attracted by the communist image of the future. To an extent the two overlapped: each gave China a special place at the forefront of world societies; each called for national unity and collective harmony; and each rejected Western individualism. The communists depicted themselves as a virtuous elite (similar to the scholar-officials?) steeped in an ideology that offered a comprehensive understanding of human history and social relations. They could substitute certainty for chaos, firm central direction for self-serving pursuit of unworthy interests, and a strong bulwark for the preservation or reestablishment of at least some ethical qualities that had long made China superior. Actual contact with communist forces often brought contradictory messages, but in wartime conditions deviations from an ideal are more readily excused.

THE FURTHER ECLIPSE OF CONFUCIANISM

In the second half of the 1940s the Occupation reforms brought liberalism into Japan in full force while the victorious Communist Party of China sought to remake China in the image of Soviet socialism. Confucianism became a prime target of both transformations. It was blamed now not only for nineteenth-century backwardness, but also for historical development in the first half of this century that had gone astray. The West and, with remarkably little dissent, the Japanese blamed the antidemocratic and militaristic character of the prior era on a way of thinking and a pattern of social relations deeply rooted in Japanese history. While some writers preferred the label "feudalism," such traits as excessive loyalty to superiors, dependence on paternalistic relations, and insufficient equality and individualism were unequivocally linked to Confucian traditions. Unlike the reforms required of West Germany after World War II, those demanded of Japan were targeted at replacing an entire way of life. The Soviets, of course, did not occupy China nor did they have direct control over Mao Zedong and other Chinese leaders. Nevertheless, their Stalinist blueprint for socialism was adopted with few major modifications before 1958. The acceptance was so complete that even in the years of the Sino-Soviet split, Maoist radicalism sustained and deepened most aspects of the Stalinist approach, particularly as it concerned traditional social relations. In contrast to the "revisionists" in Moscow, China's leaders saw themselves as the true heirs to Stalin's version of socialism. As part of their orthodoxy, they condemned Confucian beliefs and practices in ever more titanic spasms of destruction until Mao's death in 1976.

Once again, in the second assault on Confucianism, Japan's critique became intense (although limited by the majority's desire to retain the emperor system) and was followed immediately by constructive alternatives, while China's attack dragged on without establishing a viable set of new relations. The American-led Occupation lasted six years and even before it ended the Japanese government was losing interest in extending the battle against old practices. China's application of the Soviet model expanded from 1949 to 1957, and continued and, in some respects, reached new heights from 1958 to 1978. Even after Deng Xiaoping's reforms began in 1978, uncertainty existed about how much of the past system should be undone. For three decades and much of a fourth, the negative thrust of the Soviet model against China's past retained great force. If we add earlier periods, we can calculate that the total time of sharp eclipse of tradition in Japan amounted to roughly two decades, while in China it was as many as six or seven decades over the course of a century.

A common target in the two countries was the tradition of deference—at home, in the community, in the school, in the workplace, and in politics. This tradition called for honor and respect to superiors accompanied by repression of individual preferences in the face of a group consensus. In Japan the struggle against deference came under the label "democracy" and was largely limited to clearly defined targets. It reduced the emperor to human proportions, but left him in office. It took away landholdings that were not farmed directly by landlords, but tolerated other sources of wealth and some compensation to the landowners and made it possible for them to retain influence until memories of hierarchical village relations gradually faded. The attack on the authority of teachers as representatives of a centralized and politicized educational system actually helped the teachers to gain greater independence, especially when local school boards failed to assume much power. Caught up in the rising tide of Marxist thought within the intellectual community, the teachers and their powerful union became vocal critics of Confucian traditions. Yet, even as the state's hold over moral education remained a subject of dispute, the teachers retained authority in the classroom and often introduced moral training. Elder males lost some power when the family code was rewritten in the wave of postwar reforms, accelerating the already developing tendency for the Japanese wife in urban salaried families to become the dominant figure at home. This example illustrates the tendency for reform effects to overlap with the results of modernization.

There were also specific signs of the times after World War II that called traditional forms of deference in Japan into question. Mass strikes and a rise in worker activism point to the loosening grip of the firm on the worker, although increasing reliance on seniority wages, enterprise unions, and other strategies contained this divisive process. Large numbers of people swung their support behind socialist and, for a time, communist candidates for office, indicating a high level of dissatisfaction with the status quo and a search for a comprehensive historical explanation for Japan's defeat, not excluding rejection of Confucian traditions. Yet, as in the 1870s and 1880s, an increasingly conservative government succeeded in outflanking the critics of tradition. Its reform methods were not intended to arouse social disorder. Old authority figures largely remained in place, and customary forms of deference did not suddenly disappear. Change relied first of all on legal provisions, to which citizens did not normally appeal. It relied also on structural developments consistent with modernization, such as the spread of the nuclear family, which regulated its effect. Finally, it relied on public opinion, which had the power to halt it. After the end of the reform process and the Occupation, Confucian values and practices were sufficiently widespread to find new ways of adapting to a rapidly modernizing society. Reform from above only set the stage for a gradual linkage from below of tradition and modernity.

Chinese communists used very different methods to counteract deferential relations and other signs of tradition. Their response can be separated into two periods. In the first period persons who had exercised authority felt the full brunt of the attack. This period, from 1949 (and earlier in communist base areas) to 1957, followed the approved course of building socialism from land reform to collectivization and from united front to proletarian dictatorship and strict central control. While some of the targets were the same as in Japan, the Chinese campaigns against deference penetrated much deeper. Not only did landlords lose their land and other forms of livelihood without compensation, they also were humiliated and in some cases brutalized or killed. After 1956 they were forced to rely on the collective farm, or its successor, the commune, which often discriminated against them in assigning tasks and allocating pay. In trying to eliminate lineage organizations and establish party organizations at the village level, the Chinese communists had in mind nothing less than doing away with the entire network of deferential relations outside of the household and replacing it with a control system that could combine the centralization of Soviet power with the moral suasion of a dedicated elite. This hopelessly contradictory objective resulted in no more than lip service being paid to the latter, while the former took precedence. Power replaced deference, although illegitimate uses of party power readily broke down into deference linked to kinship and other traditional bonds.

A more limited assault on deference occurred in Chinese cities. Teachers and other educated persons were required to undergo reeducation, while being given a radically new set of materials for use in their work. Bureaucrats of the previous government were also treated with suspicion. Virtually all who had been treated deferentially in the past now were officially scorned as not suited and perhaps even useless to the new society; their supposedly long, clean fingernails were not dirtied by labor of service to the masses. In comparison with Japan, many more of the old authority figures were purged, killed, or had fled, while those left in responsible positions worked under a cloud of suspicion. For a time in the hectic Great Leap Forward the anti-intellectualism intensified, as harbingers of what was to come in the Cultural Revolution could already be seen, but the collapse of China's economy allowed some time for an exhausted society to recover, and leaders who did not share Mao's vision managed for a time to deflect new campaigns aimed at "class struggle."

From the point of view of the struggle against Confucianism, three reasons for the desperate pressures of the Cultural Revolution deserve attention. First, even if they had embraced the same goals, Mao would have faced a battle more difficult than that faced by Occupation reformers in Japan. China remained largely nonmodernized, and its mass Confucianism retained more of its premodern forms associated with self-sufficient village life. Traditional authority in the village had been scarcely touched by the previous half-century of change. Land reform alone was inadequate to combat entrenched lineage relationships, which created a hierarchical web in each of hundreds of thousands of villages across China. China's low literacy rates and urbanization in 1949 left Mao with a very small base from which to select new leaders and with a wide gap between the well-educated and the masses. China's low migration rate to cities and urban jobs left a strong residue of paternalistic family and community authority. The weakness of urban interest groups and the middle class prepared few people for active participation in government. Under these circumstances, it was especially difficult to drop Confucian practices. Moreover, the Chinese communist decision to join the attack on traditional authority figures as feudal to an attack on most modern authority figures as capitalist made it inevitable that destructive forces would overwhelm constructive ones.

Second, while there may be ways to combine socialism with Confucianism, Mao's adoption of the Stalinist approach together with his impatient methods meant that some of China's most valuable traditions were deprecated. To recognize that frustrations stemming from serious problems of incompatibility helped create the climate for the Cultural Revolution is not to say that what resulted actually reduced these incompatibilities. More often than not, it exacerbated the very problems the ideologues claimed to be solving. Instead of expanding egalitarianism based on a universal dedication to principle, China's new policies helped to spread traditional patron-client relations based on illegitimate sources of wealth. Criteria for promotions and monetary rewards became vague, leading to new opportunities for favoritism and currying favor. The educational yearnings and entrepreneurial talents of the Chinese people were more severely suppressed from 1967 to 1977 than at any other time in modern history, after the frustrations of not allowing these important forces to flower sufficiently in the previous decade had helped bring on the tense atmosphere of the mid-1960s.

The third special factor we want to mention in explaining the attack on Confucianism from 1967 to 1976 is that there were many Confucian elements in it. In a curious way, it was a Chinese-style response to Stalinist socialism, which, while staying close to Stalinism's core values, built on aspects of Confucianism incompatible with modernization. The Chinese synthesis took the worst of socialism and the elements of Confucianism least amenable to modernization. This can best be seen in the worldview—a fixed model of human relations not subject to social science reexamination, a belief in the moral authority of the supreme leader not subject to checks and balances, and reliance on supposedly morally upright officials unrestrained by local interest groups. Confucianism incorporated a cosmological myth that fused the human and cosmic order and imparted, in the eyes of those who accepted it (many well-educated Confucian-trained leaders did not), a degree of sacredness to the principles of behavior handed down from generation to generation; failure to maintain the right moral order threatened to create an imbalance in the natural world leading to such disasters as floods and earthquakes. Chinese communism similarly claimed universal knowledge of the laws of human development and a kind of religious certainty supporting its political platform. The resulting conceptualization of leaders as protectors of the faith left little room for legal restraints, checks and balances, local initiative and independence, and objective verification measures to reexamine the effectiveness of programs. Imperial Confucianism, we suggest, pushed Stalinism to an extreme, while the many other parts of the Confucian tradition struggled to survive in a repressive atmosphere. Just as Japanese militarism gained force by building on a part of the Confucian tradition, so too did the Cultural Revolution, but the latter—unlike the former—repudiated the bulk of the tradition.

Mao repudiated the most basic requisites for a revitalization of China's Confucian tradition. By relying on peasant communes and egalitarian means of distribution, he stifled mass Confucianism centered on family enterprise and aspirations for upward mobility; yet he did not succeed in uprooting it. In the villages Mao's alternative organization proved to be a dismal failure. Households continued to rely heavily on their own production from tiny private plots, while dependency on the elder generation for housing and other scarce resources reinforced traditional practices such as patriarchal authority and patrilocal marriage. Mass Confucianism retained most of its vitality in rural China even through two decades when the struggle for survival became the primary preoccupation.

In the urban areas the negative impact on Confucian values was more far-reaching. Japan had tapped three vital elements in its traditions while achieving rapid modernization in the cities. It had relied on (1) entrepreneurship, symbolized by merchant-house Confucianism; (2) bureaucratic orderliness and service, symbolized by samurai Confucianism; and (3) intellectualism and the application of knowledge to changing circumstances, symbolized by reform Confucianism but originally fused with samurai and mass Confucianism. Mao, and like-minded communist leaders, tried to crush entrepreneurial behavior. They disdained bureaucratic experience and methods in favor of impulsive campaigns to stir up enthusiastic participation at grass-roots levels. Moreover, from 1966 to 1977 they conducted an anti-intellectual experiment in education unprecedented in scale. In its essentials, the society that China's communist leaders were building until the end of the 1970s repudiated the very forces of Confucian tradition that might have contributed most to rapid modernization.

China's direct repudiation of tradition was harsher than that in the Soviet Union, but China's traditions are not easily overturned. The Soviets created a more durable system, although one in some ways decidedly incompatible with the needs of a highly modernized society, by relying on bureaucratism (a deeply rooted element of its own tradition) and creating more outlets for people. Vast numbers competed for educational advancement, and ambitious youths in the villages at least could usually look forward to migration to urban jobs. The Chinese communists did not put in place a viable edifice for building a modern society. In desperation after Mao's death, they turned back to Confucian traditions and outward to capitalism.

In both China and Japan the critical reevaluation of Confucian traditions in the postwar era increasingly came from a Marxist standpoint. Anti-"feudalism" in Japan's postwar reforms was led by capitalists who sought to release the energies of the individual and the competitiveness of interest groups within a market economy. After a quick burst of reforms and the shift of attention by Occupation authorities and the Japanese government to stability and economic growth, it was largely the Marxist intellectual community that carried forward the attack on so-called "feudal" elements. Yet there were virtually no policies implementing their criticisms, and gradually public opinion shifted against them.

In the first half of the 1950s, China's reforms won widespread support as a necessary program for modern development, capitalist as well as socialist. Only in 1955, with the sudden decision to collectivize agriculture and nationalize industry, and especially in late 1957, with the anti-rightist campaign and the move toward establishing peasant communes, was the capitalist potentiality of the reforms largely eclipsed. China's repudiation of Confucian traditions was more sweeping verbally, it was more fully implemented through policies, and it was of much longer duration. The most intensive verbal assault actually occurred only in 1973–1975 as part of the campaign against Lin Biao and Confucius. Nevertheless, actual conditions in China, especially in the villages, were not leading to the general displacement of Confucian attitudes by Marxist ones nor even to a stable synthesis of the two. In contrast, rapid modernization and the spontaneous operation of modernizing forces was producing a synthesis in Japan between capitalism and Confucian traditions.

Toward a Synthesis for the Twenty-first Century

Until the 1980s the Japanese were largely content to remain under
the protective umbrella of American military and foreign policy and
the no less protective umbrella of Western social thought. Each was a
holdover from the lack of self-confidence after Japan's defeat in
World War II, although each became identified with a new consensus
on the national interest. Each could readily endure because of two
factors in Japan's external environment that became increasingly
pronounced in the 1980s—the enormous success Japan enjoyed in
selling industrial goods to the West and the deep distrust of the Soviet
Union as an expansionary neighbor and world superpower. Already
in the 1970s Japanese pride was becoming visible in the burgeoning
literature about Japan's distinctive values and organizational methods. Increasingly in the 1980s Japanese doubts about new manifestations of social deviance were reflected in popular efforts to
strengthen moral upbringing. In the late 1980s the combination of
Japan-bashing and protectionist measures in the United States, confronted with an enormous trade deficit blamed largely on Japan, and
disarmament initiatives and reform programs in the Soviet Union,
overwhelmed by a stagnant economy in desperate need of the high
technology and capital that Japan possesses in abundance, was creating new prospects for an independent Japanese stance in the world.
What will Japan stand for intellectually? What image will it create?
To answer these questions we must turn to the revitalized Confucian
traditions in the highly modernized context of contemporary Japan.

Until Deng Xiaoping's rise to power in 1978, China's ideology was
an extreme variation of Stalinist socialism, and its outward thrust economically and culturally was slight. Since 1978 China has developed
an independent approach to reforming socialism and until 1989 an
open-door policy to the world. China's leaders also began to acknowledge the positive side of Confucian traditions. Yet, even as China's
"Four Modernizations" advanced, self-confidence about a new system
of beliefs leading the country away from the nadir of ideological confusion around 1980 was slow to build. The party elite stifled the
search by intellectuals for a replacement for the old dogmatism. After
the crackdown of June 1989, we can observe a vigorous official claim
to spiritual superiority coupled with a rejection of "bourgeois liberalization." The besieged leadership cannot even manage any respectability from a synthesis of socialism and China's own characteristics
based on its past, or any protection from clothing itself in the doctrine of the "new authoritarianism."

The starting point for Confucian-based policies toward the family is the presumption that it must be supported and strengthened even at great cost. Japanese in recent years have shown great concern with signs of family instability—rising divorce rates, cases of violence against parents, and the increasing abandonment of the elderly. Even indicators of change modest by world standards arouse intense concern.

Public opinion in Japan places a lot of pressure on individuals to meet high expectations for serving the family. First, girls and boys are conditioned to value marriage. Illegitimate children are rare. Cohabitation without a marriage license, made difficult by a tight housing market, is uncommon. When the expected age of marriage is reached, relatives and coworkers descend on the individual in force to make sure that action is taken. If a self-selected partner does not quickly materialize, pressure mounts to allow others to arrange meetings designed to lead to marriage. As a result, Japan boasts a high rate of persons married and a high level of conformity in age at marriage (around 25 for women and 28 for men). For the company man and the woman seeking acceptance in the general community, marriage is expected—not only marriage but the careful selection of a mate with prospects of making a stable and successful union as measured by the man's career and the woman's child-rearing aptitude. The divorce rate is rising, but remains well below U.S. or Soviet levels. Parents are especially reluctant to divorce when children might be most affected. In the 1930s Japan claimed to have a superior family system. In the 1980s such claims are more muted, but signs of greater stability than in other industrialized countries do not escape notice.

The mother-child bond is perhaps the single most important factor in modern accounts of Japanese familism. This bond takes shape through close physical proximity in the first years of life with a mother not employed outside of the home. It continues as the "education mama" helps with homework and test preparation at successive rungs on the ladder of schooling. The child is likely to remain in the parental home until at least the time of marriage.

We should also mention that the small-scale family enterprise is a long-standing variant of familism that still retains force. An extraordinary percentage of Japan's work force remains employed in this sector. Government tax and land-use policies protect this bastion of collective family endeavor, as do subsidies to farm households.

Comparisons of U.S., Soviet, and Japanese families point to the possibility that Japan has a superior system. It has fewer instances of illegitimacy, crime, lonely single persons, and other costly and disruptive social problems. Japanese children study harder and develop more responsible attitudes toward the group. American individualist attitudes toward family life and Soviet reliance on collective child-rearing and women doubly burdened are perhaps not capable of producing the same level of diligent, orderly, and knowledgeable citizens as in Japan.

Japanese do not often put on parade the Confucian credits for their present-day familism. They are only now emerging from a period in which it was respectable to look down on terms such as filial piety and ancestor reverence. In intellectual parlance Western individualism still often has the upper hand. Nevertheless, quietly, for the most part, households keep alive many traditions such as the observation of rituals before tablets within the home to honor individual ancestors. Modernization continues to elicit new accommodations. Women are working for more years outside the home. The greying of Japan will create a massive population of elderly persons within two decades. The synthesis of Western and Confucian traditions has by no means reached its final form; yet we can say with confidence that, for at least the next generation, Confucian elements will continue to play a vital part in keeping Japan distinct from the West.

In China, as in Taiwan, the family enterprise is even more common than in Japan. The dynamism of China in the 1980s is largely a reflection of the released energies of farming families and service or repair enterprises that are at their core family activities. Children start as apprentices, at first combining study for school with labor at home, and then become full-fledged contributors in their own right. On the whole, except for employees of large enterprises, the intrusive socialist state has given way to the market-oriented, corporate family. While this was not initially welcomed by many leaders (after June 1989 restrictions were again tightened), Chinese authorities find some solace in the fact that the family unit rather than the unfettered individualism of capitalism has come to the fore. With a watchful eye on the successes of Chinese family firms outside the PRC, China's leaders seem to be, to some degree, reconciled to the family unit as a dynamic force for modernization.

The Chinese state still takes an obtrusive role in protecting the moral environment of the family. It places many barriers before divorce, including the need to win the permission of the work units or community authorities, which may not be granted if it could adversely affect children or if there are other circumstances. Extramarital affairs and potential illegitimacy are matters that may lead to public rebuke, forced abortions, and even criminal proceedings. As family enterprises grow in size, they may also become the object of predatory or redistributive demands by local communist authorities.

We conclude that the government is interceding to keep state leverage over the family (which still may take the form of interference, in violation of guarantees declared in Beijing) and to strengthen the family's hold over the individual. In the 1980s the former interference declined sharply, while the latter has perhaps become less needed, since the family's own assets are now much greater.

China's "socialist spiritual civilization," as widely discussed in the 1980s, embraces the Chinese family as something almost sacred. The family emerges as the bulwark in the defense against "spiritual pollution"—sexual promiscuity, pornography, criminal greed, and the like. In this worldview, the enemy is bourgeois liberalization, which is equated with a spiritual wasteland and anarchy. The family must stand firm against ill winds from the West. In place of the old ideal of equality, one increasingly finds a Confucian-like appeal for respecting the moral authority of the leadership and its designated representatives. In place of the long-venerated bimodal emphasis on families below and bureaucracy plus scholar-official elite above, we find a new bipolarity in the family and the communist party elite— with the latter trying to gain some respect after falling into disrepute. This combination, in effect, sweeps aside some of the collectives that gained great control over individual lives in the mid-1950s and kept this control until the 1980s. Nevertheless, a desperate leadership is responding to the worldwide collapse of socialism by clinging to various forms of collectivism.

For some time to come it will be difficult to determine whether the basic framework of socialism—even in its "primary stage" of development—and the heritage of Confucianism can be combined for stable and rapid modernization. There now seems to be no uncertainty concerning the effectiveness of early reforms for family entrepreneurship and basic educational training, but there is still great uncertainty about political reform as it affects large-scale production, academic ingenuity, and continuous reform dynamism in all spheres. China's reliance on Communist Party leadership has, much more than the imperial bureaucracy of scholar-officials, led to overcentralization. As modernization continues, the Communist Party threatens to stifle the rising tide of individual diversity and interest-group formation. The intrusive socialist orientation, prior to the advent of the responsibility system, placed great strain on family functions. Simply easing that strain does not suffice, as modernization (whether capitalist or socialist) leads to the narrowing and refocusing of family ties on love relations and the shifting of group consciousness away from community identity to voluntary interest groups.

Wong Siu-lun contrasts the organization men of Japan with the family-oriented entrepreneurs of Hong Kong and other Chinese areas. Chinese would much prefer to become "the owner-manager of a small firm than the senior executive of a large corporation."[16] From early times the Chinese had been taught to set their sights on the highest status, while Japanese had learned through their samurai and merchant-house traditions to serve an organization and make gains appropriate to their status as well as their ability. The resulting centrifugal force in China leads firms to refrain from cooperation, and employees who are not bound by hierarchical family ties—even brothers, in many cases—to strike out on their own. Employers forge personalized ties with their workers to try to counter this tendency. In China in the 1980s this kind of paternalism based on personal ties was becoming widespread in private business, but a different kind of paternalism, described by Andrew Walder in his 1986 book, has kept the Communist Party active in forging dependency relations based on political patronage.[17] Can the two types be reconciled, or is China's dynamism to be limited largely to the small-scale firms in which the family is less encumbered by the party?

The first academic forum on Chinese cultural history in the People's Republic occurred in 1982. It was followed in 1986 by the first international forum. As the description of the latter in *Social Sciences in China* noted, a "cultural fever" is mounting in China. Scholars are rethinking China's traditional culture, responding to rapid changes and ideological perplexity inside China and to the search in Hong Kong, Taiwan, and elsewhere for the roots of an industrial civilization of the oriental type. The Chinese review article, like others in the mid-1980s on the subject of Confucian thought, offers a mixed assessment. On the negative side, it finds in the heritage (1) the rule of rites but not rights—while absolute subordination and fulfillment of obligations was expected, as in filial piety and loyalty, there were no terms for democracy or freedom; and (2) the danger of the revival of feudal practices in conflict with modernization and with Marxism-Leninism. On the positive side, the PRC article finds in the Confucian heritage (1) a solid foundation for modern needs such as patriotism, self-cultivation, renovation of one's family, and striving to manage the country well; and (2) an alternative to Western self-centeredness in a humanistic tradition of mutual respect and affinity with the fam-

---

[16] Wong Siu-lun, "Modernization and Chinese Culture in Hong Kong," *The China Quarterly* 106 (June 1986), pp. 306–25.

[17] Andrew G. Walder, *Communist Neo-Traditionalism: Work and Authority in Chinese Industry* (Berkeley: University of California Press, 1986), pp. 246–49.

ily and state.[18] The article makes clear that opinions on the tradition remain divided. The affirmative side holds it up as useful to China's needs. It disagrees with the once accepted analysis of Lu Xun that Confucianism produced a mentality of servility. Chinese largely agree now that, unlike 1900, the old civilization is not much of an obstruction to modernization. New techniques of production are already well established in China and, moreover, Japan's record shows that there need be no fear of total Westernization.

The dual approach to Confucian thought is also clearly revealed in a 1985 article that argues that modern China must completely disassociate itself from the Confucius who was a loyal supporter of the feudal social order, which became stagnant for a long time, and should embrace the Confucius who was a great and learned thinker, stressed humanism, and treated man as capable of resolving his own fate through a joint effort of the progressive intelligentsia and the working people.[19] A third article in 1986 made a clear linkage between the need for a spiritual civilization in China to accompany the Four Modernizations and the need to understand and develop China's traditional cultural strengths. In other words, socialist culture cannot reject all traditional culture. In Confucianism it can find creativity as well as conservatism.[20] With rethinking of this sort now popular in China, we can anticipate that not only through pragmatic policies favorable to family vitality but also through an ideological synthesis between Marxism-Leninism and Confucianism, China will become noted for its blend of two approaches. Following the campaign against bourgeois liberalization in 1987 and even more the rejection of moderation in 1989, the alternative ideological blend of socialism and Western liberalism seemed to be a more distant prospect. Yet, the complaints about the insufficiency of democracy in China's past suggest that the awareness of economic efficiency and social vitality in capitalist countries will eventually work in favor of a three-way synthesis or a total rejection of socialism.

Both Chinese and Japanese leaders were worrying in the 1980s about a loss of values among youth. They are calling for educational reform with a stress on moral training. In Japan this represents a sharp departure from the generally inconspicuous role of didactic

[18] Wang He, "Traditional Culture and Modernization: A Review of the General Situation of Cultural Studies in China in Recent Years," *Social Sciences in China*, vol. 7, no. 4 (December 1986), pp. 9–30.

[19] Zhen Ru, " 'Kongci ping zhuan' dui Kongci tichu xin jianjie," *Liaowang*, Nov. 25, 1985, p. 33.

[20] Xu Minhe, "Zhongguo xuezhe zhongxin sikao quantong wenhua," *Liaowang*, Feb. 10, 1986, pp. 23–24.

upbringing in the public realm since the postwar reforms, while in China it is a compromise after the Maoist reliance on political education had been discredited. Both countries seek in this way to counteract excessive materialism and to cultivate a willingness to dedicate oneself through hard work and sincere belief to socially approved goals. This path reminds us of the Confucian appeal to cultivate one's mind, to set one's inner self in order, and to learn high moral principles in order to put them into practice. While the focus on individual self-examination and dedication had become a popular theme in late imperial China, its actual application was far greater in Japan, where the samurai spirit of total commitment was embodied in organizations. The Japanese concept of seishin, although seen in the immediate postwar era as undemocratic, remains an ideal, combining such traits as loyalty, discipline, esprit de corps, frugality, clearing one's mind of distractions, and working to exhaustion. Its rejection of selfishness and egotism and its acceptance of authority clearly deviate from Western individualism.[21] From this perspective, life appears as a series of battles (one's weapon is now the pen or the computer and one's battlefield is the examination room or the office), and the preparation and mental state of the combatant largely decides the outcome.

China's moral education remains in disarray in the 1980s even as its premier students become more successful in mastering modern knowledge. The leadership has retained many outdated and simplistic communist teachings that seem to have little relevance to current policies. The instructors are often holdovers from the Maoist era. Only haltingly has a new fusion of values been permitted to reach the classroom. Distracted by decades of blatant contradictions between proclaimed values and reality and by the absence of opportunity to realize the fruits of their labor, the Chinese will not easily rebuild a value system that extends beyond family-oriented aspirations. It is also unlikely that they will embrace Western individualism in large numbers. In one form or another, they will share the Japanese view that the superiority of their civilization lies in the relationship of individuals to each other and to their society. The ideal relationship implies a degree of loyalty, filial piety, family solidarity, and suppression of individuality that is uncommon in the West. Whereas China's school teachings and public institutions in the mid-1970s seemed largely Stalinist, by the mid-1980s the personal relationships were be-

---

[21] Robert Frager and Thomas P. Rohlen, "The Future of a Tradition: Japanese Spirit in the 1980s," in *Japan: The Paradox of Progress*, ed. Lewis Austin (New Haven: Yale University Press, 1976), pp. 255–78.

coming traditionally Chinese. Yet, the intrusion of lingering Stalinism could not but arouse sympathy, especially in the middle class, for Western democratic values.

In the workplace we find a more personalized pattern of relationships in East Asia than in the West. The model of the paternalistic firm has become predominant among large-scale firms in Japan only after World War II, although its roots and social predispositions can be found much earlier. The Chinese application of the Soviet model broke down into relations of personal subordination. Although with the expansion of performance-based material incentives in the 1980s one reason for cultivating contacts has declined, there is still no impersonal labor market that could give a big boost to Western-type labor relations. Observers have rightly contrasted the Western ideal of impersonality, individual calculation of self-interest, and management by contract to the Eastern ideals of human emotional bonds, regard for group harmony, and management by status or by consensus. The gap is narrowing, but will likely remain for a long time.

CONCLUSIONS

Japan's greater success in modernization can be attributed partially to its greater ability to harness Confucian traditions to modern needs. Compared with China, it was less critical of the traditions and, except for short intervals, consciously adopted policies to reinforce them. Japan's ability to harness Confucian values may be traced to the different character of Confucianism in the two countries, as seen in the comparison of five types of Confucianism in this chapter. Various explanations can be offered for this difference.

One explanation may be the timing and suddenness of Confucianization in premodern times. The later its adoption, the more distant its practices from native customs, the more social engineering required in its dissemination for mass usage, the more administrative measures resorted to in its implementation, the more Confucianism became associated with an intensely, impersonally administered system. In nineteenth-century Japan, Confucianism represented a dynamic force finding new application to the current needs of the society.

A second explanation may be the extent to which Confucianism combined with an indigenous and increasingly military organization. The more militarized the setting, the more Confucian relations were conceived in terms of strict hierarchical controls. Hideyoshi and the Tokugawa shoguns who followed fostered a Confucian system concerned with clear lines of authority, behavior according to fixed status, and collective community responsibility. Some of these results may also be attributed to the pre-Confucian social structure; in Japan, village-based Shintoism of the seventh century A.D. supplied a more ascriptive setting than the already partially urbanized and literate China, in which land had already become a market commodity when Confucius and his disciples expounded their views 1000–1200 years earlier. Along with this backwardness, Japanese were exclusively oriented toward local ties. They seemed to be unable to accept universal philosophies; after Confucianism was introduced as part of a large cultural package, it was soon particularized.

Geographical factors account for some differences in the interpretation of Confucian values in each country. Although China's central bureaucracy is famous for its early professionalism, it in fact remained small (and in per capita terms grew smaller) relative to the vast population governed and extended its reach into an enormous number of local areas largely through nonbureaucratic means. The smaller scale of Japan and the possibility of forgoing a powerful central or regional government for a long time because of the unlikelihood of foreign invasion led to a competition among bureaucratizing forces scattered in local areas around the country and then to a re-Confucianization to bolster the newly established center and maintain the social order that had been built largely from the bottom up.

Another factor enabling Japan to harness Confucianism quickly was the early success of the Meiji Restoration and the subsequent reform program. A stable environment with a centralized government was quickly established, while the status of Confucianism was soon divorced from concerns of social-class conflict and national independence. Traditions of control and coordination were reinterpreted to promote imperial authority, nationalism, and self-sacrifice for family, community, and state. This setting permitted Confucian values in favor of education, hard work, and public service to operate with few restrictions. Capitalism in its liberal interpretation, which entered Japan with the Meiji reforms, accentuated concerns that helped to balance traditional values of Japanese Confucianism. The value of equal opportunity worked against the tradition of ascriptive social classes, in which position at birth had often taken precedence over ability. The value of individualism limited the impact of collective responsibility. Above all, widespread reliance on market mechanisms reduced the scope of tight administrative controls prevalent in the Tokugawa era. The depersonalized, intensely administered Japanese Confucian tradition combined with the individualistic, market-oriented liberal tradition to produce a combination of forces that proved to be favorable for modernization in a latecomer seeking through state initiative to catch up to already modernized countries. Yet, taking advantage of new means for building state authority and controlling opponents, Japan turned toward militarism and—together with postwar Korea and cases of Chinese capitalism—showed the potential danger of the authoritarian side of the Confucian tradition for democratic development.

China's more personalized Confucian traditions initially combined with capitalism in a different manner. Inadequate, personalized, or corrupt administration often stifled entrepreneurship. Personalized, factional ties were not easily redirected from warlordism or, on a smaller scale, self-interest harmful to community needs. Lacking the stability of the Meiji political order, China found that liberal values in the context of a nonmodernized society without much of a middle class could not solve the problem of state-building or overcome factionalism. Attitudes favorable to education, public service, and family firms contributed to pockets or spurts of modernization, but it was only after problems of control and depersonalization were resolved that a generally supportive environment materialized. The Japanese occupation in Taiwan, British rule in Hong Kong, and American postwar aid all played some positive role in building institutions to this end. Even after a dosage of state-centered development or colonialism, the personalized character of the Confucian tradition remains strong. Instead of, or in addition to, contractual relationships, *guanxi* (personal ties relying heavily on kinship bonds) are used to promote economic transactions. In the world of politics, too, ties that date back to school connections, common place of origin, or early socialization in an organization are carefully cultivated. In Kuomintang China, the state was often ineffectual in establishing counterweights through an efficient bureaucracy, but in Kuomintang-led Taiwan and in Hong Kong and Singapore, the family firm has prospered, with balance coming from the colonial tradition of state regulation and the liberal tradition of sanctity for the market. The Meiji reforms are the factor that accomplished for Japan what took many decades to achieve in China.

Together these explanations may help account for the different intensity of the five types of Confucianism discussed in this chapter. Whatever the historical explanation, the different character of Confucianism at the imperial, elite, and merchant levels gave Japan a different and, we believe, superior basis for modernization.

Confucian traditions are making a comeback across East Asia in the final decades of the twentieth century. In Japan, because the periods of decline had been brief and largely under the control of reformers with a strong government mandate, the adaptation of Confucian values to modern needs has occurred over a long period. Japan has a mature synthesis of Confucian approaches to family, education, the work community, and the state applicable to a highly modernized society. In South Korea, Taiwan, and Hong Kong (to the extent its development remains independent), where modernization is still recent and political transitions are in progress, we can anticipate more adaptations of tradition. Even so, the basic shape of the future already seems clear. In the People's Republic the alliance between Confucianism and socialism is still at an early stage; after lengthy periods of decline of Confucianism, the rebuilding process may be arduous and time-consuming. It is too early to conclude that socialism can combine with Confucianism to form a stable foundation for rapid modernization. The result in China may be the displacement of socialism or a substantial infusion of liberalism, leading to convergence with other East Asian countries. Leaders opposed to either outcome may use "neo-authoritarianism" drawing on elements of Confucianism to buttress "proletarian dictatorship."

In the next few decades we expect two contradictory trends to shape the continued adaptation of Confucian values and behavior. On the one hand, internationalization will continue at an accelerated pace and work to break down national distinctiveness. As people become more educated, urbanized, and informed about the world, they lose much of their distinctiveness. Through multinational firms and satellite transmissions, regional differences among modernized countries will lose much of their meaning. Japan's homogeneity and deeply rooted "societal exclusionism" will continue to be a buffer as it absorbs much from the rest of the world, but Japan is internationalizing rapidly in most respects, and the younger generation is already abandoning many traditions. Even greater leveling effects from internationalization may be expected in China because the gap between its largely rural and meagerly educated population and the modernized peoples of the world remains enormous. There is no escaping the conclusion that the advancing force of internationalization will play a role along with modernization in continued de-Confucianization.

On the other hand, a self-confident East Asia is likely to strengthen its self-image as a Confucian region and separate countries with advantageous national traditions. We have yet to see the peak of self-conscious pride and its dissemination through moral education and a budding self-congratulatory ideology. As tensions continue to mount with trading partners in other regions, and domestic problems become more serious owing to modernization and other factors, the urge to bolster the national self-image will grow. Also, growing international consciousness of the regional tradition will have a feedback effect. Losing ground to internationalization, Confucianism will gain some ground back and take on new forms through self-consciousness.

In the emerging period of modern transformation, the alternating cycle of decline and revival of Confucianism is likely to be broken. In place of war and revolution, rapid modernization will set the tone for popular awareness. Governments will become articulate in identifying themselves with the growing pride in the past. Just as socialism and liberalism are controversial labels that are widely discussed, often misunderstood, and distorted for political ends, the Confucian label for East Asia will undoubtedly be drawn anew into similar dispute.

Chapter 5

PERCEPTIONS OF CONFUCIANISM IN TWENTIETH-CENTURY KOREA

MICHAEL ROBINSON

SINCE 1900, Korea has undergone a fundamental reordering of its political and social system. In spite of this, observers of contemporary Korea continually point to the importance of the Confucian tradition while explaining the peculiarities of political patterns and values as well as social organization. While differing in intensity, Korean attitudes toward political and social authority, interpersonal relations, social mobility, and education all remain informed by Confucian values. As previous chapters have made clear, Confucianism as a body of political, social, and quasi-religious ideas has been subject to a diverse array of interpretations and applications in East Asia. Nevertheless, these ideas also provided a substantial source of continuity among the different East Asian societies. It is not surprising, therefore, to find Confucian ideas and values alive and well in twentieth-century Korea.

Confucianism continues to influence modern Korean society, but its impact is very different from that in the past. Moreover, since 1900 the legitimacy of Confucianism has been challenged by Westernized intellectuals, nationalist iconoclasts, and social revolutionaries alike. Thus, it is important not only to understand where the remnants of the Confucian tradition reside, but also to know how Koreans themselves have perceived Confucianism in this century, and what effect this has had, if any, on these traditional values. Confucianism as an organized political/cultural orthodoxy has disappeared in modern Korea. Although it no longer dominates Korean political and social life as a prescriptive orthodoxy, it has gone underground and continues to covertly shape behavior and social organization in Korea. In this sense, the Korean Confucian tradition has proved remarkably resilient.

In order to focus our discussion, some definitions are necessary. For the purposes of this paper we will divide Confucianism into political and social values. Confucianism as a political system envisioned a harmonious state in which monarchical authority was articulated through civil bureaucrats governing society. This concept legitimated kingly authority, but it also stressed, at least in theory, the rule of virtuous men and the importance of selecting officials on the basis of merit. Confucian ideologues conceived of a hierarchical society in which authority was tempered by benevolence downward and reciprocal loyalty and submissiveness to the state from below. Politics, therefore, were thought to form a part of a universal social system regulated by certain values and harmonized by adherence to well-defined norms.

It followed that social values in Confucianism would be closely related to its political goals of harmony. This makes it difficult to separate politics and society. Confucian social values revolve around the idea of the five primary social relations; three of the five relations are familial—father-son, husband-wife, and elder and younger brother. Indeed, the emphasis on proper family relations mirrored the ideal of benevolent authority and harmony in the political realm. If families were stable, patriarchal authority upheld, and proper relations between generations and sexes maintained, then society at large would be harmonized. Therefore, the Confucian value system and its emphasis on upholding ceremony developed as a means to regulate and maintain the key relationships that underlie social order and political stability.

Confucianism in Korea supported key institutions in the political and social spheres.[1] One example of a Confucian-inspired institution was the censorate. While the office of the Censorate was not new to Korea, it assumed great importance during the Yi dynasty. The Censorate was charged with monitoring the behavior of the monarch and bureaucrats. Such an office used the traditional right of remonstrance to ensure adherence to Confucian norms in both personal and official conduct. Another institution closely tied to Confucian values was the civil service examinations. With its aim to select officials on the basis of merit, the state civil examinations became a prime avenue of social mobility in Yi dynasty Korea. Both state and private schools developed as a means of preparing students for the examinations and became an important transmitter of Confucian values in society.[2]

[1] Chai-sik Chung, "Chŏng Tojŏn: 'Architect' of Yi Dynasty Government and Ideology," in *The Rise of Neo-Confucianism in Korea*, ed. Wm. Theodore de Bary and JaHyun Kim Haboush (New York: Columbia University Press, 1985), pp. 59–88.

[2] For a detailed discussion of the Korean civil examinations see Ch'oe Yong-ho, "The Civil Examinations and the Social Structure in Early Yi Dynasty Korea: 1392–1600" (Ph.D. diss., University of Chicago, 1971). Also: Edward Wagner, "The Ladder of Success in Yi Dynasty Korea," *Occasional Papers on Korea* 1 (1974): 1–8.

Ancestor worship and family law supported key Confucian values in society at large. By the late nineteenth century these values, originally the preserve of elites, had been accepted by all levels of society. As Professor Haboush has pointed out in Chapter 2, in the eighteenth and nineteenth centuries Korea was a Confucianized society, as measured by the diffusion of these norms. The general effect was to weaken the position of women, strengthen patriarchal authority in the family, and entrench aristocratic privilege in government.

Confucianization, however, did not mean that Korean society became a copy of China. Particularly with regard to politics and the recruitment of officials, Koreans adapted Confucian principles to indigenous patterns. Confucianism contains within its canon contradictory impulses that support centralization of political power around a merit-based bureaucracy while also affirming ascriptive class distinctions in society. During the Yi dynasty, these contradictions were maintained by the development of an aristocratic/bureaucratic hybrid system that preserved certain ascriptive privileges while concurrently recruiting officials on the basis of merit through examinations.[3] Moreover, Korea's relative isolation, the long period of peace and concomitant atrophy of its military institutions, and the absence of a strong commercial class preserved this system up to the late nineteenth century.

The system was stable, but it was also highly resistant to change. The forces that made up the Yi political system were counterpoised in a finely tuned mechanism of checks and balances. Although the system was centralized, the Yi monarch had little of the transcendent power of the Chinese emperor. A relatively closed pool of aristocratic lineages dominated official posts in the central bureaucracy, but the maintenance of this closed elite did not develop regional political autonomy.[4] Thus Korea faced the multiple threats of the late nineteenth century unable to cope with either the scope or pace of change demanded by imperialist-power politics.

CONFUCIANISM AND THE LATE NINETEENTH-CENTURY CRISIS

The political crisis of the late nineteenth century that ultimately toppled the Yi system in 1910 signaled a significant change in the fortunes of Confucianism in Korea, the bedrock of politics and society. The intrusion of Western commercial and military power after 1840

[3] James B. Palais, "Confucianism and the Aristocratic/Bureaucratic Balance in Korea," *Harvard Journal of Asiatic Studies* 44, pt. 2 (1984): 427–66.

[4] James B. Palais, *Politics and Policy in Traditional Korea* (Cambridge, Mass.: Harvard University Press, 1975), pp. 13–18.

into China and, later, Japan was relatively slow to affect Korea. Ultimately, however, Korea was forced to recognize the changing world order. After the signing of the Kanghwa treaty with Japan in 1876, the failing Yi dynasty was buffeted by the increasingly acrimonious competition of imperialist powers in East Asia.

The traditionalist response to the mid-nineteenth-century crisis was to shore up the system. Confucian reform philosophy posited that social and political malaise were products of nonadherence to the Way; hence, reaffirming the state orthodoxy and isolating Korea from corrosive heterodox foreign values were seen as positive steps toward preserving society. After the opening of Korea in 1876, however, it became increasingly difficult to accomplish this, as the Yi state demonstrated neither the will nor the power to maintain its autonomy. In the 1880s, under the influence of Meiji Japan, progressives began to discuss the wholesale reform of Korean political institutions and social practices; for the first time, they questioned the appropriateness of Confucian ideology in the modern world.[5]

With regard to key political values within the Confucian tradition, the tentative iconoclasm of the early progressives turned to a torrent of criticism with the rise of Korean nationalism after 1900. Rejecting the universalism of Confucian political theory, nationalists focused on how to develop state power, politically and economically. In Korea's case, the particularistic imperatives of nationalism precipitated an attack on Confucianism's external Chinese origins. Despite the fact that Confucian precepts had been a part of the Korean intellectual tradition for over a millennium and had become thoroughly Koreanized, nationalists blamed the plight of the failing Yi political system on its excessive veneration of a foreign cultural system.[6]

Beginning with the Independence Club (1896–98), the issue of Confucianism as an alien—hence bad—tradition gained currency among nationalist modernizers.[7] The principle of *sadae* (serving the great), an idea that had been used for centuries to describe Korea's relationship with China, was excoriated as an affront to Korea's national independence and sovereignty.[8] Nationalists wanted to sepa-

[5] Martina Deuchler, *Confucian Gentlemen and Barbarian Envoys* (Seattle and London: University of Washington Press, 1977), pp. 151–52.

[6] Sin Il-ch'ŏl, *Sin Ch'ae-ho ŭi yŏksa sasang yŏn'gu* (Studies on the historical thought of Sin Ch'ae-ho) (Seoul: Koryŏ taehakkyo ch'ulp'anbu, 1981), pp. 56–86.

[7] Vipan Chandra, *Imperialism, Resistance, and Reform in Late Nineteenth-Century Korea: Enlightenment and the Independence Club* (Berkeley, Calif.: Institute of East Asian Studies, 1988), pp. 126–48.

[8] Michael Robinson, "Nationalism and the Korean Tradition 1896–1920: Iconoclasm, Reform, and National Identity," *Korean Studies* 10 (1986): 35–53.

rate their vision of a modern, autonomous (culturally and politically) Korea from the Yi dynasty's cultural and political dependence/subservience to an outmoded and decadent universal order centered in China.

It is difficult to separate political and social aspects of Confucianism within this debate. This is because early twentieth-century reformers had to grapple with an integrated system of thought that resisted compartmentalization. Early nationalist critics of the Confucian tradition were forced to make a totalistic assault in order to clear the way for new institutions and values upon which to ground a modern Korean nation. Therefore, it is obvious why the *sadae* issue became *cause célèbre* at the time.

Transitional intellectuals (classically trained, yet active in early twentieth-century progressive causes) such as Chang Chi-yŏn, Pak Ŭn-sik, and Sin Ch'ae-ho were at the front of the *sadae* debate. Chang, classically trained and well respected in conservative circles, reexamined the Korean and Chinese classics of Confucianism in light of Social Darwinist principles. Translating the works of Liang Ch'i-ch'ao, Chang offered a compromise position in the *sadae* debate. At the very least, room for new ideas, new concepts of social organization and behavior, had to be found, according to Chang.[9] The consequences of inaction were dire. Indeed, in the 1900–1910 period, when Chang was writing, the Yi dynasty was in its death throes.

Sin Ch'ae-ho, influential intellectual, journalist, and historian, attacked what he considered the Confucian political tradition's corrosive influence on Korean national identity. The Yi dynasty's adoption of Confucianism as state orthodoxy had inhibited the development of a strong national identity. Supported as it was by Confucian ritual that affirmed Korea's subordinate status, obeisance to the Chinese, no matter how important in *realpolitik* terms, had bred a weak Korean identification with the nation.[10] Sin's early journalism pounded away at this theme; he believed that the nation could survive only if its people were reconnected with its national history and culture, both obscured by 500 years of excessive veneration of the alien Confucian tradition.

The reaction of nationalists to the issue of *sadae* was certainly self-serving, and it overemphasized the causal role of Confucianism in the declining fortunes of the traditional Korean political system. Nevertheless, modern nationalist reformers linked the failure of the Yi po-

[9] Sin Yong-ha, "Chu Si-kyŏng ŭi kyoyuk sasang e taehayŏ" (The patriotic enlightenment thought of Chu Si-kyŏng), *Han'guk hakbo* 1, pt. 1 (Fall 1975): 50–75.

[10] For Sin Ch'ae-ho's early journalistic pieces stressing this theme, see *Tanjae Sin Ch'ae-ho chŏnjip* (Collected works of Sin Ch'ae-ho) (Seoul: Ulso munhwasa, 1972).

litical system to its failure to meet the late nineteenth-century crisis. According to this general critique, a *sadae* mentality weakened the legitimacy of the Korean monarch, thereby circumscribing his authority. In retrospect, the weakness of central authority was more a product of indigenous political patterns than it was an outgrowth of strict obeisance to Confucian norms. In the early twentieth century, nationalist intellectuals also began a tradition that endures to the present—that is, they asserted that Confucianism, as defined by their generalized usage, was a barrier to modernization. Without rejecting Confucianism, so some argued, Korea could never hope to become modern.[11] Ironically, this facile thinking was based on a very Confucian style of reform thought that insisted on reforming men's thought as a fundamental precondition to broader social change.

The general perception among progressive intellectuals that Confucianism represented a barrier to modernization caused many to reject Confucian learning as the basis of Korea's educational curriculum. For centuries, ambitious students had crammed for rigorous state examinations based on the Confucian classics. Mastery of the classics was the sine qua non for success on the examinations and, by extension, an official career. Although over time the examinations became less important, families wishing to rise socially or maintain political prominence continued to educate their sons according to the Confucian canon. The abolition of the state examinations in 1895 precipitated a revolution in education. New schools advertised Western languages, science, philosophy, and mathematics as the "new learning." After 1900, the Confucian classics increasingly became the subject of specialized scholarly study. With the demise of the state examinations and transformation of the state- and private-school curriculum, the burden of transmitting Confucian precepts and knowledge of the classics fell to private tutors of families interested in maintaining high traditional standards. Formal study of Confucianism was decisively separated from official career, heretofore the main vocational aspiration of the Korean elite.

Although Confucianism no longer defined education in twentieth-century Korea, it continued to influence the style and self-image of the intellectual elite. The Confucian tradition in Korea, with its decidedly humanistic bias, continued to influence students to choose major courses of study in history, politics, law, and literature while at the same time hypocritically decrying the perceived anti-science, anti-technology obscurantism of the classical Confucian curriculum. Long

---

[11] Yi Kwang-su, "Minjok kaejoron" (Treatise on the reconstruction of the nation), *Kaebyŏk* 5 (May 1922): 18–72.

after the demise of the Yi dynasty, students eschewed technical studies for the liberal arts. In the early 1920s, Korean nationalists mounted a massive nationwide campaign to raise money for a national university. The master plan for the university called first for the creation of a liberal arts college, and only if the second and third phases of fund-raising were successful would a medical school and engineering school be established.[12]

Western learning became the core of the curriculum, but well-rounded men of letters continued to define cultivation and refinement. Knowledge of Japanese or a Western language replaced fluency in classical Chinese as a "requisite" skill of the well-educated man. Knowledge of Western books, authors, history, and political theory in whatever depth helped create the illusion of cosmopolitanism. What had changed was the content of what defined the cultivated man, not the reverence for learning and cultivation nor the belief that these attributes marked men for social status and political leadership.

While much of the early twentieth-century critique focused on the enervation of Korean politics caused by excessive adherence to Confucian values, nationalist intellectuals also attacked the Confucian social system. This critique was aimed at the Confucian conception of human relations as well as the ritual observances that perpetuated these values. At the core of the assault was a belief that Confucianism, with its reliance on hierarchical and male-dominated relationships, imprisoned individual will and stifled creativity. Convinced that individual freedom was an important component of Western social dynamism, Westernized intellectuals viewed the Confucian insistence on the hierarchy of generations, the absolute authority of the father, and the particular evil of arranged marriage as special forms of social tyranny. Early modern novels presented these themes to an avid and growing readership among the literate middle class.[13] Some felt that liberating individuals from the confining web of familial and generational obligation was an important step toward reinvigorating Korean society. Although Confucian social relations were based on reciprocal benevolence downward and obedience upward, progressives charged that the inherent authoritarianism of the Confucian social scheme was antithetical to the creation of a society of free and dynamic individuals.

Just as progressive critics of Confucianism decried the authority of

[12] Michael Robinson, *Cultural Nationalism in Colonial Korea, 1920–1925* (Seattle and London: University of Washington Press, 1989), pp. 82–92.

[13] Kim Yun-sik, *Yi Kwang-su wa kŭ ŭi sidae* (Yi Kwang-su and his times) (Seoul: Han'gilsa, 1986), pp. 528–70.

father over son, they lashed out at the unequal treatment of women in the Confucian tradition. The position of women in Korean society had gradually deteriorated after the adoption of Neo-Confucianism as state orthodoxy and the basis for family law at the beginning of the Yi dynasty. Critics pointed to the subordination of wives to husbands, daughters to all men in the family, the loss of inheritance rights, inequitable marriage laws, and unequal treatment in genealogical records (*chokbo*) as proof of the sexual inequality fostered by the Confucian tradition.[14] Certainly, Confucian law supported patriarchy and the general subordination of women in Korean society, but it should not have been singled out as the only source. Nevertheless, early feminists and other supporters of women's rights focused on well-known Confucian precepts as the main underpinning for sexual inequality. More positive sources for the reexamination of the position of women in Korean society came from the spread of the Tonghak (Eastern Learning) faith, a native religion of mid-nineteenth-century origins, and Christianity. Both religions stressed equality for the sexes in worship. When combined with the attack of Westernized elites, the attitudes of the new religions in Korea helped to challenge the traditional position of women.[15]

Confucian ritual also came under attack. In particular, ancestor worship was singled out as a pernicious and wasteful custom. In terms of human relations, ancestor worship affirmed the dominance of the older generation over youth. Moreover, to many modernizers it also symbolized an unhealthy attachment to the past. Finally, it was considered a purely wasteful custom in economic terms. In attacking ancestor worship, progressives hit Confucianism at its heart. Filial piety is perhaps the cardinal principle of the entire Confucian social system. Ancestor worship and its ritual socialized people to the natural hierarchy of age, patriarchal authority, the primacy of the eldest son, and—by excluding women—the proper roles for the sexes.[16] Modernizers, therefore, cut to the heart of the tradition by attacking these values as wasteful, backward-looking, authoritarian, and superstitious.[17]

[14] Martina Deuchler, "The Tradition: Women During the Yi Dynasty," in *Virtues in Conflict: Women in Traditional Korea Society*, ed. Sandra Mattielli, Laurel Kendall, *et al.* (Seoul: Royal Asiatic Society, 1977), pp. 1–48.

[15] Donald Clark, *Christianity in Korea* (New York and London: University Press of America, 1987).

[16] Roger Janelli and Dawnhee Yim Janelli, *Ancestor Worship and Korean Society* (Stanford: Stanford University Press, 1982), pp. 61–65.

[17] Ch'oe Hyŏn-pae, *Chosŏn Kaengsaeng ŭi do* (A Way for the rebirth of Korea) (1926; rept. Seoul: Chŏng'ŭmsa, 1962).

Confucianism and the Japanese Occupation

It is clear that by the fall of the Yi dynasty in 1910 Confucian ideas had already been under assault for several decades. In the period of Japanese rule (1910–45), the general critique of Confucianism was sustained and broadened. During the period of Japanese occupation, intellectuals—both nationalist and social revolutionary—continued, rather unfairly, the general attack by equating Confucianism with the entire political and social tradition of the Yi dynasty. Since Korea had fallen under Japanese colonial rule, this Confucian tradition had become a scapegoat for the political malaise that had brought Korea down. The linking of Confucianism to the general political fortunes of the nation found its ultimate expression in a very influential publication that has set the tone for perceptions of Confucianism in Korea up to the present day.

Hyŏn Sang-yun's *History of Korean Confucianism* (Chosŏn yuhaksa), published in 1949, crystalized the general critique of Confucianism begun in the late nineteenth century and sustained through the Japanese occupation. The product of a lifetime of scholarship, Hyŏn's history linked Confucian thought to the political enervation of the Yi dynasty and the tragedy of the Japanese occupation. His analysis was decidedly influenced by his own career as a nationalist politician and influential educator before 1945, and the publication of his magnum opus after liberation influenced an entire generation of Korean intellectuals.[18] This history, in addition to being a study of Korean Confucian thought, was also an attempt to assess the relevance of Confucian ideas for contemporary Korean politics and society. Therefore, Hyŏn attempted to assess the "good and evil" aspects of Confucianism with a mind to preserving the good and expunging the bad. He listed the beneficial influences of the Confucian tradition: industry of men of virtue, high regard for virtue and humaneness, and respect for law. His list of pernicious elements included envy (veneration of China), factionalism, clanism, class conflict, literary effeminacy, disparagement of commerce, reverence for titles, and reverence for the past.

A cursory glance at Hyŏn's list of pernicious elements is sufficient to determine that he has overstated his case. Veneration of China (*sadae*) was hardly a requisite aspect of the Confucian tradition. That Confucianism became the basis of a universal culture that spread throughout East Asia did not mean that it required obeisance to

---

[18] Hyŏn Sang-yun, *Chosŏn yuhaksa* (A history of Korean Confucianism) (Seoul: Minjung sŏgwan, 1949).

China politically. In fact, it was not Confucian ideas but power politics, geographical proximity, and a long tradition of cultural borrowing that had encouraged Korea's veneration of China. Moreover, factionalism was also difficult to interpret as an evil of Confucianism. The factional struggles of the Yi dynasty might have been fought out in the lexicon of Confucian virtue and immorality, but their primary cause was the struggle of competing groups for advantages within Korea's unique political system. Another of Hyŏn's pernicious elements, clanism, also does not ring true. Confucian filial piety demanded loyalty to the family unit in an age of agricultural communalism, and its extension of filial loyalty to the king as father of the people was largely symbolic. In Hyŏn's world of fervid nationalism and patriotic movements, to uphold family over national identity might have seemed disloyal, but in its traditional context this was never an issue.

Central to Hyŏn's critique was his belief that Confucianism upheld an inequitable class ideology. In this sense he echoed leftist contemporaries, who interpreted Confucianism as an ideology that supported a feudal class system and the dominance of a bureaucratic elite. There is no doubt that class conflict, bureaucratic dominance, and inequality were features of the Yi system, but to attribute these factors to Confucian thought requires a leap of the imagination. If anything, in an earlier period Confucianism had been a progressive force behind the destruction of the feudal class structure in China. In later periods, class structure evolved in East Asia with reference to control of land and resources. The dominance of scholar-officials and the general attitude in Yi dynasty Korea of "revere officials, despise people" (*kwanjon minbi*) corrupted the original Confucian ideal of the rule of men of virtue and the responsibilities of officials to serve the interests of the people.

Finally, Hyŏn charged that the Confucian tradition was responsible for a general literary effeminacy among the Korean people, or, more concretely, an excessive valuing of pacifism. Writing at a time of Japanese dominance in Korean affairs, Hyŏn was painfully aware of the weakness of the martial tradition during the Yi dynasty. With Korea having fallen victim to the machinations of imperialist powers, each wielding superior military force, Hyŏn tried to blame the Confucian insistence on the dominance of civilian authority and its disparagement of technical and military arts. That Confucianism stressed civilian dominance in government is not the issue in dispute; the problem was that Korea had somehow gone to an extreme in allowing its military forces to atrophy to a point of complete ineptitude. Yet in another breath Hyŏn had already praised the Confucian virtue of humaneness as worthy of preservation.

Hyŏn's critique of the Confucian bias against commerce and industry also rings false. Certainly, in the ideal social scheme, Confucianism valued scholars and peasants over merchants and artisans, but this artificial hierarchy had not inhibited Chinese and Japanese societies from developing significant commercial power in the eighteenth and nineteenth centuries. Indeed, Confucian social mores did not seem to constrict the development of a small but important class of entrepreneurs during the colonial period. To blame Yi dynasty adherence to Neo-Confucian orthodoxy as the cause of economic weakness in twentieth-century Korea seems a gross oversimplification of a very complex problem.[19]

Although Hyŏn's argument is flawed in many areas, the point remains that his ideas reflected a general consensus among intellectuals at the end of the colonial period, and postwar social critics continue to advance similar arguments. Despite elaborate refutation of Hyŏn's argument, critics continue to blame the Confucian tradition writ large for the persistence of authoritarian political patterns in South Korea.[20] While the economic success of the last two decades has diminished the relevance of the commercial-weakness thesis, the Confucian legacy remains a convenient explanation for the continued dominance of the central bureaucracy and factional politics in Korea.

While intellectuals continued to grapple with the presumed ill effects of the Confucian tradition on twentieth-century Korea, the Japanese state (1910–45) selectively played upon Confucian values to further their own policies. This was particularly true with regard to the issue of loyalty and the natural legitimacy of the state. Therefore, whenever possible, the Japanese authorities chose to use the residual power of Confucian values to win support for their rule. In their design of the curriculum for the colonial education system, the Japanese paid close attention to cultivating values of loyalty and submissiveness to the state. In doing so they also played upon the deepseated respect for the value of filial piety. The following passage from *Rules for Teachers* published in 1916 illustrates how state loyalty and filial piety were intertwined:

---

[19] Yi Sang-un, "Han'guk e issŏsŏ ŭi yugyo ŭi kongbiron" (A reevaluation of Confucianism in Korea), *Asea yŏn'gu* 9, pt. 4 (Dec. 1966): 1–20. For a summary of this article in English see Yi Sang-un, "On the Criticism of Confucianism in Korea," in Korean National Commission for UNESCO, *Main Currents of Korean Thought* (Seoul: Si-sa-yong-o-sa Publishers, Inc., 1983), pp. 112–46.

[20] Ibid.

The fostering of loyalty and filial piety shall be made the radical principle of education and the cultivation of moral sentiments shall be given
special attention. It is only what may be expected of a loyal and dutiful
man, who knows what is demanded of a subject and a son—that he
should be faithful to his duties.[21]

In this way, the Japanese authorities manipulated the cultural sensi-
bilities of their Korean subjects to bolster the legitimacy of their rule.

What separated this manipulation from the past was the difference
in the nature of the state to which allegiance was owed. The colonial
state was powerful, highly centralized, intrusive, and efficient. It had
at its disposal a large police force and enormous bureaucracy. As
such, it was very different from the Yi dynasty state and even more
removed from an ideal version of the Confucian state with its benevolent monarch and loyal officials. It was the Japanese who created the
first modern, centralized state in Korea, and its authoritarian excesses, in combination, perhaps, with the long-lived Confucian political tradition, must be blamed for patterns that have endured into the
contemporary period.

The Japanese also attempted to preserve useful aspects of the traditional Korean class system and in doing so became official patrons
of Confucianism. The cultural policy of the 1920s sought ways of co-
opting various segments of Korean society into supporting the colonial state. Having already given stipends to high officials of the Yi
dynasty in the immediate aftermath of annexation in 1910, ten years
later Governor General Saitō began to patronize individual Confucian scholars and provide financial support for organizations devoted
to the preservation and maintenance of Confucian values. This support took the form of underwriting formal ritual observance of Confucius' birthday and memorial rites to famous Korean Confucians.[22]
This policy, while not as extensively publicized as the "concessions"
to the new intelligentsia (for example, broader permission for vernacular publishing and political organization after 1920), sought to
win over conservative and upper-class elements of Korean society. At
the same time, it reinforced the public educational doctrine of loyalty
to the state.

Another aspect of Japanese colonial rule that reinforced Confucian
values in Korea while intertwining them with the fortunes of the
modern state was the ideology of the family of empire. Particularly

---

[21] Government General of Korea, *Rules for Teachers* (Keijō: Chōsen sōtokufu, Mom-
busho, 1916).

[22] Kang Tong-jin, *Ilche ŭi Han'guk ch'imnyak chŏngch'aeksa* (A history of Japanese imperialist policy in Korea) (Seoul: Han'gilsa, 1980).

after 1931 and the broad advance of Japan in Asia, the Japanese enjoined the Koreans to think of themselves as part of the family that constituted the Japanese empire. The entire language of the assimilation program after 1931 was couched in familial terms. The general rubric for the assimilation policy was *nissen ittai* (Korea and Japan as one body). Official rhetoric notwithstanding, it was made abundantly clear that the Koreans remained younger brothers in the greater imperial family. The Japanese emperor was father, Japanese citizens elder brothers, Koreans younger brothers, and later additions to the empire younger still. Indeed, the Japanese empire was portrayed as a family and Confucian values were trotted out to support the political mythology of assimilation into this hierarchical system.[23]

Certainly not all Koreans believed in this portrayal of imperial politics. For collaborationist elements, however, the language was irresistible. In particular, the tiny Korean capitalist elite, an elite who saw themselves as junior partners with the Japanese in the development of Manchuria and who profited in their participation in the Japanese war economy after 1937, embraced the Confucian language of imperial family. If anything, Korean economic leaders wanted to strengthen the symbolism of younger brother and gain true acceptance in the Japanese system.[24] After the outbreak of war with China, economic elites as well as prominent intellectuals were mobilized to lead Korean mass organizations in support of the war effort. Speeches given by such leaders to student groups enjoined them to give the ultimate sacrifice to the empire and join the armed forces. Their appeal was to the loyalty a son would feel toward a benevolent father (here, the Japanese emperor). Although not the rule, such appeals even on the part of a small group of collaborators illustrated to what depths appeals to traditional Confucian virtues could sink in the service of the state.

CONTEMPORARY KOREAN SOCIETY

In the first fifty years of the twentieth century, the entire Confucian tradition came under assault. At the same time, selected values from this tradition were mobilized toward the service of the modern state. The attack of progressive intellectuals discredited the Confucian tra-

[23] Peter Duus, "Backward Imperialism: The Japanese in Korea, 1894–1910," unpublished paper, Japan Seminar, USC-UCLA Joint Center for East Asian Studies, December 1987.

[24] Carter Eckert, "The Origins of Korean Capitalism: The Kochang Kims and the Kyongsong Spinning and Weaving Company, 1871–1945" (Ph.D. diss., University of Washington, 1986), pp. 485–516.

dition on political and social developmental grounds; and the perverted appeals of loyalty and filial piety in the service of the state made in the context of political and cultural repression undoubtedly bred cynicism and distrust of such lofty values. Although the idea of state Confucianism was swept away by Japanese colonial rule, Confucian interpersonal values proved more difficult to efface. While intellectuals railed against the "defects" and "evils" of the Confucian tradition, people quietly continued to adhere to Confucian norms in their private lives. Arranged marriages, ancestor worship, respect for elders, filial piety, and subordination of women remained the norm for Korean society. It took the shocks of postwar division, civil war, and an unprecedented economic revolution to accelerate the process of altering such deeply held beliefs.

The process of structural change in Korean society began during the Japanese occupation period. Particularly after 1931, living and working patterns began to change. Even after the limited industrialization of the 1930s and 1940s and the rapid growth of the Korean urban labor force, Korea (South Korea) remained a predominantly agrarian nation into the 1950s. Rural society was significantly altered by land reforms in 1948 and 1950. Over 70 percent of eligible land was redistributed, benefiting over one million of a total of two million rural households.[25] The Korean war had an even more decisive effect in leveling class differences and stimulating demographic change. Finally, the rapid economic growth after 1962 precipitated a massive shift of the entire demographic base. In the last twenty-five years, purposeful industrialization has spurred a massive shift of population from farm to factory, village to city. Korea is now 65 percent urban and 35 percent rural, a reversal of the percentages of 1945. With this change in the way Koreans work and live have come pressures on the traditional value system. But in spite of what one might predict, Confucian values, although under assault, remain deeply ingrained in the body politic and private personas of the Korean people.

Since liberation, politics has been consumed with the problem of nation-building in South Korea. This has led to a subtle shift in the dialogue about the Confucian past. While Confucianism and its hold on Korean society is still scapegoated as a barrier to the creation of a modern society and economic system, postliberation leaders continue to use the language of Confucian loyalty to bolster the identification

[25] Hagen Koo, "The Interplay of State, Social Class, and World System in East Asian Development: The Cases of South Korea and Taiwan," in *The Political Economy of the New Asian Industrialism*, ed. Fredrick Dayes (Ithaca: Cornell University Press, 1987), p. 170.

with the state. For example, government authorities have been willing
to exploit the value of loyalty, now in the guise of modern patriotism.
Confucian themes of subordination to benevolent authority, loyalty
to the state, or the natural legitimacy of the state bureaucracy are
prominent in many presidential speeches. State-controlled textbooks
feature biographies of loyal soldiers and statesmen extolling the virtues of service and patriotism as qualities just as valuable in a modern
democracy as in an ancient Confucian monarchy. The value of individual cultivation and search for virtue is presented to Korean students from the very beginning of their education in the guise of exhortation to study hard for their own self-advancement as well as for
the benefit of the nation.[26]

The state also continues to patronize grand rituals serving the
memory of Confucius, but there is a peculiar motive behind such
support.[27] With regard to the formal state ritual of Confucianism
(sacrifice to Confucius as well as separate memorial services to the Yi
kings), the tradition of state Confucianism is sanitized by placing it in
a context of performance and exhibition. In a sense, this subjects the
tradition to taxidermy—preserving the outer trappings while ignor-
ing the political and social ideology behind the ritual. Indeed, the
Ministry of Culture and Information supports a number of projects
that control the interpretation of the past. Such institutions as the
National Academy for the Performance Arts and designations for
"living" national treasures provide a particular control over the sub-
sidization of traditional arts. In another example, official patronage
of the performance aspects of shaman dance and costuming divorces
shamanism from its spiritual and psychosocial context. The state pa-
tronizes the memory of a political/cultural tradition as two-dimen-
sional—therefore "safe"—art, so that, as in a museum, modern Koreans can view, safely behind glass, the trappings of the past.[28]

Although the modern South Korean state is willing to indirectly
use Confucian values of loyalty and service, it is reluctant to endorse
the tradition itself. This is because there is a tremendous antipathy to

[26] Overseas Information Service, Republic of Korea, *A Handbook of Korea*, 4th ed.
(Seoul: Ministry of Culture and Information, 1982), pp. 672–73.

[27] For a description of these rituals see Spencer Palmer, *Confucian Rituals in Korea*
(Berkeley, Calif.: Asian Humanities Press, n.d.).

[28] The Ministry of Culture and Information of the ROK is responsible for a wide
assortment of programs. These include propaganda overseas and support for research
on Korea both by Korean and foreign scholars. In addition, it supports the maintenance of monuments and architectural remains as well as traditional fine arts, crafts,
and performance arts. For a description of ROK cultural policy see Kim Yersu, *Cultural
Policy in the Republic of Korea* (Paris: United Nations Educational, Scientific and Cultural
Organization, 1976).

the Confucian tradition, which is seen as an obstacle to economic development. The purposeful economic program of the Park Chunghee years, continued under his successors, Chun Doo Hwan and Rho Tae-woo, leaves no room for aspects of the Korean tradition that are considered to inhibit economic growth. In Park's 1962 speech, "Reflections on Our Nation's Past," he adopted the language of early twentieth-century progressives, criticizing the corruption, irrationality, venality, and waste of the Confucian tradition.[29] Park's critique went on to catalogue the abuses of the Confucian tradition as encouraging a mentality of vassalage, lack of independent spirit, indolence, lack of enterprise, malicious selfishness, and lack of sense of honor in the Korean people. Here he echoes the analysis of Hyŏn Sang-yun; in the very long document only two positive aspects of the Confucian past were mentioned—loyalty of certain officials and the pragmatism of the seventeenth- to eighteenth-century Sirhak scholars (Practical Learning school).

Therefore, no less a personage than the ROK president weighed into the debate over the legacy of the Confucian tradition in modern Korea. While adopting many aspects of Park's line, Chun Doo Hwan was more sophisticated in his treatment of the Confucian tradition. Chun identified "discipline" and "public interest" with the good aspects of Confucianism. Going further, he asserted that the Confucian spirit was the basis of Korean culture; therefore, to not maintain discipline in the name of economic development and national security was a breach of traditional values. Moreover, Chun's analysis of excesses in modern Korean society illustrated his idea of the useful aspects of the Confucian tradition:

> The prevalence of toadyism, a blind admiration for all things foreign, a pervasive notion that money is everything, unbridled egoism and the like is indicative that for some, at least, spiritual and cultural interests have taken a back seat to monetary ones. We must rectify perversion and confusion in values . . . only then can a new era be forged.[30]

This statement shows to what extent Korean political leaders are ambivalent about the Confucian tradition. Toadyism and *sadae* consciousness have long been associated, rightly or wrongly, with the Confucian past. But in decrying the blind struggle for wealth and unbridled egoism Chun argues the other side of the coin. Here, what Westernizing progressives had argued was a necessary development

---

[29] Park Chung-hee, *Reflections on our Nation's Past: Ideology of Social Reconstruction* (Seoul: Dong-a Publishing Co., 1962), pp. 34–107.

[30] Chun Doo Hwan, *The 1980s Meeting a New Challenge: Selected Speeches of Chon Doo Hwan* (Seoul: Korea Textbook Co., Ltd., 1981), p. 184.

(i.e., the creation of economic power and the encouraging of individualism) seemed to President Chun to be borrowed values run amuck in modern Korea. Moreover, Chun adopted a Confucian reformist attitude in admonishing citizens to rectify moral values as a precursor to behavioral change.

The state has traditionally taken a strong role in shaping and guiding public values and morality. Campaigns to change public habits of consumption, public courtesy, and rural self-help (the well-known "New Village Movement") exemplify this commitment. What has changed in contemporary Korea is the mix of values the state deemed appropriate for public emulation. The centralized school system, indoctrination in the armed forces, and public campaigns all exhort the people to adhere to values that will support national solidarity and economic growth.

It is clear, at least at the level of national politics, that there is an ambivalent attitude toward the Confucian tradition. Political leaders wish to support the memory of traditional grandeur and state pomp by patronizing the symbolic and artistic legacy of Confucian ritual. Moreover, they want to use Confucian lexicon regarding loyalty and service to the state. They will even, at times—when it serves their purpose—enjoin the citizenry to adhere to traditional values of asceticism and moral virtue. Yet, when things go wrong, the Confucian tradition can always be represented as an evil, obstructionist legacy, a mind-set to be rooted out and put behind modern society.

According to one official government handbook, Confucianism disappeared from the stage of Korean history in 1910 with the fall of the Yi dynasty. The reason given for this is that Confucianism is no longer the basis of government and administration in Korea. While it is no longer the basis, as we have seen, it still preoccupies government leaders. The same source asserts, however, that Confucianism does live on in the customs, habits, and thoughts of the people. Those elements of Confucianism that are to be encouraged are reverence for age, social stability, and respect for learning and culture. In contrast, what needs to be rooted out in Korean society are idolization of the past, social rigidity, and abstract unworldliness.[31] It is debatable whether or not these are true Confucian categories; the point remains that they have been labeled as such.

In recent years, there has been an explosion in anthropological and sociological studies of modern South Korean society. The rapid economic development of the last two decades and its attendant social change have provided the main impetus for this surge of interest.

[31] Overseas Information Service, *A Handbook of Korea*, p. 204.

Although there has been a dramatic exodus from the countryside, village life remains very much influenced by Confucian patterns. The family remains the economic and ethical universe for villagers. *Hyo* (filial piety) and *ŭn* (parental grace) still govern relationships between children and parents.[32] Although the ritual of ancestor worship might be truncated and streamlined, it is carried on as an important part of family life. To older Koreans, certainly, these values are an important means of maintaining generational solidarity and reciprocity as well as proper roles for parents and children.

Roles in the family have changed. The new family registration law of the revised Civil Code (1950s) reduced the power of household heads and improved the position of women with regard to inheritance and rights in divorce cases.[33] The size of families is decreasing as younger sons more frequently move away from the natal home. Yet the general structure and pattern of family solidarity remains, and it is shaped by Confucian values. The government has at times enjoined families to simplify family ritual in order to encourage savings, but such pronouncements have fallen on deaf ears. Lineage ritual, including ancestor worship, is too important to ignore; it reaffirms agnatic ties and family status, and provides a source of continuity in a rapidly changing society.[34]

The rapid growth of the urban sector in South Korea has changed the physical environment for families. Apartments have replaced single-family dwellings, and families are separated between rural and city branches. These changes have lessened the relevance of the older generation's experiences to younger Koreans; elders cannot maintain their prestige and authority as easily as in the traditional rural setting. Community-centeredness and values that support it have faded. The urban-centered, nuclear, conjugal unit has become the norm in Korean society.

Nevertheless, the hold of Confucian family values remains very strong. While the structure of families has been extended geographically, it has evolved into a "modified stem family"—that is, sons do not live with their parents after marriage, but remain in close proximity.[35] Moreover, even though ancestor ritual in the city tends to be

---

[32] Clark Sorensen, *Over the Mountains Are Mountains: Korean Peasant Households and Their Adaptations to Rapid Industrialization* (Seattle and London: University of Washington Press, 1988).

[33] Ibid., p. 169.

[34] Jannelli and Jannelli, *Ancestor Worship and Korean Society*, p. 145.

[35] Lee Kwang-kyu, "Confucian Tradition in the Contemporary Korean Family," in *The Psycho-Cultural Dynamics of the Confucian Family*, ed. Walter H. Slote (Seoul: International Cultural Society of Korea Forum Series, n.d.), no. 8, pt. 5.

less elaborate, it is carried out with more enthusiasm. Roles within the family have altered. Authority and privilege of the elder generation is, perhaps, no longer unconditional, but offered to parents as a reward for providing. The idea of filial duty has been transformed toward a concept of intergenerational compromise. The focus of modern families also tends to be children-centered rather than husband/wife-centered.[36]

The Confucian tradition has shaped other modern sectors of Korean life. In the 1950s and 1960s government service continued to be a prime goal for educated elites. The expansion of higher education (from 60,000 college students in 1960 to over one million in 1985) in the postwar era was matched by an increase in the size of the state bureaucracy. Based on its ability to attract the best and brightest students, the relative efficiency of the South Korean bureaucracy, in spite of its many flaws, has been singled out as a major contributor to economic growth.[37] The intrusion of the military into politics after 1961 challenged the primacy of the bureaucracy. Charging the bureaucracy with moral effeminacy, the military revived a centuries-old enmity engendered by Confucian bias against military officials. In spite of this, the bureaucracy remains an important avenue of mobility in Korean society, and the prestige of a civil service career can be linked directly to traditional values.[38] Yet, the esteem traditionally ascribed to the college graduate can also cause problems when suitable employment opportunities cannot keep pace with the supply of job-seekers with degrees. This has been the case during the 1980s, and high levels of resentment and frustrated ambition have been cited as a contributing factor to the political unrest of recent years.

When analyzing the economic success of South Korea, development economists continually stress the high level of education and trainability of Korea's work force. This fact is a logical outgrowth of the Korean tradition that education is the principal avenue to social mobility. Although the expansion of the modern education system

[36] Lee Kwang-gyu, "Changing Aspects of the Rural Family in Korea," in *Family and Community Change in East Asia*, ed. K. Aoi and K. Morioka (Tokyo: Japan Sociological Society, 1985), pp. 158–87.

[37] Leroy P. Jones and Il Sakong, *Government, Business, and Entrepreneurship in Economic Development: The Korean Case* (Cambridge, Mass.: Council on East Asian Studies, Harvard University, 1980), pp. 256–57.

[38] The military is not alone in its critique of the state bureaucracy. See Pyong-choon Hahm, "Toward a New Theory of Korean Politics: A Reexamination of Traditional Factors," in *Korean Politics in Transition*, ed. Edward R. Wright (Seoul: Royal Asiatic Society, Korea Branch, 1975), pp. 322–23. A more sanguine analysis of the bureaucracy's role in the modern era is contained in Edward R. Wright, "The Bureaucracy," in *Korean Politics in Transition*, ed. Wright, pp. 71–84.

preceded the economic takeoff and consequently produced an over-supply of college graduates in the 1960s and again in the 1980s, this did not deter Koreans from spending a large portion of their savings educating their children. So strong is the belief in education's role to enhance social mobility that families have always made great sacrifices. The rapid expansion of industry has been plagued by a shortage of skilled labor, but there has almost always been an oversupply of liberal-arts-trained college graduates. This indicates that, although weakened, old attitudes toward manual labor and technical positions remain strong.

In the main, however, traditional Confucian values have supported Korean growth. The focus on education and self-cultivation within the Confucian tradition as a means for improving both individual and family position in society encouraged the expansion of mass education. The values of hard work, diligence, and self-discipline have helped to shape a trainable, hard-driving industrial work force that for many years was willing to postpone financial rewards for security during the post-1960 boom. Thus the general values and attitudes toward education, not specific skills, have been a major Confucian influence on the character of the modern blue- and white-collar work force.[39]

Primary Confucian values of loyalty to the family, trust among friends, acceptance of hierarchy, and obedience to authority also resonate with the requirements of modern corporate life. While stronger than that of their American counterparts, the loyalty of Korean white-collar employees to their company (those working in the large conglomerates [chebŏl]) seems more conditional than that exhibited by Japanese workers. The pressures fostered by the important relationship between government and business have encouraged, according to recent research, a less paternalistic and more authoritarian style in large Korean companies. With the fortunes of the company so closely tied to its relationship with government authorities, managers closely guard their autonomy in decision-making. Thus the manager's authority does not emulate the benevolent authority of a father, and employees are less reluctant to leave companies for employment elsewhere.[40]

Our understanding of Korean corporate culture is still sketchy. Al-

[39] Edward S. Mason et al., The Economic and Social Modernization of the Republic of Korea (Cambridge, Mass.: Council on East Asian Studies, Harvard University, 1980), p. 378.

[40] These comments are based on as yet unpublished research by Roger Janelli. He has completed the field-study phase of his project "Management, Authority, and Tradition in the Korean Firm" and is currently preparing a monograph based on his research during a one-year residency at the Lucky Corporation in Seoul.

though many of the great conglomerates are privately owned and family networks dominate their leadership, this does not mean that the patterns of authority necessarily follow traditional family, or Confucian, values. Indeed, it can be posited that precisely because families dominate corporate leadership, the general rank and file feels less identification with the fortunes of the company. In fact, tight family control has led to the anomaly of younger family members occupying important posts in large *chebŏl*, in which they direct employees of greater age and experience. When considering authority patterns and loyalty structures, however, a distinction must be made between the giant *chebŏl* and medium- and small-sized firms. It is clearly easier to extend familial values to a small work force than to a rapidly created megacorporation. In addition, large-firm management relations with labor in Korea are notoriously authoritarian.[41] In this case Confucian reciprocity does not inform worker welfare. Nevertheless, interpersonal behavior of white-collar workers within the company remains consistent with predominant values in society at large.

The Changing Present and Uncertain Future

In the final analysis, Confucian values in twentieth-century Korea remain strong, but in altered form. The formal state ideology of Confucianism has long since disappeared, yet the terminology continues to survive in corrupted form in government propaganda and mobilization campaigns. Respect for Confucianism as a system of values integrated into politics has been destroyed by the unremitting hostility of modern intellectuals and nationalists, who have blamed Confucianism for Korea's political and economic woes in the twentieth century. However unfair to the Confucian tradition this may be, Confucianism-bashing has become an integral part of modern Koreans' view of their recent past.

At the state level, the ideals of incorruptible officials serving a benevolent monarch were crushed under the weight of Korea's political experience since 1910. The modern state came to Korea in the form of the draconian Japanese colonial administration. Its use of Confucian ideology to buttress its legitimacy, and Koreans' association of Confucian political ideology with the hated language of assimilation, have also undoubtedly undermined these values. In postliberation Korea, the image of the bureaucratic state has fared no better, tar-

[41] The most comprehensive study of Korean labor unions is contained in Choi Jang-jip, "Interest, Conflict, and Politics in Control in South Korea: A Study of Labor Unions in Manufacturing Industries, 1961–1980" (Ph.D. diss., University of Chicago, 1983).

nished as it is by a history of corruption and inefficiency in the 1950s and authoritarian abuses since the 1960s. The government has attempted to place the tradition in the museum, to take the good and expunge the bad. In the end, it has been largely successful in divorcing the modern nation-state from its Yi dynasty Confucian precursor.

Confucian interpersonal and family values, however, remain strong in modern Korea. Although they survive in changed form, filial piety, respect for elders, reciprocity in human relations, and the importance of education and cultivation remain key characteristics of modern Korean behavior. The focus on family and community has been transformed by modernization, but the values have been transferred to new structures and groupings. Group loyalty in village Korea has transformed into loyalty to one's work group, whether it be office or shop floor. Respect for education and individual cultivation lives on in the modern Korean drive for advanced degrees and the phenomenal expansion of higher education. Interpersonal relations remain guided by a strong sense of reciprocity; intergenerational authority and respect, although weakened, remain important values in Korean life. Thus the Confucian tradition has faded with the advent of the twentieth century, but remains alive in the background of a vastly changed Korean society.

INDEX